1987

THE STRATEGIC
DEFENSE DEBATE

CAN "STAR WARS"
MAKE US SAFE?

Edited by

CRAIG SNYDER

THE UNIVERSITY OF PENNSYLVANIA PRESS
Philadelphia · 1986

THE WORLD AFFAIRS COUNCIL OF
PHILADELPHIA

THE STRATEGIC DEFENSE DEBATE

CAN "STAR WARS" MAKE US SAFE?

Library of Congress Cataloging-in-Publication Data

The Strategic defense debate.

   At head of title: The World Affairs Council of
Philadelphia.
   Based on a conference sponsored by the World
Affairs Council of Philadelphia, held Oct, 3–4, 1985.
   Includes index.
   1. Strategic Defense Initiative—Congresses.
I. Snyder, Craig.   II. World Affairs Council of
Philadelphia.
UG743.S76 1986   358′.1754   86–25057
ISBN 0–8122–8040–7 (cloth)
ISBN 0–8122–1233–9 (pbk.)

For Lois

ABOUT THIS BOOK

The World Affairs Council of Philadelphia is a private, nonprofit, nonpartisan organization devoted to the promotion of a more informed citizenry on U.S. foreign policy and global issues. The Council takes no positions on issues and does not endorse candidates for public office. Membership in the organization is open to all who share its purposes.

This book is based on a conference sponsored by the Council in Philadelphia on October 3 and 4, 1985, titled "Strategic Defense and American Security: Can 'Star Wars' Make Us Safe?" This meeting was convened for the broad examination by leading commentators, widely differing in their views, of the defense of the United States in the nuclear age.

The project of the Council on strategic defense began with Ambassador Paul Nitze's presentation on our podium of the major address "On the Road to a More Stable Peace." This speech marked a turning point in the national debate about President Reagan's "Star Wars" initiative by thoroughly and clearly explaining the administration's strategic concept.

At the conference itself, more than two dozen noted experts spoke and debated before a diverse audience of over 1,000 concerned citizens from across the nation.

In addition to this book, the conference resulted in the documentary film "Shielding America" which was televised nationally on the Public Broadcasting System.

This book, made possible in part by grants from RCA Corporation and the Boeing Company, is designed to allow more sustained consideration by a wider public of the vital question of nuclear policy which affects us all. We hope it proves interesting and useful.

Buntzie Ellis Churchill
President
The World Affairs Council of Philadelphia

CONTENTS

FOREWORD

President Reagan's announcement of his Strategic Defense Initiative on March 23, 1983 opened up one of the richest debates we have experienced on the purposes and possibilities of any military strategy in the nuclear age. Following the criticisms of the morality of mutual deterrence, or mutual assured destruction (MAD), as expressed in the Letter of the Roman Catholic Bishops, and the projections of a possibility of a "nuclear winter" global ecological disaster (conceivably triggerable by the nuclear warheads on even a single SLBM submarine), the President's proposal for "rendering these nuclear weapons impotent and obsolete" still raises as many questions as it answers.

Is it indeed even possible to protect cities against nuclear attack? Would it too much increase the chances of nuclear war if either side were to come close to such a capability, as the other worried about what would follow if a nuclear monopoly was about to be recreated? But if we do not find some alternative, such as SDI, can we count on mutual deterrence to persist into the future? Is substantial disarmament a preferable alternative to any space-based weapons intended to stop an adversary's missiles? Or is such disarmament fraught with all the same perils, also perhaps making nuclear war more likely if the world was approaching total disarmament?

The collection of analyses presented here considers this array of issues, and illustrates the variety of responses the President's proposals have drawn, as the critics of SDI have almost from the outset appended to it the alternative and derisive label of "Star Wars." The authors here are nothing less than experts on the subject: the principal spokesmen for the administration as it moves ahead with one notion or another of SDI, and the most experienced and articulate spokesmen for avoiding any investment in this kind of anti-missile preparation. Novices may despair of the subject, if authors who are so expert and have the very best of credentials seem to be so much in disagreement; but this merely shows that the issues of war and peace in the nuclear age are intellectually very rich, as well as monumentally important.

The debate in this book does not affect just Americans, but also U.S. allies (whose views are presented in the book), allies whose cities may be more difficult to protect than the cities of the United States. It similarly affects the nonaligned countries (who would also inexorably suffer in any superpower nuclear exchange), and, of course, it affects the Soviet Union in particular. One irony of this enrichment of the American debate is that the Reagan administration is at times voicing the same moral and strategic arguments which were commonplace in Moscow fifteen years ago, or even five years ago, thus illustrating what critics of the administration sometimes call a "Sovietization of American strategy." And a matching irony is that Soviet complaints about SDI suddenly now sound strikingly like the mutual deterrence analyses U.S. officials were voicing in the mid-1960s and early 1970s. At least some of the blame for the unsettled nature of the American strategic debate, illustrated so well in this book, must therefore be directed at Moscow, for all the confusions of intent that have been signalled in Soviet strategic pronouncements.

Critics of SDI can point to the failure of the Space Shuttle as just one more sign that so massive a technological undertaking can never work so perfectly as to satisfy President Reagan's declared intentions. Defenders of SDI conversely sometimes lament its "I" for "initiative," contending that the Soviets have been ahead of us in declared intentions for the very same kind of program, and have indeed invested more than we in space defenses and space research.

This debate will go on without quickly being settled. Since the debate will be prolonged, this book will amount to an important contribution to it.

George H. Quester

College Park, Maryland
July, 1986

PREFACE

In the essay "Nuclear War, Nuclear Peace," Leon Wieseltier, the Literary Editor of the *New Republic* and a contributor to this volume, writes:

Whatever else the bomb is, it is a practical problem. It demands solutions, not merely sentiments; and it demands solutions that are not sure to be simple. There comes a point in the discussion of this very grave subject when eloquence is egregious, when it must be replaced by a cool and careful consideration of the danger in all its details.

To advance a bit this process of replacing heat with light on nuclear issues in general and "Star Wars" in particular, the World Affairs Council of Philadelphia undertook the project "Strategic Defense and American Security," which this book completes.

First a few words about scope and tone. Genuine nonpartisanship requires balance and thoroughness, but comprehensiveness is impossible. The emphasis here is on issues of *policy*, on the "live" choices to be made. It is therefore deliberate that all of the contributors—notwithstanding their real disagreements—are not too distant from the center in their views on "Star Wars" and related subjects. This book is an invitation into the circles of thought in which decisions about the security of the nation and the world have the greatest chance of being made. It is less a work of scholarship, than a political document, a snapshot of the evolving debate on the nature and purposes of American security policy. It aims to be a reference for concerned citizens.

Undoubtedly, some honorable and intellectually distinctive approaches to this subject have been left out of this work, including the variants of pacifism that might call for unilateral disarmament and a posture of "nonviolent" defense. Many aspects of the arguments within the mainstream community of political ideas are also underrepresented here, including elaborate analyses of the costs of strategic defense, the views of the Russians and our allies on "Star Wars," the economic and military implications of strategic defense for American conventional military power, and the impact of "Star Wars" on the international political environment in peacetime.

Even rigorously balanced debate, however, requires honest selectivity about issues and materials, and also requires decisions on acceptable language. In this book the terms "Star Wars" and "strategic defense" are used interchangeably, despite the objections to the first term raised by some proponents of the idea. No prejudice is intended by this choice; it is surely true that "Star Wars" is a very unfortunate name for so important an issue. Nonetheless, "Star Wars" is simply the name with the widest currency. While we hope to raise the level of debate a notch or two, we must begin from where it is now.

Our primary purpose is to make available, in clear and compact form, the central views of knowledgeable Americans on whether Star Wars enhances the security of the United States. Beyond this, we also look at the context of the Star Wars debate. Our aim is to clarify the positions in a vital national debate and to make them more accessible to a broader public.

All expressions of fact and opinion are, of course, the responsibility of the authors alone.

Craig Snyder

Philadelphia
May 1986

ACKNOWLEDGMENTS

A book like this is obviously the product of many people's work. First, there are the authors themselves. They have not only written well and in the spirit of public education on which this project is based, but they have also kept to deadlines and have been wonderfully tolerant of the folding, stapling, and mutilating of their work required to package it in this form. An editor's dream.

There is another quite extraordinary group to thank—the staff of the World Affairs Council of Philadelphia. The entire staff deserves credit for the great success of our "Strategic Defense and American Security" conference, this book's parent project. Buntzie Churchill, the organization's president, does not simply run the place, she does so with imagination and guts. These qualities were the sparks that ignited our Star Wars program.

Invaluable efforts for the conference were also made by Lisa Hayden and Laura Shell. Laura's efforts made the conference possible.

For the book itself, I am indebted to Tom Rotell, Alison Anderson, Jean Sue Johnson, and the staff of the University of Pennsylvania Press, who taught a toddling editor to walk and persuaded various naysayers of the value of publishing this text. I am also indebted to Andy Jickling and Martha Keon, Council staff members sentenced to the hard labor of it. Without Martha's kindness, patience, and dedication, there would have been no book.

Finally, though weaknesses remain that are solely my responsibility, my dear friend Bart Gellman, my brother Robert, and especially my wife Lois have insisted on clarity and rigor in the face of my tendency to be obscure and mushy. And, of course, my parents are owed everything.

PART ONE

INTRODUCTION AND OVERVIEW

STAR WARS
AND NUCLEAR IDEOLOGIES
Craig Snyder

The nuclear age has reached middle age. The bomb is forty. It has been more than forty years since the atomic weapon was made and first used. But it has also been more than forty years since it was last used.

How can we best deal with the threat posed by nuclear weapons? This question is both technically and morally complex, a truly serious problem, even if often a source of black humor.

Nuclear weapons will simply not go away. Though many argue that they have actually helped keep the peace among the major nations these past forty years, the very existence of such instruments is the central burden of this generation. And, like individuals who discover their own mortality at forty and begin to shift their attentions from the shorter to the longer term, recently millions in the West—both ordinary citizens and the nuclear elite—have come to regard old questions of strategy and ethics with new urgency. The image of the mid-life crisis does much to explain the intensity of the debate about strategic defense: the bold idea and program, commonly called "Star Wars," that aims to eliminate, or at least to reduce, the nuclear threat.

This chapter is an effort to outline the principal arguments about Star Wars as the central debate on American security policy

Craig Snyder is the Program Director of the World Affairs Council of Philadelphia.

and to sketch some of the context. This last task is necessary because what lies behind the specific discussions, and what infuses them with meaning, is the debate among contending schools of thought on America's goals in a dangerous world. Perhaps it is presumptuous to attempt to lay out a conceptual road map of such difficult intellectual terrain, or to describe clearly opposing ideologies about living in the nuclear age, when the subtlety of individual commentators defies such neat categorization. But maps—with their keys or legends to translate abstract symbols into meaningful representations—make up in usefulness what they lack in precision of detail. Thus, even with all that is overlooked here, there is much to be said.

MARCH 23, 1983

This is not a generation of great orators or great speeches. Today, pictures seem to matter more than words. But among the exceptions must surely stand the concluding remarks of President Reagan's television address of March 23, 1983, entitled "Peace and National Security," when he announced the vision of the Star Wars project. In a single important moment, the President reaffirmed that expressing an idea can be a powerful act, at least in the political life of a democracy. He said:

Let me share with you a vision of the future which offers hope. It is that we embark on a program to counter the awesome Soviet missile threat with measures that are defensive. . . .
   What if free people could live secure in the knowledge that their security did not rest upon the threat of instant U.S. retaliation to deter a Soviet attack, that we could intercept and destroy strategic ballistic missiles before they reached our own soil or that of our allies? . . .
   I call upon the scientific community in our country, those who gave us nuclear weapons, to turn their great talents now to the cause of mankind and world peace, to give us the means of rendering these nuclear weapons impotent and obsolete.

The President's action was bold in form and substance. The central idea of the Strategic Defense Initiative (SDI)—that the United States would accelerate and focus public attention on research into technologies to defend against nuclear attack, to shoot down nuclear weapons before they could reach their targets—stood on its head the still young, but quite widely and deeply accepted, doctrine of the deterrence of nuclear war through offensive weapons alone. And that orthodoxy, which has legal support in the Anti-Ballistic Missile (ABM) Treaty, was called into question by the President without his even observing the political sacrament of "prior consultation." President Reagan made his speech without first informing, much less seeking guidance from, either our allies, the Soviets, the Congress, or indeed most foreign policy and defense officials within the administration itself.

Though there is something delicious, almost celebratory, about the President's method of unveiling Star Wars, few today would argue that it was wise. The March 23 announcement, in the midst of the Euromissile controversy in the Atlantic Alliance and the related Soviet "peace offensives," quickly became a problem in U.S. relations with the Soviet Union and Europe. It was also a less than auspicious launch for Star Wars at home, because the administration seemed ill-prepared to defend the President's vision against the many critics who immediately attacked it. The idea seemed half-baked.

But several years have passed. The arguments have sharpened, and the acrimony has passed on. As the essays in this book make plain, there is now a policy on strategic defense and a coherent opposing position. It is now reasonable to ask what the Star Wars proposal really consists of and what are its primary intellectual roots.

THE STAR WARS POLICY

In the March 23 speech, President Reagan explained the first step toward implementing his vision: a "comprehensive and intensive effort to define a long-term research and development program to begin to achieve our ultimate goal of eliminating the threat posed by strategic nuclear missiles." The commission set up to accomplish this—commonly called the Fletcher Commission, after its Chairman, NASA administrator James Fletcher—yielded in short order the SDI organization in the Pentagon, under the direction of Lt. Gen. James Abrahamson.

So today SDI is a research program, constrained by the ABM Treaty as the administration reads it, in search of technologies for the destruction of ballistic nuclear missiles in flight.

On February 20, 1985, Paul Nitze, the President's senior arms control advisor, explained the administration's "strategic con-

cept," the rationale for this research, in an address to the World
Affairs Council of Philadelphia. Nitze said:

During the next ten years, the U.S. objective is a radical reduction in the
power of existing and planned offensive nuclear arms, as well as the
stabilization of the relationship between offensive and defensive nuclear
arms, whether on earth or in space. We are even now looking forward to
a period of transition to a more stable world, with greatly reduced levels
of nuclear arms and an enhanced ability to deter war based upon an
increasing contribution of non-nuclear defenses against offensive nuclear
arms. This period of transition could lead to the eventual elimination of
all nuclear arms, both offensive and defensive. A world free of nuclear
arms is an ultimate objective to which we, the Soviet Union, and all other
nations can agree.

Nitze's explication of that four-sentence text did much to
define a consensus approach within the administration on a policy
emphasizing Star Wars.

In particular, Nitze outlined criteria for evaluating the feasibility of the Star Wars technologies that embodied responses to
the first round of criticism of the program. Nitze said:

The technologies must produce defensive systems that are *survivable;* if
not, the defenses would themselves be tempting targets for a first strike.
This would decrease rather than enhance stability.

New defensive systems must also be *cost-effective at the margin—*
that is, they must be cheap enough to add additional defensive capability
so that the other side has no incentive to add additional offensive capability to overcome the defense. If this criterion is not met, the defensive
systems could encourage a proliferation of countermeasures and additional offensive weapons to overcome deployed defenses instead of a
redirection of effort from offense to defense.

As I said, these criteria are demanding. If the new technologies
cannot meet these standards, we are not about to deploy them.

In addition to assuming this new posture in the debate about
the technology of Star Wars, Nitze's text provided answers to the
questions about the political and doctrinal stance of the United
States in the envisioned transition to a strategic environment
dominated by defensive weapons. Saying that "we would see the
transition period as a cooperative endeavor with the Soviets" that
would be "tricky," Nitze stressed that "we would have to avoid a
mix of offensive and defensive systems that, in a crisis, would give
one side or the other incentives to strike first."

Nitze further argued that:

the concept is wholly consistent with deterrence. In both the transition and ultimate phases, deterrence would continue to provide the basis for the U.S.-Soviet strategic relationship.

Deterrence requires that a potential opponent be convinced that the risks and costs of aggression far outweigh the gains he might hope to achieve. The popular discussion of deterrence has focused almost entirely on one element—that is, posing to an aggressor high potential costs through the ultimate threat of nuclear retaliation.

But deterrence can also function if one has the ability, through defense and other military means, to deny the attacker the gains he might otherwise have hoped to realize. Our intent is to shift the deterrent balance from one which is based primarily on the ultimate threat of devastating nuclear retaliation to one in which non-nuclear defenses play a greater and greater role. We believe the latter provides a far sounder basis for a stable and reliable strategic relationship.

DETERRENCE

Deterrence. A "holy word" in the vocabulary of nuclear policy but a somewhat strange idea. Thinking about deterrence can produce a strong feeling that the nuclear world is a world of mirrors.

What is deterrence? In its broadest form, deterrence is simply the idea that one party in a dispute can assume a posture that preemptively dissuades the other party from acting in some undesirable way. But nuclear deterrence has come to be associated with a particular kind of posture designed to persuade potential enemies not to attack us.

Two adversaries face each other across a table. Each holds a loaded pistol aimed straight at the other's heart. Each can certainly kill the other, but each knows that to fire is suicide, for if one fires, the other's weapon will surely discharge, leaving both dead. This is the classic image of the nuclear balance of terror in which the United States and the Soviet Union have become trapped. It is called "mutual vulnerability" these days, but the more familiar name for this posture is "mutual assured destruction," or MAD.

Some in this volume argue that MAD is not a military strategy—a plan for the use of nuclear weapons in war to obtain a desired gain—but simply a name for the reality of our age. They believe that the weapons themselves determine their own singular function—to prevent others from using similar weapons against us. Our nuclear arsenal exists and must be maintained in a state as convinces any potential aggressor that an attack with nuclear weapons on the United States or our allies would produce unacceptable consequences in the form of retaliation.

So our offensive nuclear weapons are our defenses. This is deterrence by the threat of punishment. In some sense, this approach to war prevention in the nuclear age does seem an irreducible consequence of the nature of the weapons themselves. Thus MAD has been with us since each side had enough bombs and delivery systems to destroy the other's society regardless of who struck first. However, the "strong sense" of MAD—the idea that nuclear war would amount to two massive spasms of firepower, Armageddon pure and simple—has never been American policy. As nuclear strategist Colin Gray argues, every American president in the nuclear age has wanted an alternative to indiscriminate retaliation against an aggressor's civilian population as the basis for our security.

From the beginning, there have been ideas and efforts—extending even to efforts for strategic defense at times when technology was much less advanced—to make the world less MAD. The doctrine of "counterforce" was the main alternative to emerge before Star Wars. Called "nuclear war-fighting" by critics who fear it makes war more likely, counterforce is a strategy in a way that MAD is not. It is about plans for the use of nuclear weapons against an adversary's military and political targets, not its society as a whole. Advocates of counterforce argue that the only real way to deter nuclear aggression is to have the capacity to respond with flexibility and against targets of specific military value. They contend that as only a credible threat can deter, the threat to use nuclear weapons in relatively limited ways is more likely to keep the peace because it is more likely to be believed.

The opponents of counterforce respond, however, that the threat to use nuclear weapons in ostensibly limited ways is more believable because it appears to make this kind of nuclear use less dangerous. But such a belief, they argue, is baseless—MAD cannot be avoided. Thus they say that raising the credibility of the nuclear threat also raises the prospect of nuclear destruction.

THE INTELLECTUAL ROOTS OF STAR WARS

Where did the idea of Star Wars come from? In part from attacks on both MAD and counterforce, the principal forms of offense-dominated deterrence, meaning deterrence through the threat of punishment.

Numbers on both the political Left and Right have advanced the view that it is simply wrong to hold hostage millions of civilians in another society. Deterrence through the threat of annihilation is immoral, even if the threat is intended to keep the peace and even if the mass destruction would be only "collateral damage" in strikes aimed at military targets.

The argument is that nuclear weapons are not usable weapons at all. Any use of them is likely to produce destruction on a scale disproportionate to any provocation, however great. Thus, by ignoring the moral requirement to punish only the guilty and to use only as much force to resist attack as is compatible with the protection of the values under attack, the use of nuclear weapons would violate the ancient and honored "just war" tradition in moral philosophy. Furthermore, there is the derivative claim that it is wrong to threaten to do what it would be wrong to do.

In their 1983 pastoral letter, the American Catholic bishops laid out the view that deterrence is morally questionable. On the one hand, they said that the maintenance of nuclear retaliatory forces can be credited with having prevented a third world war while protecting the values of democratic society, but these benefits have been achieved by means of a willingness to use nuclear weapons—to participate, on this view, in genocide. Ultimately, the bishops endorsed traditional deterrence as a lesser evil among bad policy choices but offered little comfort on the basic question of the morality of the policy.

Like its morality, the very rationality of MAD can be questioned. What sense does it make, some have asked in recent years, to rely for the security of everything we value on the good judgment of our opponents? In the peculiar logic of MAD, our safety rests on other parties being dissuaded from attacking us because they fear for their own safety. But what if they do not believe we will retaliate? What if they are simply crazy and do not care whether we will retaliate? Then we have no safety at all.

Compounding these moral and logical difficulties is a growing recognition of the actuarial riskiness of MAD. Nuclear deterrence must work twenty-four hours a day, seven days a week, year in and year out, forever, or at least until the world is remade in some profound way. If it ever fails, the consequences may well cancel out decades of apparent success. Even if deterrence seems robust today and there is no need for great worry about its collapse tomorrow, the simple fact that it must work perfectly for so long in so many unforeseen circumstances creates unease.

Beyond these abstract concerns about MAD, there are several more immediate strategic problems. First is the general dissatisfaction with the process of arms control. Though attacks on the nuclear arms limitations regime that has been negotiated since the 1960s have come much more from the political Right than from the Left, there is no dispute that in the period of arms control, the nuclear arsenals of the superpowers have grown dramatically bigger and more sophisticated. While many believe that the world is at least somewhat safer than it would have been without arms control, few believe that the arms control years have contributed to safety in any absolute sense.

Though schemes have always existed for the negotiation of radical reductions in the nuclear arsenals, in the period before the Star Wars debate they always seemed implausible, whatever their potency today. The argument against arms control as a savior is simply that if the degree of trust and cooperation required to pull off substantial agreements were possible, the agreements might well not be necessary and the arsenals might well not exist. The overall political relationship between the superpowers controls their arms; arms control does not dictate their politics.

The second strategic factor contributing to the push for Star Wars is the view that has grown up in the last decade that the Soviet Union is seeking, and may be achieving, "nuclear superiority." Most of the impulses that combine to produce a broad frustration with MAD are felt across the political spectrum. Not so the fear of nuclear inferiority, which resides on the Right. In more conservative quarters, there has been concern for some time about a nuclear "window of vulnerability" for the United States, a specific weakness in our nuclear posture that undermines deterrence by making our threat to retaliate less convincing.

The argument goes like this: The Soviets have relentlessly

increased the size and technical capability of their arsenal of the most threatening form of nuclear weapons—land-based missiles. Some believe the Soviets now possess the right combination of weapons numbers and accuracy to launch a militarily effective surprise attack against the strategic forces of the United States— a nuclear Pearl Harbor. Using just a third of their intercontinental missiles, the Soviets might be able to destroy 90 percent of our land-based missiles and that portion of our bombers and submarines caught on the ground or in port.

What would an American president do if such an attack were launched against the United States? It is argued that being even "technically" vulnerable to such a potent preemptive attack is unacceptable because it would leave us with no choice but suicide or surrender. The President could order retaliation against the Soviet Union by the surviving American nuclear forces, mostly the submarines at sea when the attack came. This would utterly destroy the Soviet Union but would not avoid the utter destruction of the United States by the yet more massive Soviet second strike against us. Why would the President do it? Retaliation would be futile, but the only alternative would be acquiescence to whatever demands were made by the other side.

But the counterpoint is that the window of vulnerability is not really open wide enough for the Soviets to get through. In an essay that follows, former Defense Secretary Robert McNamara comments:

Those who accept this first-strike scenario view the Soviet ICBMs and the men who command them as decoupled from the real world. They assume that Soviet leaders would be confident that these highly complex systems, which have only been tested individually in a quiet environment, would perform their tasks in perfect harmony during the most cataclysmic battle in history; that our electronic eavesdropping satellites would detect no hint of the intricate preparations that such a strike would require; that we would not launch our missiles when the attack is detected; that the thousands of submarine-based and airborne warheads that would surely survive would not be used against a wide array of vulnerable Soviet military targets; and finally, that we would not use those vast surviving forces to retaliate against the Soviet population, even though tens of millions of Americans would be killed by the Soviet attack on our silos. Only madmen would contemplate such a gamble. Whatever else they may be, I do not believe the Soviet leaders are mad.

Whether the Russians would ever launch a first strike against us cannot ultimately be known. McNamara's view, echoed in large measure by President Reagan's own Commission on Strategic Forces, headed by Gen. Brent Scowcroft, gives good reasons for believing that a Soviet first strike is not imminent, even that the Russians are not purposefully planning to attack us. The Soviet development of a force with such a capability, however, remains extremely troublesome. Given the vast expense of first-strike weapons, building them is nonsensical if it is not intended to provide some sort of advantage.

Recently, the debate about what the Soviets intend their formidable nuclear arsenal for, about whether they believe they can "fight and win a nuclear war," has been tied into growing discussions of a Soviet strategic defense program. As illustrated in the contribution to this volume by Secretary of Defense Caspar Weinberger, some argue that our efforts in the field of strategic defense research are not so much an initiative as a response to the Soviet's own work in this area.

The Soviets have the world's only operational ABM system. They spend enormous sums and devote many thousands of their men in uniform to air defense. They have long demonstrated a commitment to passive or civil defense, including bomb shelters and the like. They are widely felt to be in violation of the ABM Treaty in the construction of a large phased-array radar at Krasnoyarsk in Siberia. Finally, they have already put in years of work on the exotic technologies associated with Star Wars.

There are also strategic concerns that have helped to lay the intellectual foundation for Star Wars that relate to threats other than that of deliberate Soviet attack, namely, accidental war and the use of nuclear weapons against the United States by some nation other than the Soviet Union, or even by terrorists.

Thus, Soviet nuclear doctrine and capabilities, especially the potential vulnerability of our land-based forces to Soviet missiles and their own apparent attraction to the concept of defense against nuclear attack, add to a range of concerns about a world where nuclear weapons may spread. These concrete fears combine in people's minds with sharp criticism about the morality and rationality of deterrence in its traditional offense-dominated form, the stability of the deterrent regime in the long term, and the effectiveness of arms control in substantially reducing the nuclear danger. As a result, the structure on which we have based our security and the protection of our values seems to many to be weakening at its very foundation.

Finally, in addition to the intellectual impulses that have spurred the search for an alternative to the present strategic order, there are political factors as well. It is surely no coincidence that President Reagan's Star Wars speech came in the midst of the largest groundswell of public concern about the nuclear danger in decades—the freeze campaign. The political ingenuity of the speech was to take much of the wind out of the sails of the President's critics on both the Left and the Right, both in the peace movement and among those principally concerned with the window of vulnerability. On the one hand, Star Wars puts the President himself on record as a supporter of antinuclear goals. On the other, it quiets the fears of those who have questioned whether he could muster the political strength to do, on the offensive side, what it would take to enhance our retaliatory capabilities—to put mobile missiles in someone's backyard. The almost comic-opera quality of the debate about basing the MX missile reveals the President's need to find some fundamentally different approach to reducing our vulnerability to Soviet ballistic missiles.

The greatest single source of energy driving the idea of strategic defense is, however, less abstract. It is technical advance, the simple fact that, despite the enormous difficulty of the project today, some sort of defense against nuclear attack is clearly more nearly possible than it has ever been.

TECHNICAL FEASIBILITY

Strategic defense as a project, rather than a doctrine or vision, is a problem for scientists and engineers. Can they do it? The answer is no, yes, and no one knows yet, depending on what is meant by "it."

In the first months after the President's March 23 speech, the debate about Star Wars focused on the technical aspects of the idea. The loudest critics of the proposal seemed to be within the scientific community. Since then, the strategic implications of Star Wars have become prominent, and the sharpness of the technical debate has been somewhat blunted. Clearly, there is much real disagreement about the feasibility and the cost of technologies designed to defend against nuclear attack, but some degree of consensus is worth noting.

Ballistic missiles and the nuclear weapons they carry can be intercepted and destroyed at various phases in their flight, so at least some of the weapons of Star Wars could work. But nothing human beings do is perfect. One need not be a scientist to endorse the scientific consensus that a leak-proof shield is not possible in the foreseeable future.

The "no" about strategic defense technology is thus about fulfilling literally the President's call to render nuclear weapons "impotent and obsolete." Project head General Abrahamson has said, "A perfect astrodome defense is not a realistic thing." On the other hand, the consensus "yes" is that a partial defense should prove possible from the research program now underway. Along these lines, leading Star Wars critic Robert McNamara has said, "technology today is capable of shooting down offensive missiles."

Under the heading of whether it can be done, then, the primary questions are about the degree of effectiveness, short of perfection, that strategic defense systems can be expected to attain and the costs and difficulty of achieving this level.

The proposals for strategic defense systems begin with descriptions of the attacking force at work. It takes only a half hour for a nuclear missile to travel from Siberia to a target in the United States. During this time the weapon passes through a number of distinct phases of flight. First, the boost phase. At present there are several minutes from the time a missile leaves its silo until its main engines are spent and it has left the earth's atmosphere, entering orbit. It is generally believed that for the overall system to be substantially effective, the technology for intercepting enemy missiles in the boost phase is the most vital. It is at this point that missiles are easiest to detect; they are like ten-story buildings rocketing off the ground with the intense heat of their engines trailing behind. Also, in the boost phase one "kill" destroys all the warheads carried.

Next the missile enters the postboost phase, a stage also lasting several minutes. The main engines having fallen away, the vehicle, called a "bus," maneuvers through space powered by a smaller engine. The bus drops off its cargo of multiple, independently-targeted reentry vehicles (MIRVs), each carrying a nuclear bomb directed at a separate target. The bus may also carry hundreds of decoys to confuse the opponent about the nature of the attack.

The midcourse phase follows postboost as the warheads and decoys begin their twenty-minute fall back to earth. Finally, there is the terminal phase, when the bombs and decoys reach the earth's upper atmosphere approximately 60 miles above their targets. The flight of a nuclear warhead ends two minutes later when its bomb detonates.

The primary approach currently under study to intercept these weapons is one of a layered defense, or defense-in-depth. Different sorts of weapons would attack the enemy missiles throughout their flight, destroying some percentage in each phase. If there was one layer of defense corresponding to each of the four phases of missile flight, each 70 percent effective, the overall system would stop 99 percent of the warheads.

A defense system of this sort would certainly involve several different kinds of weapons, but the weapons are only the hands of the full organism. Equally important are the information collecting and processing components—the brain and nerves of the system.

An overall strategic defense system must include machines for (1) surveillance, to locate potential targets; (2) discrimination, to determine which threatening objects are real targets and which are decoys; (3) pointing and tracking, to aim and guide the weapons; (4) kill assessment, to determine whether a target has been destroyed; and (5) battle management, to coordinate all of the information necessary for the total system.

Little of this technology exists today, but work is underway in each of these areas. The weapons concepts that are being considered are varieties of directed-energy and kinetic-energy devices.

Beam Weapons

LASERS

Among the directed-energy, or beam, weapons are several types of lasers and neutral-particle beams. Lasers are devices that produce high-powered, concentrated beams of light along a single wavelength. Potentially, they can be focused over great distances to burn holes in enemy missiles or, in the case of pulsing lasers, to hit the target with a great instantaneous impact.

The most powerful lasers that now exist are chemical lasers, beams produced by the reaction of gases such as hydrogen and fluorine. Chemical lasers as usable weapons, however, would have to be ten times more powerful than any that exist today. Further, because their beams diffuse somewhat over distance, they must be kept locked on a target for several seconds in order to destroy it, during which time an enemy missile would move approximately twenty miles. In addition, chemical lasers would require perfectly smooth mirrors perhaps thirty to fifty feet in diameter in order to remain focused. Because they do not require huge power plants, chemical lasers could be parked in low earth orbit in order to keep constantly in range of Soviet missiles on the ground.

The question of the required number of such laser battle stations in orbit has raised great controversy among scientists. Based on different assumptions about the launch sites of Soviet missiles, the power of the lasers, and the required time for re-aiming from one target to another, among other things, estimates have ranged from 100 to 1,600, at a cost of perhaps one billion dollars each.

Alternative beam systems, such as electron and excimer lasers, use shorter wavelengths. Free-electron lasers pass huge numbers of electrons through vibrating magnets, generating ultraviolet light. Excimer lasers use combinations of rare gases to generate their ultraviolet beams. Because of their shorter wavelengths, these beams can be fired through the earth's atmosphere. This is essential, because the enormous power requirements of such devices would dictate that they be based on earth. In order to destroy 2,000 targets, these weapons might need as much energy in a few minutes as New York City consumes in several hours.

These short-wavelength lasers are said to have become the favored Star Wars weapons system in the Pentagon because of the rapid advance of this technology. In principle, they could be fired from mountaintops to mirrors in high orbit. These geosynchronous mirrors, kept hovering over one spot on the earth's surface, would reflect the beams to battle mirrors in low earth orbit, where they would be aimed at missiles or warheads.

This concept looks more cost-effective than space-based chemical laser satellites because there is much less weight to carry into orbit and because the constraints of power supply are less pressing. It suffers the same defect, however, regarding the need for giant and flawless mirrors in space and the even more intractable problem that, to date, these high-powered beams have destroyed mirrors instead of reflecting off them.

Last in the laser category is the X-ray laser. This weapon would, theoretically, use the energy of a hydrogen bomb explosion to create powerful beams of X-rays. These "third-generation" nuclear weapons are the defense concept preferred by hydrogen bomb physicist Edward Teller, one of the men who first brought the idea of Star Wars to the attention of President Reagan.

Among the advantages of X-ray lasers is that the beams generated are so powerful that they need no "dwell time" on a target, as do the other lasers; they destroy what they hit immediately. Also, they would require less precision in aiming, because such a beam would be powerful at a width of perhaps several hundred yards.

But an X-ray laser is a one-shot weapon. It consumes itself in its operation. It is also fratricidal, destroying even "friendly" objects nearby when the beam-generating bomb goes off.

Equally important, the X-ray laser has a political problem. President Reagan has spoken often of his desire to base our defense on nonnuclear technologies, and this is a requirement that X-ray lasers cannot meet. Further, the stationing of hydrogen bombs in low orbit above the Soviet Union, even for ostensibly defensive purposes, might be highly provocative. As a result, X-ray lasers have been primarily discussed as "pop-up" weapons, which would be launched from the earth at the earliest sign of an attack. They are the only Star Wars weapons that might be suitable in size and firing speed for such a procedure. However, in order to reach space quickly enough to fire down on Soviet missiles during boost, the launchers would have to be located in submarines kept close to the periphery of the Soviet Union, perhaps making the submarines themselves vulnerable to preemptive attack.

Additionally, X-ray lasers may not be able to penetrate deeply into the atmosphere. If the Soviets shorten the boost phase of their missiles by developing "fast-burn" launchers that would complete their work in under 100 seconds and inside the atmosphere, the popped-up laser would have neither sufficient time nor range to be effective in the boost phase.

Even if the Soviets do develop fast-burn boosters, X-ray lasers may still have a place in a defensive system. They would be effective in the postboost and midcourse phases, but perhaps not at a reasonable cost. A one-shot weapon might be impractical if used against the large number of targets present in the middle phases of the attack.

PARTICLE BEAMS

Besides lasers, there is another variety of directed-energy weapon—the particle beam. Particle beams could penetrate a missile's skin and destroy its internal mechanisms. Because they would so penetrate, they would not be susceptible to some of the countermeasures anticipated against lasers, such as coating missiles with reflective material or spinning them to increase the dwell time necessary to kill. However, precisely because a particle beam destroys its target internally, it is difficult to assess when the job is done so that the beam can be retargeted.

Most particle beams are even less effective in the atmosphere than X-rays, making them primarily useful as postboost and midcourse weapons. Furthermore, even in space, charged-particle beams would be bent off course by the earth's magnetic field, so the beams would have to be made neutral. But the neutral-particle beam weapon has another difficulty. These machines might well be eighty feet long and weigh fifty to one hundred tons. At present there is no means to lift such machines into space. The cargo capacity of the space shuttle, for example, is thirty-three tons.

There is one type of charged-particle beam, the electron beam, that can (actually must) operate inside the atmosphere. This is a possibility for terminal defense, but such beams can now be controlled only over very short distances, much less than the several-mile range required for a terminal weapon.

Looking down the road, SDI researchers are exploring even more remote beam technologies, such as gamma-ray lasers and plasmoids. For the present, while the directed-energy weapons are lethal in principle, it is uncertain whether such systems could be relied on as the key instruments of a strategic defense.

Kinetic-Energy Weapons

Much more likely as first-generation weapons for the purpose of defense against nuclear attack are the kinetic-energy weapons, or "cannons in space." These technologies are more readily at hand, though major difficulties remain.

The most developed kinetic weapons are ground-based or airborne interceptors carrying "smart rocks," precision-guided projectiles that destroy their targets by smashing into them. Because of the limitations of speed, however, such weapons could only be used for terminal defense. Thus they are merely an updated version of the antiballistic missile weapons that the United States decided not to build in the 1970s on grounds of cost-effectiveness. This kind of defense could perhaps be overwhelmed by increased numbers of offensive weapons.

To use smart rocks against missiles earlier in their flight would require orbiting launch platforms. Like space-based lasers, these weapons would be subject to attack by the full range of antisatellite technologies. Further, Soviet adoption of fast-burn boosters would make it much more difficult for the relatively slow smart rocks to reach the missiles before they released their warheads.

Potentially, the most effective kinetic-energy weapon would be one that is not yet in hand—an electromagnetic railgun. This weapon would generate magnetic fields to accelerate smart rocks to much greater velocities than possible today—ultimately, perhaps, twelve miles per second, compared, for example, to 3,000 feet per second for a bullet fired from an M-16 rifle.

At present, however, railgun technology suffers from many of the defects of the different varieties of beam weapons: the machines are too large, they require too much power, and they tend to self-destruct in firing, all of which makes space basing impractical.

Sensors

As already noted, a strategic defense system would have to be much more than weapons, however potent they might be. Targets that cannot be found and tracked cannot be hit. Thus, sensors are required to accomplish wide-scale and detailed identification of objects in the enormous reaches of space. Ideally, devices must be created that will not only locate objects but discriminate between real targets—the enemy's nuclear warheads—and decoys such as balloons and metallic chaff. Present technology is not up to these tasks. Today's sensors are too heavy to be space based and are not powerful enough to work under the conditions required for application to strategic defense, when, beyond the boost phase, many small, cold, dark objects are spread out across thousands of miles.

Naturally, SDI researchers are at work on the problem. Parallel to the overall concept of the defense system, they are banking on sensors of different kinds working together to locate possible targets and discriminate among them. Radars may find objects coming up from the ground while infrared devices may search for traces of heat and—the major exotic idea in this field—lasers and particle beams may be bounced off space objects to determine if they are warheads or lighter-weight decoys.

Data Processing

It is often argued that the single most difficult piece in the puzzle of Star Wars technology is in the area of information management. The ultimate battle the defense system is supposed to fight would be of unprecedented scale and occur at extraordinary speed. The hardware, or computer machinery, to handle the volume of data involved in such a situation does not yet exist. It has been estimated that the main Star Wars computers would have to process somewhere between 600 million and well over one billion computations per second. Yet, while the usual unclassified description of the best of present technology is 500 million computations per second, most experts seem to agree that the hardware for Star Wars battle management can be built.

It is the software, the programmed instructions, that seems to be the highest hurdle. The task may need from 10 to 100 million lines of software. Critics argue that no one knows how to write such a computer program, that the SDI advocates are counting on leaps in the infant area of artificial intelligence so that computers themselves can help write the software for the Star Wars computers. Moreover, how to test or "de-bug" such a system to allow for confidence that it can be trusted is, at least, unclear.

Power Sources

Many of the complex machines in space that would form the strategic defense system would have voracious appetites for electric power. The battle-management satellites—including sensors, computers, and communication links—might each require as much power as the largest space machine we have yet orbited, Skylab—about seventy-five kilowatts. If, like Skylab, they were powered with huge solar panels, they might be highly vulnerable. The weapons of Star Wars would demand far more energy. Railguns might need one million kilowatts in each discharge, and some of the beam weapons might well have power requirements many times greater than this.

Research is underway to develop chemically powered electric generators and extremely high capacity batteries, but it seems clear that nuclear reactors in space would not be avoidable. Needless to say, this last likelihood is political dynamite.

Space Transportation

Getting the many devices into orbit that may have to be there for an effective strategic defense may pose a major problem. At present, using the space shuttle, the price per pound to orbit is estimated at $1,400 or more. This must be reduced by at least 90 percent in order to make the costs of space basing affordable.

Beyond cost, the likely size of some of the instruments of strategic defense makes them difficult to lift into space. The shuttle would be far too small, so a new "super booster" with 100 tons of cargo capacity would have to be developed.

Soviet Responses

In sharp contrast to the other large-scale technical projects that Star Wars is often compared to—most notably the moon landing—the greatest obstacle in the way of effective strategic defense is not nature but a clever and determined human adversary. Of course, physics provides the ultimate limit on what both the Soviets and we can do, but the much more immediate limits on an American Star Wars program may well be Soviet countermeasures.

First, the Russians can alter the manner of an attack against us. They can cluster their missile launches both in time and place. Most obviously, and at the least cost, they can attempt to overwhelm the defense by producing far more warheads. Their SS-18 missile, for example, is today limited by arms control to ten warheads each but has a capacity of perhaps twenty.

They can also attempt to deceive the defense by a proliferation of decoys. Or, they can try to shield their missiles by coating them with certain materials or spin them in-flight, making them more resistant to many beam weapons. In time, and at considerable expense, they can also replace or supplement their existing offensive missiles with a new generation of fast-burn boosters that, as already indicated, might render far less effective many of the defensive weapons designed to operate in the crucial boost phase.

The Soviets can also seek to turn the Star Wars defense into a kind of high-tech Maginot Line. They can attempt to outflank the defense—in this case go under it—with bombers, cruise missiles of various kinds, low-flying submarine-launched weapons, and perhaps, in the long run, entirely new forms of delivery systems.

There is another whole category of response: to attack the Star Wars system itself. There is an intense debate about how safe space is as a medium for military operations. The advocates of Star Wars argue that the objects that the system will require in space can be made survivable because in the weightless environment they can be armored; in the huge environment they can be maneuvered to evade threats; and in the openness of the environment they can guard themselves, being prepared to shoot in their own defense. But the opponents of Star Wars argue that objects in space are far more vulnerable than any on earth. They are "sitting ducks" following precisely calculable orbits that take them over enemy territory.

Many varieties of antisatellite weapons have been suggested. Some, like space mines for the Soviets and air-launched homing projectiles for the United States, are already operational. Others, such as ground-based lasers and nuclear-tipped rockets, are readily at hand.

Finally, and most ominously, most of the Star Wars weapons themselves would seem far more certain to be effective against the other side's defenses than against offensive weapons. In other words, World War III might begin with a first strike by one superpower against the other's defensive shield.

Technical Conclusions

For every suggested Soviet response to an American strategic defense effort—from offensive countermeasures to antisatellite weapons systems—there are suggested responses, or, if you will, counter-countermeasures. Thus, in no area of the technical debate is there anything approaching conclusive evidence. Clearly, neither side can be assured of victory.

The proponents of Star Wars like to quote the unfortunate statements some have made in the past that now-familiar technologies would be impossible. For example, Albert Einstein said in 1932, "there is not the slightest indication that [nuclear] energy will ever be obtainable. It would mean that the atom would have to be shattered at will." The opponents, however, speak in terms of Star Wars as "clearly a fallacy." They review the state of the technology and conclude that defenses that would meet Nitze's criteria are beyond reach.

Both sides might benefit from a dose of humility.

THE POLICY DEBATE

Four questions dominate the policy debate about Star Wars: two about whether strategic defense can make a positive contribution to the goal of avoiding nuclear war, and two about its effect on the conduct of a war should deterrence fail.

First, what does Star Wars do to deterrence? Does it make the overall military capability of the United States stronger or weaker as an instrument of war prevention? Second, what does Star Wars do to the prospects for arms control, to efforts to find at least a partial substitute for the prevention of war through military preparation in the form of political accommodation?

Turning to the prospective impact of Star Wars on the waging of a nuclear war, there is, first, a question about the relationship between offensive and defensive forces: What kinds of offensive arms are logically and morally compatible with defense? Second, there is the question of nuclear outcomes. In the event of war, would strategic defense save lives or cost them and, beyond "damage limitation," would it make the postwar world more or less acceptable?

So, should it be done? Notwithstanding President Reagan's vision of a posture of pure defense—assured survival—these questions arise from the one essential certainty about the technology. Since the shield cannot be perfect, it is difficult to foresee how we could put down our sword. That is, defense will not replace offense but will be added to it in some way. It is as though, to return to an earlier metaphor, one or both of the two adversaries pointing pistols at each other across a table put on a bulletproof vest. The kind of pistol or the way the weapon is aimed may also change, but it is the relationship between the pistol and the vest that creates dramatic new concerns.

What follows is a sketch of the four fundamental questions of the debate about imperfect defense. The responses presented are intended to represent the major arguments of both the proponents and opponents of Star Wars. Each side's affirmative case is aired and each is given the opportunity to rebut the critique of its contender.

Star Wars and Deterrence

Proponents: Star Wars would vastly complicate the planning of an attacker. The aggressor would be uncertain how many of his offensive weapons would get through the defense and where they would strike, uncertain, in other words, of the military effectiveness of any planned attack. Further, defense constitutes a far more credible basis for deterrence. Available defenses would certainly be used to deny an attacker his objectives, whereas retaliatory offensive forces might not be used as punishment.

Opponents: The acquisition of defenses by an armed adversary will seem to the opponent like preparation for an attack. Further, in a defended world, even upgraded offensive forces might seem useful only as first-strike weapons. At full strength and with the opponent's defense taken by surprise, military success would seem far more likely as an aggressor than as a retaliator, when remnant forces would face a fully alerted defense. Thus, each side, fearing that the other was seeking a cover from behind which to attack with relative impunity, would have itchy fingers on its offensive nuclear triggers. Moreover, the new basis of deterrence through defense, denial, is more credible only in principle. In practice, the technology will not support sole reliance on defense.

Proponents: The relative premium on a first strike is meaningless if the defense makes a first strike itself militarily ineffective. Thus, a cost-effective Star Wars program makes any use of ballistic missile weapons obsolete.

Opponents: The threat of a first strike is great during the building phase in a defensive transition, because each side knows that the utility of its offensive weapons will be reduced by the completion of the other's defenses.

Proponents: The defensive transition can be managed cooperatively and is not incompatible with simultaneous negotiated reductions in offense. Even if each side pursues defenses unilaterally, each can do so in phases such that they are stabilizing rather than destabilizing, namely, beginning with defenses of military assets. This means that the premium on a first strike is at its highest before the construction of any defenses, which is to say, now. This threat is, however, answered when one takes account of the continuing robustness of the present order of offense-only deterrence. The point of Star Wars is to shift to a sounder basis for the prevention of war in the long term, not to answer an immediate likelihood of the failure of the present system.

Opponents: A negotiated transition is preposterous on its face. One of the driving forces behind the appeal of Star Wars is dissatisfaction with the arms control process to date, but the level of cooperation required for the superpowers to manage the introduction of defenses jointly is many orders of magnitude greater than that needed for limitations of offensive arms alone. If such a degree of cooperation were possible, it would not be necessary for these two nations to defend themselves against each other at such expense.

Similarly, it is hypocritical for the advocates of Star Wars to rely on the robustness of the present deterrent regime as the answer to the first-strike premium created during the transition period. They suggest great weaknesses and vulnerabilities that require the enormous and admittedly dangerous effort of strategic defense to replace offense-only deterrence, yet they believe that this same flawed system is sufficiently reliable to handle the obvious risks created by the provocative nature of Star Wars.

Star Wars and Arms Control

Proponents: The United States could not persuade the Soviets to accept MAD as a doctrine by reason alone (the Russians pursued militarily useful weapons systems despite the logic of MAD) but perhaps we can persuade them to reduce their offensive weapons by the force of a new technological situation in which the cost advantage clearly favors the defense. Historical analogies are relevant. It did not become physically impossible following World War I to use horses in combat, it just became clearly irrational to do so. Nations stopped using what had been for centuries a most formidable weapon.

Opponents: It is unclear at present whether there can be any cost advantage to the defense, much less one that is great enough to make it clearly counterproductive to produce augmented offenses. Indeed, in an environment of only partially effective defenses of uncertain reliability, one of the most reasonable responses is to attempt to overwhelm them by simply adding numbers to the offense.

Further, defense creates enormous technical obstacles to arms control. Simply by virtue of the greatly increased complexity of the strategic environment, the work of even well-meaning negotiators might well be made nearly impossible. And verification, the Achilles heel of arms control, is made yet more difficult by Star Wars.

Proponents: The first of the Nitze criteria for deployment of strategic defense is cost-effectiveness at the margin. If a technological restraint on the continued reliance on ballistic missiles is not created, there will be no strategic defense. Thus the defense that can be overwhelmed is a straw man. So are negotiations that are too complicated to be concluded when the parties have a sincere desire to reach agreement.

Opponents: Nuclear deterrence seeks to influence the perceptions and intentions, as well as the capabilities, of one's opponent. Star Wars will create increased fear in the wake of the offense/defense weapons spiral that is its likely consequence. The minimum requirement for political accommodation as a substitute for military preparation in working toward the goal of preventing a war is building trust and breaking down the psychological barriers that divide the powers.

Proponents: Arms control is not based on trust. It is based on what can best be characterized as objective common interest.

Thus, if strategic defense alters the objective rationality of offensive weapons, arms control to limit these weapons becomes more likely.

Opponents: Even if Star Wars created objective common interest, it might not be visible enough to overcome the psychology of destabilization bred in the vastly more complex strategic environment.

Star Wars and Offensive Forces

Opponents: There are two trends in technological advance and doctrinal revision that attempt both to increase the credibility of the deterrent—that is, to raise the certainty that the means of deterrence would actually be used in the event of war—and to allow a more morally acceptable course of action in the event of war. These are counterforce and strategic defense. They are incompatible. One attempts to make offensive weapons useless, while the other attempts to make them more potent and precise instruments.

Proponents: The ratio between the effectiveness of the offense and of the defense may not be the same between the United States and the Soviet Union. Either their defense may not be as good as our defense, or our offense may be better at getting through their defense than theirs is at getting through ours.

Further, a question must be raised about the time horizon at issue. Perhaps ultimately, defenses would reach the point where it would no longer be possible to target accurately, but this is only to say that at some point effective defenses would render all offensive ballistic missiles obsolete. This is the end point for Star Wars.

Opponents: First, to presume a long-lived American technical superiority over the Soviets in defense—at least to any militarily significant degree—is wishful thinking, contradicted by the record of the Soviets' catching us in field after field of military know-how.

The second argument of the proponents on this point again relies on a degree of obvious advantage in defensive effectiveness that is extremely unlikely, but a defense of almost any effectiveness would be sufficient to make it impossible to be confident of one's ability to conduct limited or discriminant attacks. How would a planner know which of his weapons would survive and which targets they would hit? Thus, ironically, Star Wars restores MAD, and in an even more dangerous form.

Proponents: The Soviet Union has never accepted the vulnerability of its homeland, and certainly not of its military and political assets. It has done everything that is technologically possible to develop strategic defenses ranging from civil defense to air defense to ABMs and to research on exotic technologies. Despite what the Russians say, there is no reason to think that they would not deploy Star Wars systems if and when they could construct them. It is naive to believe that our program in this area is showing them the light about defense.

At the same time, they have developed counterforce-capable offensive systems and continue to improve them. Thus in the short run we must improve our offensive capabilities (which means making them both more survivable against Soviet attack and more flexible for retaliatory purposes), and we must move ahead with defense as technology permits.

In sum, our counterforce may be incompatible with Soviet defense, but it is not incompatible with our having a defense, and we must have that defense because of their counterforce capability and their potential defensive capability.

Opponents: The American Star Wars system cannot be justified on the basis of a hypothetical Soviet Star Wars system. First, they do not yet have one, and there is little doubt that the Soviets' much-discussed present capabilities for defense against nuclear attack would be utterly ineffective. Furthermore, their fear that we might outpace them technologically (not by any means a guarantee that we *would* outpace them) and their desire to avoid the costs of such a new arms competition (which we should share) might well enable us to negotiate verifiable arms control that insures that neither side deploys defenses—simply a reinvigoration of the ABM regime.

The American Star Wars system also cannot be justified on the basis of the present window of vulnerability because, however widely the window is open, it can be closed with more certainty and at much lower cost by other means. Examples are the mobile

Midgetman missile, which could also improve our ability to strike Soviet offensive targets, or even earth-bound defenses directed at the terminal phase of missile flight in order to protect our offensive forces. Nothing is gained by our taking the front line of strategic competition into space.

Proponents: If the Soviets would agree to a comprehensive ban on defense technologies, it would represent a fundamental judgment on their part that we could develop an effective system, indeed a more effective system than theirs. Why should we think less of ourselves than they think of us? Further, cost is hardly an issue for the Soviet regime. In any event, the argument about such an agreement begs the issue at hand; we would only want such a treaty if Star Wars were not in our interest, that is, if it did not make the world safer. But that is what we are debating.

Further, the Midgetman, the submarine missile D-5, and other counterforce weapons cannot substitute for defense as a means of fundamentally and permanently reducing American vulnerability, but they are a logical bridge to defense from the technology of orthodox MAD.

Star Wars and Nuclear Outcomes

Opponents: More weapons would go off in a nuclear exchange if both sides had defenses than in the present offense-only situation. It is in the nature of military planning that each superpower will overestimate the effectiveness of the other's defense and will underestimate the reliability of its own offense. In compensation, both by adding offensive forces and by utilizing redundant countermeasures, each will overwhelm the other's defense and cause more weapons to fall than otherwise would have been the case.

Proponents: In this argument the critics of Star Wars again rely on unprovable assumptions about technology. They assume both that the decision will be made to augment offensive forces rather than decrease them in the face of a clearly effective defense, and that countermeasures will restore the advantage to the offense. But a clearly leaky and fragile system will not be built. It is a straw man.

Opponents: One need not be a technological pessimist to believe that defense would make a bad situation worse. Improvements in offensive systems and other countermeasures are themselves feats of high technology. At present, the burden of proof is on those who argue that Star Wars can be survivable and cost-effective, because at present the advantage is clearly with the offense both on earth and, because of antisatellite technology, in space.

Proponents: Star Wars seeks to change the outcome of a nuclear conflict, and it is largely through this means that it seeks to increase the likelihood of preventing one. The system offers the only hope of avoiding "nuclear winter" in the event of a full-scale nuclear exchange—if indeed the worst of the calculations about such a world-ending phenomenon are correct. It also offers the only direct and common-sense approach in the effort to attain the goal of a politically and morally acceptable outcome for nuclear war. The goal is to save lives and protect the values and institutions of a free society.

Moreover, what are the alternatives to defense in the event of a failure of deterrence? Schemes for "war termination" are entirely implausible. Whether the parties are fighting "rationally," believing it is in their interest to do so, or because they are insane, there is no reason to believe they would follow prenegotiated rules for stopping the war. The real choice would be suicide or surrender.

Opponents: Even if the defense technology worked as well as ardent supporters foresee in the reasonably near term, the consequences of nuclear war would remain unimaginably awful and in no way morally tolerable. Star Wars is thus another in the war-fighting delusions that ignore the irreducible reality that unacceptable destruction is the only likely consequence of the use of nuclear weapons.

Proponents: While the possibility of mass destruction certainly remains beyond the ability of any presently conceivable defensive system to eliminate, this is not the issue. The issue is the effect of defenses on the likelihood of such destruction. If defenses would make war less likely and/or the technology would permit some damage limitation in the event of war and some enhancement of chances for an acceptable political order in the postwar world, then we would be safer than we are today.

SCHOOLS OF THOUGHT

Nuclear issues act like a powerful whirlpool. Thinking about the bomb draws a person in—through the shallows of analyzing the past and present capabilities of the superpowers, to the moderate depths of questions about technology and strategy, deeper still to judgments about the fundamental effect of the nuclear danger on international relations and military preparation and to judgments about the world roles of the Soviet Union and the United States and, ultimately, to great depths at which a primary moral decision must be made: What is right in the nuclear age, given what is possible? It is essential, then, in talking to, rather than past, each other on these issues, to adopt a policy of full-disclosure. Commentators must be willing to argue explicitly for whatever hierarchy of values they start from when they begin to study this area and that guide them to whatever policy conclusions they reach.

The Star Wars debate is not resolvable on its own terms, from within. One spins from argument to counter-argument to counter-counter-argument. Most seem plausible. At the level of thought represented in this book, genuine errors of reasoning are rare. Yet, while either side may be correct in a formal sense, neither at present can prove enough of the components of its position to dispose the issue plainly.

Much of the argument about Star Wars rests on conclusions about technology. It almost seems that the policy debate should be put on hold, that the fundamental question is whether the SDI research program can produce systems that meet Nitze's criteria of cost-effectiveness at the margin and survivability. On this level, the debate will have an empirical answer; someday it will be known who is right. But this is entirely too happy a way to phrase the issue. On the one hand, it is highly unlikely that the answer will be known with sufficient certainty to quiet all dissent, regardless of the effectiveness of whatever defense technologies are developed. On the other hand, the very scope and scale of this debate produce a strong sense that more is at issue than can be laid to rest by even quite definitive technical answers.

So, why do the two sides think what they think? Here the issues get deeper. A clarification of the larger worldviews into which the Star Wars camps fit, and the fundamental moral judgments that lie behind these worldviews, does not so much demystify the question as reveal the mystical character at its heart.

The first level down from the policy debate about defense is that of the schools of thought on nuclear policy in general. For all the unavoidable weaknesses of paradigms, it is a valuable exercise to describe them.

Reformism

How much does the bomb change the nature of international relations and military preparation? The "reformist" school would say, a great deal. Comparing the past forty years to the prenuclear world, while much of the life of nations has gone on as usual, there has also been a crucial departure. Despite their quite deeply rooted status as adversaries, the political objectives of the superpowers have been moderated, each has been forced to give weight to the interests of the other.

On the purpose of military power in the nuclear age, the argument in the reformist camp is one for sufficiency, a threshold concept of power that sees more than "enough" as dangerously provocative. Nuclear weapons have no military use. Their only purpose is to prevent others from using them. Naturally, there are many shades of difference between those with either a more or a less elastic definition of enough, between those who are either more or less willing to seek security through redundancy, but the basic point remains.

Classicism

In the view of the "classicist" school, however, while the destructiveness of nuclear weapons clearly raises the stakes of international life and creates an obvious need for caution and restraint in pursuit of political objectives, the bases of relations between nations and the purposes of military preparation are essentially unchanged. Wars are prevented by military advantage, by strength. Nuclear policy must aim at a credible threat, which means—independent of what one "wants"—the threat to fight and win. Naturally, there is a spectrum within this camp as well; there is either more or less stress on the possibility of victory in a nuclear war.

Both the reformist and classicist schools of thought are, of course, subject to further division along many axes. Perhaps the most significant subcategories are the Right and the Left on each side. A split in the thinking about nuclear issues described by Leon Wieseltier can be overlaid on this outline. The Left, among both the reformists and the classicists, is made up of the "idealists," those who seek and believe in the possibility of final and complete release from the nuclear danger. The Right is made up of the "realists," those who believe the best we can do is to manage the great threat from which there is no real escape.

How does Star Wars fit in? There is an emotionally powerful vision of strategic defense that is an idealist concept: perfect defense. Perhaps this was the President's initial vision. If perfect defense were possible, the reformist-classicist division would be transcended. In terms of the policy debate that has been sketched here, however—the debate about imperfect defense—Star Wars appears as a classicist idea. Military balances between competing nations have always had elements of both offense and defense. The idea of agreed mutual vulnerability simply is a reformist notion.

The worldviews into which the Star Wars camps fit also differ in their judgments of the nature of the Soviet threat and in the basic principles they favor for the role of the United States in the world.

Russians

While across the entire mainstream of our politics there is, on the one hand, an understanding of and opposition to Soviet domestic repression and Soviet expansionism and, on the other hand, a widely shared understanding that the Russians "love their children too," still there are potent disagreements. Some see the Soviet regime as an "evil empire" and believe that Soviet foreign policy is *essentially* aggressive, even if cautious. Others see the Soviets as *essentially* defensive, even if opportunistic.

What is the locus of conflict between these two nuclear giants? Some paint the relationship primarily in moral colors, others primarily in the colors of interest, seeing it as essentially a clash over power.

Star Wars is not logically connected to either of these per-spectives on the Soviet Union in any strict sense, and given the degree of consensus about the nature and purposes of the Soviet regime, the search for a decision about strategic defense might not seem to be advanced much by this outline of differing views on the Russians. Nonetheless, there is more of a connection in fact than in the abstract. Those most concerned by the Soviet threat tend to support Star Wars. They wish for the means for our security to be more firmly under our physical control than in the present nuclear relationship. Those more sanguine about Soviet intentions are far less likely to be supporters of Star Wars.

Americans

Then there is the flip side of the dispute over Soviet objectives in the world, the one over the American place. In the wake of Vietnam, some stress the limits of military power as a means of achieving our international ends. Many stress, as well, limits on the very ends of our foreign policy. This is the stance of noninterventionism, called neo-isolationism by its critics. Just now, in what Charles Krauthammer of The *New Republic* has described as a "three-cornered debate," this approach is countered by two alternatives, known as realism (or realpolitik) and neo-inter-nationalism. Both tend to favor a more broadly activist American posture and both are more congenial to military power, though they divide on the rationale for our role. They also share a rela-tively high priority for competition with the Soviet Union.

NUCLEAR IDEOLOGIES

Could one be a non-interventionist and favor Star Wars? Of course. Indeed, this combination is a high-tech version of the old "Amer-ica First" school. But while some certainly hold this position, it is not prominent in the debate.

Why? Because the dominant views about Star Wars seem to have been combined with other views in much the way disparate symptoms compose a syndrome. Perhaps this is an overstatement; there are some logical connections among the views. But the metaphor does have power. As Wieseltier has written in *Nuclear War, Nuclear Peace:*

The nuclear debate has been infected by ideology. . . . Political positions come in packages. . . . According to *The Nation,* it follows from your opposition to the war in Vietnam that you oppose the free market, or the patriarchal family, or Camp David. According to *Commentary,* it follows from your opposition to the Soviet Union that you oppose environmentalism, or Jacobo Timmerman, or homosexuality.

These packages of positions may certainly be found, despite their apparent randomness. But, at least from the specifics of Star Wars to the level of generality relevant here, are the connections really so obscure? Are the correlations between the contending views on Star Wars and wider ideological positions on security and foreign policy themselves senseless? Perhaps not.

Like the debate about Star Wars, the competing claims about the changes wrought by the bomb, the nature and purposes of the Soviet regime, and the American global role are not susceptible of proof. Neither side can win the argument, at least not in the strict or formal sense. Yet there are forces that, on the one hand, unite the positions that form the two nuclear ideologies, and, on the other hand, keep them apart.

Looking deeper still, at plainly moral judgments and, if you will, prerational impulses rooted in character, the broader structure of the debate may well make sense after all. Beyond the unresolvable technical arguments on nuclear issues, there are still things to be decided. Prior to making policy, we must make peace with ourselves about the fundamental basis of our views.

Across the lines of division both about Star Wars and about the larger related questions, there would certainly be agreement about the following. American nuclear policy should:

1. Make it as unlikely as possible that nuclear war will occur.
2. Make it as likely as possible that, if nuclear war does occur, the outcome will be as favorable as possible.

Put another way, the first goal is to prevent war. The second goal, though, is much more difficult to encapsulate in a simple phrase. For some, the goal is simply to limit physical damage in the event of war. For others, it is to conclude a war on favorable political terms. Obviously, the first of these interpretations belongs to the reformist school, the second to the classicist. The difference may indicate the ultimate source of the two camps. It certainly suggests the roots of the familiar alternate phrasing of goals for nuclear policy: if we do what is best, we should remain "neither red nor dead."

Both the advocates and the critics of Star Wars argue that the policies they favor are best suited to the achievement of all these goals. Perhaps one side is correct, right across the board. It could be. But is it not more likely that the reason there are competing nuclear ideologies is that the pursuit of all the good things we want, at once and in the same way, is not possible?

The orthodox doctrine of the nuclear age, MAD, allowed as an article of faith that our military capabilities, in concert with other instruments, of course, would avoid the need for choice. The belief in "existential deterrence"—that the very existence of such powerful weapons would keep the peace—produced another belief: that there is no substantial conflict in addressing both of the principal threats to our security—war itself and the evil of totalitarianism. Thus, there has been strong confidence that we could avoid having to choose, even in emphasis, between preventing war and limiting damage if war occurs, on the one hand, and being "red and dead" on the other.

Technical advances—the development of counterforce and the possibility of strategic defense—may call this confidence into question. Now that there is more than one thing we can do with and against nuclear weapons, the questions of what really keeps the peace, what kind of peace is worth keeping, and what we want should war occur, all seem more open.

If neither side in the Star Wars debate is completely right, if neither side's view will both best preserve peace and best conduct war, and will best ensure in both peace and war that we remain neither red nor dead, then where are the tensions? Where are the required trade-offs?

Return to the debate about Star Wars itself. The issues about which there is disagreement run parallel to the goals for nuclear policy numbered here—preventing war and conducting it correctly. It is often said that discussions of nuclear issues are complex in the way of images in a house of mirrors, nothing being quite what it seems. But if we remove the mirrors, what is the effect on the debate?

A reasonable and certainly potent argument (even if, like the others, uncertain) is that, on the face of it, the opponents of Star Wars "win" the dispute about the effect of strategic defense on

war prevention. Is it not common sense that advanced and elaborate preparations for war in an environment of political rivalry are
provocative?

On a day-to-day basis, the United States and the Soviet Union
surely overdeter each other greatly. Neither side wakes each
morning to consider as a serious issue whether war would be
rational that day. Whatever the impact of Star Wars on precise
calculations about relative capabilities, and thus on this business
of routine deterrence, strategist Colin Gray has argued that the
real issue on this point is the impact of Star Wars at that one
moment in some crisis when one or both sides actually ask, in fear
and anger, "Am I deterred?" Put another way, is it not likely in a
situation where the superpowers have built weapons intended to
limit the damage from a conflict, that at an instant when war seems
more than possible, the likelihood of conflict is increased?

On the other hand, by the same common sense, do not the
advocates of Star Wars "win" the argument about the effect of
strategic defense on war-fighting? Should deterrence fail, more
flexibility and more resources under our own control seem plainly
preferable.

If nuclear war should occur, is there a strategy for its conduct
other than to seek some sort of victory? There is, of course, the
argument that the goal in a nuclear war is simply to end it. But
this is a moral argument—in effect, a view that just staying alive
would constitute the limits of a nuclear victory. It may be true,
but it is by no means the only possible view. So the point remains
that as Star Wars increases options beyond deterrence, it can look
desirable from this vantage point.

If there is indeed a tension between the best approach to
preserving peace and the best approach to restoring it favorably
in the event of war, how can we decide which to concentrate on?
For what seems the thousandth time, there are questions of fact
the answers to which could help break the impasse. If we could
know how likely war is, even when we do what is best to prevent
it, and if we could know how likely a favorable outcome of war is
when we do what is best to secure it, then we would know far
better how to approach the question of what ends deserve emphasis. But we cannot know such things.

Is there also a tension between the goals of preserving peace
and protecting freedom, a need to rank being red and being dead?

There is an argument that such a decision about priorities is necessary because of a powerful linkage to the prima facie opposition between war prevention and preparation for war. In the abstract, the logical conclusion of the pursuit of peace—the surest way to avoid war—might be surrender. On the other hand, the logical conclusion of the pursuit of freedom—the surest way to eliminate the threat to our values—might be victory.

Thus, preventing being red seems to involve an emphasis on preparedness to fight, while preventing being dead seems to involve an emphasis on preventing war. So there is a haunting possibility that the argument for Star Wars and the ideological position into which it fits—a position that gives priority to the threat of conflict with the Soviet Union and the wisdom of preparing to conduct it favorably—creates greater risks of war, and that the contrary school of thought—focused on preventing war—creates greater risks to freedom.

Naturally, these conclusions are not reflections on the motives of the advocates of either school of thought. In the mainstream of the American political debate at the level of serious thought, there is no one who is "pro-war" and no one who is "pro-communist." Nonetheless, the point is important, for several reasons. First, this line of reasoning reveals the most likely distortions that will occur in the inevitable popular reductions of the competing perspectives. This is just how our politics work. Second, the point carries weight because of the possibility that—even independent of the exaggerating, self-fulfilling effects of the popular versions of these ideologies—it might be true. In other words, the consequences of adopting the dominant packages of attitudes that surround either advocating or opposing Star Wars may well be to make more likely one or another unhappy circumstance.

The end of thinking about Star Wars seems, therefore, to be the same as its beginning: explicitly moral reasoning about ordering our most basic values, about the meaning of life in the nuclear age. Starting from the ancient traditions on what makes a war just, the question must be asked whether a nuclear war could ever be just. From the traditions on the purpose of statecraft, the question must be asked about the value of peace in the face of assaults on the quality of life.

Can nuclear war ever be a proportionate response to another evil? Can the use of nuclear weapons ever be discriminant? Can we decide who among our enemy are guilty and confine the damage we inflict to them alone?

In a broader sense, can nuclear war be limited? Clearly, without some limit on destruction there can be no victory, and thus no righting of a wrong. Yet some would argue that even without the possibility of victory—perhaps even without the possibility of survival—nuclear war might remain a just alternative.

How might the possibility of Star Wars change the answers to these questions? It is, after all, Star Wars that, in great measure, creates the urgency for an open, honest, and full consideration of them. Compared to the discussion of nuclear strategy and other technical subjects, however, these issues of nuclear ethics have received little attention. Surely these fundamental questions about what is right given the twin threats of mass destruction and tyranny have not become a part of practical political discourse. They must.

CONCLUSION

The evaluation of the present debate about Star Wars points toward the need for a more basic debate. But even what has already been widely and deeply argued creates, among other visceral reactions, a sense of irony.

First, it seems difficult to be decisive and humble at the same time. How can we be activist in any direction once we are aware of the risk that we may be wrong in whatever choice we make, and with such potentially fearsome consequences? This agony is a testament to the rigor and integrity of the system our security policy is designed to protect, but though it is hard, nonetheless it must not be permitted to produce paralysis. Inertia, omission, or any other form of unconscious decision making is intolerable.

Why? Because of another irony: While this issue seems too important to decide, it is clearly too important not to. On this point it may be useful to remember how well we as a nation have decided other great issues: creating the nation, opening the frontier, fighting the Civil War, opening our shores to immigration, harnessing the forces of modern invention, participating in the world wars, reforming our social system in quite basic ways, and perhaps one or two others. Notwithstanding Churchill's quip that "Americans can always be counted on to do the right thing—once they have exhausted all the possible alternatives," we have done rather well. And in considering Star Wars, though there are limits to the analogy, we should keep in mind the American mastery of great projects: the phone system, the highways, electrification, Apollo. All pharaonic tasks in their day.

Finally, there is the ironic possibility that the most likely moment for the confusion and uncertainty about the right nuclear policy to lift is in the midst of a nuclear war. But it will then be far too late to correct any mistakes we may have made.

Perhaps the best we can do, as we go on in our confusion, is to hope for the strength to abide its strains and for the wisdom to make good use of the time we have. Then we may pass this mid-life crisis and see the nuclear age grow old successfully, if not gracefully.

PART TWO

THE CONTEXT

SOVIET STRATEGY AND AMERICAN RESPONSE
Richard Pipes

In the United States there exist two groups which share common liberal values and hold a similar view of America's national interest, and yet advocate different policies toward the Soviet Union. Such disagreement is perfectly legitimate and healthy. What I find less attractive is that one of these groups should have pinned on it the pejorative label "conservative," while the other is flattered as "moderate"—labels which are strictly partisan, betraying the bias of those who use them and beclouding the issue.

There has been an enormous surge of interest in the United States about the Soviet Union in the past year or so. I have never had such huge classes at Harvard as I have had since the recent change in the directorate of the Soviet Union. There are great expectations generated by the shifts in the Soviet leadership, or at least in the person of the leader. The question is: Are we engaged in wishful thinking, and are our expectations likely to be disappointed? I am afraid this is so.

REFORM IN THE SOVIET UNION?

The political system of Russia is exceedingly rigid. Its leadership is and always has been conservative. This antedates the Bolshevik

Dr. Richard Pipes is a professor of Russian history at Harvard University.

seizure of power in 1917. They fear change. It is almost axiomatic in Russian history that change comes only when the government is so hard-pressed, either from the inside or the outside, that it has no alternative. And even then, as soon as it is able to do so it reverts to the old policies. There are many reasons for this, two of which require particular attention.

One is that the leaders of the Russian state tend to regard the mass of the Russian people as wild savages, lacking in self-discipline and respect for law, who, if given half a chance, will tear the country apart. This view held true of Russian conservatives before the revolution and explains why Tsarist Russia was so reluctant and slow to reform itself. I believe that it is still true today. I have spoken with Russian officials on this subject, and every time one begins to press them and ask why they refuse to change even though they realize that change has become necessary, they come up with the same answer: "You know, this country is not Hungary or even China; the moment you start easing up, the Russian people perceive this as a sign of governmental weakness and we lose control."

The other factor has to do with the nature of the Soviet ruling elite—the so-called *nomenklatura*—with its 500,000 to 750,000 people, the heart of the Communist Party, who, by virtue of the system put in place by Lenin and perfected by Stalin, enjoy not only total power, but also the ownership of the Soviet Union with its people and resources. Reform threatens to weaken the authority of this group, to reduce its privileges, and, someday, perhaps even to cause its fall from authority.

The unwillingness to reform thus stems from a deep-seated anxiety rooted partly in historic experience and partly in the self-interest of the *nomenklatura*. This anxiety paralyzes the will to make changes which a good part of the Soviet leadership has come to recognize as desirable and, indeed, unavoidable.

GORBACHEV

Neither I nor anybody else in this country can know what goes on in Gorbachev's mind, or what went on in the minds of the people who chose him for high office. But I think it is a safe assumption that he was appointed because he promised to reinvigorate the leadership which for many years had become old and absurdly ineffective and, at the same time, to maintain the status quo: that is, to reinvigorate the system without altering it in such a way as to challenge the prerogatives of the ruling elite. Therefore, on the face of it one has to assume that he is not a "liberal," and the observed facts of his suits being properly pressed and his being able to walk without support on both sides cannot serve as indications of a progressive temperament.

But we also have bits and pieces of concrete evidence pointing toward a conservative outlook of the man. So far, Gorbachev has concentrated on placing his people in positions of power—in the Politburo, the Secretariat, the various ministries, the armed forces, and the provincial party apparatus. That, of course, was to be expected. But the people whom he puts in these positions are not, as far as we know, liberals; some of them even come from a KGB background. They are relatively young, energetic, effective people, likely to infuse the existing system with a new zeal, which it has been lacking for some time, but not to alter it in any substantial way.

The nuggets of concrete evidence that we have on Gorbachev's thinking on economic and political matters are not very encouraging, either. The great debate in the Soviet Union about the system focuses on the economic regime. There are many calls for decentralization of decision making in the economy and improvement of incentives. Such measures would take power away from the party and entrust it to the managers. They would also enhance the economic independence of private citizens and thereby make them less manipulable. Those who oppose reforms, for reasons stated, will argue that there is nothing wrong with the system, one only has to imbue it with greater efficiency and discipline. What does this mean in practice? Importing computers to refine the methods of decision making by means of artificial intelligence, as well as cracking down on alcoholism and absenteeism. The talk about discipline and hard work, the drive against drinking, absenteeism, and so on, emanating from Gorbachev's Russia are antireformist in spirit. They do not promise liberalization.

Gorbachev has also been cracking down on dissenters. Particularly ominous are the results of an encounter which Gorbachev had with General Jaruzelski in 1985, which was followed almost immediately by the tightening of the screws in Poland. One can only guess what Gorbachev said to the General, but I suppose that we are not far from the truth (judging by the results) when we assume he complained that things had gone too far in Poland and pressed him to reassert the power of the Polish Communist Party.

Gorbachev's policy on arms control, despite some dramatic recent proposals, suggests to me that the Soviet Union is still not serious about it, that it still prefers to apply pressure on the American administration through Congress, public opinion, and our allies to paralyze our defense effort, rather than to pursue realistic, equitable trade-offs.

None of this looks terribly encouraging. Now, it cannot be excluded that Gorbachev is indeed a hidden liberal, simply biding his time to put his people in power, a man who does not yet wish to alarm the conservatives and reactionaries in his own regime, and that once safely ensconced, he will introduce a variety of liberal reforms. One should keep one's mind open on this. It is possible, but the evidence is not there yet.

THE MAKING OF AMERICAN POLICY TOWARD THE SOVIET UNION

Turning to the broader issue of the conduct of our relations with the Soviet Union, I am convinced that the Soviet leaders do have a political strategy. By that I do not mean that they have a blueprint or timetable for world conquest, or anything of the sort. This whole notion is terribly naive. No country ever had such a thing. Even Hitler, who operated on timetables, had to make all kinds of adjustments to changed situations because of military exigencies. What I mean to say is that by virtue of the regime they have, the Communists are able, indeed compelled, to coordinate all the elements of their foreign policy—the diplomatic, the military, the propagandistic, the economic, and so on—toward a single objective which the party at any given moment decides is both advantageous and feasible. We on the other hand, find this most difficult to do. For one thing, our executive does not control the economy. Further, the President has to contend with a Congress and public opinion which influence and limit policy. American foreign policy, therefore, has to maneuver itself continually into situations which enable it to gain the support it requires. By the very nature of our democratic constitution, we cannot adopt a long-term strategy. A democratic regime is able to conduct a coordinated strategy only in time of war. But even conceding this, we should be able to conduct a more consistent strategy than we have been—if it only were not for the fundamental dislike on the part of our policy makers in both the executive and legislative branches for programs and ideologies, which, of course, are what the very concept of strategy postulates.

I served for two years, during 1981 and 1982, as the Soviet expert on the National Security Council, and during these two years we prepared a variety of documents meant to formulate a comprehensive policy toward the Soviet Union for the duration of the administration's tenure in office. People in the White House and the State Department fought over every word, every comma, in these documents. The process took interminable sessions—interagency meetings, senior interagency meetings—to produce, at last, a document that was approved by the National Security Council in December 1982. But I do not see that it is being implemented. I suspect that it is sitting in some drawer and nobody ever consults it. That is the nature of the beast. We make policy on an ad hoc basis. Decisions are made on the basis of a given situation as assessed by the various government agencies and as driven by our cultural and psychological predispositions. I do not know if the same held true of other administrations, but I suspect it did.

I am reasonably confident that it is not done like this in the Soviet Union. This puts us at a great disadvantage. Thus we are at a disadvantage not only because our system is not as coordinated as theirs, but also because we are psychologically unwilling to conduct a long-term policy in any event. I recall raising this matter once with someone in the State Department. I said, "They do have an ideology; they do have a long-term program," and the reply was, "How can they? We don't." This is very typical.

Now, one only has to look at the handicaps we suffer in regard to imports and exports in competing with the Japanese. The Japanese engage in long-term economic planning on all levels. They are not concerned with quarterly returns, and thus they place us at a tremendous disadvantage, as they plan years ahead. When you go to China you see advertisements for Panasonic, Seiko, and Toyota everywhere. They are not selling any of these goods in China yet, but they are planning for future years when they will, and then the Chinese market will be theirs. Our unwillingness to emulate them has placed us at a demonstrated disadvantage in world trade.

It is no different in world politics. We must develop the habit of deeper thinking and longer-term planning in our relations with foreign powers, especially the Soviet Union and its bloc, if we are to promote our national interest. To say this is not to make a "conservative" argument, but to think realistically, indeed "moderately."

THE NECESSITY AND POSSIBILITY OF DETENTE
Stephen F. Cohen

The conjunction of two major events—the rise of Gorbachev and the advent of the American program of Star Wars, or SDI—compels each of us, and the United States as a nation, to make a decision: What kind of relationship do we really want to have with the Soviet Union? That is the fundamental question which is rarely confronted.

If you leave aside the monstrous possibility of nuclear war, there are only two possibilities. One is cold war, whose most recent variant has prevailed since the late 1970s. The other is loosely called detente, which has a history going back to 1933 and which has been in almost complete disrepute in the United States for the last five years.

I am an advocate of detente, indeed an advocate of far-reaching detente, because detente is both necessary and possible. It is necessary, and I know this as a citizen, because cold war means an increasingly militarized relationship with the Soviet Union. It means both the ever-present threat of nuclear war and, because we are spending almost $400 billion a year on defense-related pursuits, it means a steady deterioration of the quality of American life.

As a scholar of Soviet affairs, I think that detente is possible

Dr. Stephen F. Cohen is a professor of politics at Princeton University.

because the majority of the Soviet political establishment—not all of it, but the majority—believes that detente is also in its domestic and international self-interest.

All of you know that the issue of detente versus cold war has divided American political life for a very long time. But most of you probably do not know that this same issue divides the Soviet political establishment, that the Soviets also have an acrimonious debate over relations with the West and specifically with the United States. One side says cold war with the West is a virtue and a necessity. The other side says the Soviet Union must establish some kind of political cooperation with the West. In other words, a dispute similar to that between Professor Pipes and myself exists inside the Soviet political establishment. And therefore the fateful outcome will be decided by a struggle on both sides. Either a cold war policy will win on both sides or a detente policy will win on both sides.

What is the meaning of an American policy of detente? It is not, as too many uncivil tongues in America assert, a policy of appeasement. Nor is it based on some unrealistic concept of what the Soviet Union is at home or abroad. Instead, thoughtful advocates of detente understand clearly that the Soviet Union is a profoundly undemocratic, authoritarian political system at home, and an overarmed superpower with the capacity to threaten our national interests and security in the world, just as we have the capacity to threaten its security and its survival. Moreover, detente is based on a clear recognition that the Soviet Union would like to expand its power abroad, just as the United States would like to expand its power abroad. That is not "moral equivalence;" it is simply a political fact.

Above all, detente is both a realistic policy and a policy of hope. And yet, in one respect I agree with Professor Pipes, or at least I share his pessimistic outlook. But I am pessimistic precisely because Professor Pipes' cold war outlook prevails in the United States. That is, as the opportunity for a full-scale political detente unfolds inside the Soviet Union at this very time, the United States remains either blind or indifferent to that opportunity, or inadequately resolved to seize it.

There are at least two reasons for this American myopia. One is that American thinking about the Soviet Union has become so utterly militarized that we no longer can think *politically* about our major political problem. All we can do when it comes to the Soviet Union is to think about and build weapons. The other reason is that too many of our own advocates of detente, who spoke openly in the 1970s, have now fallen silent or have muted their voices, either out of despair or out of anxiety caused by the new cold war climate of political intolerance in this country. No one wants to be called an "appeaser" or "soft on communism," as was once a reckless practice in our country.

THE DETENTE OPPORTUNITY

Let me illustrate the present detente opportunity we are ignoring by turning briefly to the new political situation inside the Soviet Union. It is very different in my perspective from the picture presented by Professor Pipes. Everything we know indicates that a reform leadership headed by Mikhail Gorbachev is struggling to take shape in Moscow. Since the early 1980s, the twenty-year conservative Soviet consensus on domestic policy inside the ruling elite has been breaking down. And ever since Yuri Andropov's death in 1984, reform groups and sentiments inside the Soviet political establishment have rallied around Gorbachev.

What about Gorbachev himself? In speech after speech he has indicated clearly that his program is one of far-reaching economic change or reform. Even if he is completely successful, such economic changes will not, of course, bring democracy, liberalism, or capitalism to the Soviet Union. But those changes, if carried out, would inescapably improve the everyday lives of millions of ordinary Soviet citizens, and they would improve, modestly liberalize, the political atmosphere inside the Soviet Union today.

But—and here is the key—Gorbachev and his group in the leadership are far from being complete masters of Soviet power or policy. American commentators have radically exaggerated the amount of power over domestic policy Gorbachev currently has. There is enormous elite and bureaucratic opposition to any such changes in the Soviet system. Every Soviet General Secretary since Stalin has tried to carry out some modest economic reform and has failed. Gorbachev may succeed, but he will not succeed without a very long political struggle at home that has only begun.

AMERICAN POLICY AND SOVIET REFORM

If Gorbachev prevails, what might we hope for? We can hope that he and the Soviet officials of his generation, people in their fifties, will seek their generational destiny in reform at home rather than more power abroad. That is the hope and possibility before us today. The outcome will be decided by a number of internal Soviet factors. But history and common sense tell us that no reform-minded leadership stands a chance in Soviet political life in conditions of increasing cold war tensions between the Soviet Union and the outside world, particularly the United States.

There are two reasons why this is so. First, a cold war approach in the United States always reinforces and redoubles Soviet conservative opposition to domestic change. Opponents say, "Yes, General Secretary Gorbachev, perhaps a good idea, but too risky because of 'the American threat.'" Second, economic reform, as both sides in the debate openly admit, requires a major increase in Soviet nondefense investment, particularly in the consumer goods sectors. But that necessitates reducing Soviet military expenditures, and that requires durable arms control with the United States that, in turn, requires a lasting political detente.

In short, a persistent American policy of cold war will almost certainly destroy any opportunity that now exists inside the Soviet Union for political and economic reform. And though an American policy of detente will not and cannot guarantee a victory of Soviet reform, it will at least give it a chance.

So, let me end by asking this question: Do we, should we, care about change in the Soviet Union? We say that we do. We have said so for years. But the fact is that the prevailing American cold war attitude greeted Gorbachev like this: "He is more dangerous and thus worse than the rest." Why? Because, our cold warriors say, "He is slick and he has domestic reform on his mind. And if he succeeds, that will make the Soviet Union an even more powerful and dangerous American adversary around the world." Such has been the prevailing American view. Anything the Soviets might want—detente, arms control, trade—by definition must be bad for the United States. Therefore, we must be against it.

Everything is wrong with this type of obsessive cold war strategic thinking. It epitomizes the way we have militarized our thinking about the Soviet Union. It means that the United States would become the enemy of domestic reform in the Soviet Union and thus the opponent of even marginal changes that might improve the everyday life of ordinary Soviet citizens. Is that a morally fit policy for a compassionate nation?

Politically, it means that we will ignore this potentially historic opportunity for a lasting detente. During the last two episodes of political and economic reform in the Soviet Union—in the 1920s and the 1950s—the Soviet Union embarked upon detente-like policies abroad. Now we seem to be saying that we are not interested. If so, it will tell us something terribly important, and something terrible, about ourselves. It will say that we really do not want better relations with the Soviet Union. It will say that Americans, as a nation, actually prefer cold war and the nuclear arms race forever—or something even worse. And that is the real political context, and the real political issue, of the debate over SDI.

THE CONCEPT OF DETERRENCE

THREE NOTES ON DETERRENCE
Adam Garfinkle

This essay makes three modest, logically related points about deterrence. These points may seem obvious—even definitional—but it is the mastery of the obvious that allows the appreciation of the sublime.

THE BREADTH OF DETERRENCE

The first point is that deterrence is not properly defined as a narrow, monolithic concept but can, and does, mean many things. When the typical citizen hears talk of deterrence, the most obvious meaning of the term is the prevention of nuclear war between the United States and the Soviet Union. But specialists and decision-makers sometimes speak of deterrence as meaning the prevention not only of nuclear war, but of any direct armed clash between the United States and the Soviet Union, because of the inherent danger of escalation to the nuclear level. When one speaks of *extended* deterrence—the nuclear-encrusted security promises that the United States has made, for example, to its NATO allies—deterrence means not only the prevention of a U.S.-Soviet war, but also the prevention of all direct conventional and nuclear

Dr. Adam M. Garfinkle is a research associate and the coordinator of the Political Studies Program at the Foreign Policy Research Institute, Philadelphia.

armed conflict in Europe involving, theoretically at least, non-U.S. and non-Soviet armed forces.

And there is still more. The political shadow of deterrence is believed by some to shore up the general balance of political will. In the case of Europe, this enables those Western European countries that fall under the protective wing of the U.S. nuclear umbrella to conduct a more vigorous and unencumbered foreign policy than might otherwise be the case in the abutting shadow of Soviet military power. Thus, the nuclear weapons of the United States are believed capable by some of deterring political blackmail of nonnuclear weapons states by nuclear weapons states. And outside of Europe, where the power projection capabilities of the United States and the Soviet Union overlap, as they do in the Middle East, the existence of nuclear weapons may also deter risk taking that might lead to a direct collision between U.S. and Soviet forces. Such *peripheral* deterrence, let us call it, very likely affects the calculations of local actors who are allied with one superpower or the other, and even the calculations of those not directly allied. The political shadow of nuclear weapons stretches far indeed.

Thus, while the prevention of nuclear war is undoubtedly the essence of deterrence, serious debate over deterrence is of necessity a much broader topic. If it were not, then the bonds of history and logic between things military and things political would be severed at our considerable intellectual and practical peril.

This does not mean that there is not considerable disagreement among honest men over all this. Some observers feel that *central* deterrence—the prevention of a major U.S.-Soviet nuclear war—is relatively plentiful, others think it is relatively scarce (to employ an economic metaphor), or at least too scarce at those tense times of international crisis when we need it most. Some think extended deterrence is relatively plentiful; others think it scarce. It is also possible for someone to think central deterrence plentiful but extended deterrence scarce (the likely position of a Fortress America neo-isolationist), or for someone to think central deterrence scarce but, having been achieved, extended deterrence then *relatively* plentiful (the posture of a realpolitik Atlanticist).

Finally, some observers take very seriously the political shadow cast by nuclear deployments; others take it less seriously, or take it seriously but differently. There are those who are quite certain that nuclear weapons will never be used—who believe in what is called by some, *existential* deterrence—and that, because of the presumed universality of that belief among the U.S. and Soviet elites that matter most, there is no significant political shadow cast by nuclear weapons. They believe that as long as even a few nuclear weapons exist on both sides to guarantee the basic deterrence relationship, their political influence is negligible. There are others who also believe in existential deterrence but who nevertheless take the political significance of perceived balances and military trends very seriously indeed—Eugene V. Rostow's views are an example of this.

What these disagreements boil down to is whether the traditional linkage between military force and the pursuit of diplomatic agendas, formulated classically by Karl von Clausewitz in *On War* (1833), has been irrevocably severed in the nuclear age, only partially severed, or not severed at all. That nuclear weapons are in fact seen by policymakers on all sides as having effects beyond that of simply deterring all-out nuclear war suggests very strongly that the age-old craft of squeezing political advantage from the possession of instruments of coercion has yet to depart from this earth.

Soviet spokesmen tell us, for example, that even a limited nuclear attack on the military forces of the Soviet Union originating from U.S. forces in West Germany would be treated as if the attack originated from the United States, and would draw a response on that level. Perhaps. But a Soviet decision to escalate a nuclear exchange to involve the U.S. homeland would clearly carry with it risks of much more extensive attacks against the Soviet Union that might otherwise be avoided. The decision to accept such risks could not be automatic and would depend on the fuller politico-military context, which is intrinsically unknowable in advance. The deployment of U.S. nuclear weapons in West Germany, then, might conduce to limiting nuclear war to Europe if war ever began. The knowledge that the U.S. homeland might be spared at once increases the credibility of U.S. nuclear forces in Europe—whatever the Soviets say—and unavoidably annoys a great many Europeans.

Rotating the terms of engagement slightly, a marginally less speculative question is this: Is the Soviet assessment of the risk of attacking West Germany with conventional arms changed if there are operational U.S. nuclear weapons located in West Germany? Believers in existential deterrence and the political irrelevance of nuclear weapons deployment would have to say no if they were logically consistent, but there is no question that the putative existence of Soviet nuclear weapons in Cuba in October 1962 did decisively change the Kennedy administration's assessment of the risks involved in a U.S. conventional assault. More likely, the answer is, yes, the Soviets *are* more reluctant to attack West Germany with conventional weapons just because U.S. nuclear weapons are deployed there.

Here we are brought face-to-face with what seems to be the central and most bedeviling paradox of the nuclear age: There is an inverse relationship between raising the nuclear threshold and raising the threshold of the outbreak of major war in general. In other words, as one lowers the nuclear threshold by constructing more plausibly usable nuclear weapons (i.e., very accurate weapons with low yields), one makes the outbreak of *any* war less likely because few, if any, political programs are worth running the risks of any nuclear use and the unmeasurable but very real possibility of uncontrolled nuclear escalation. But as one raises the nuclear threshold by deliberately possessing only counter-value weapons of mass destruction that have no plausible military use whatsoever (i.e., relatively inaccurate weapons with high yields), one increases the chances of war waged conventionally for less-than-ultimate— but hardly trivial!—stakes. Who, after all, could be counted on to take seriously a threat of ultimate consequence over a less-than-ultimate stake? That is why U.S. government policy has assumed for over a decade that, absent conventional parity in Europe, the credibility of extended deterrence is inconsistent with an exclusively counter-value U.S. strategic capability. That is also why there have been battlefield, or tactical, U.S. nuclear weapons in Western Europe (and elsewhere) since the early 1960s: essentially to threaten the nuclearization of *any* war in order to prevent *all* war. It has worked, and this is not an insignificant accomplishment; it hardly needs stating that people killed by conventional ordnance are just as dead as those killed by nuclear ordnance. But we have had to run sobering risks to make it work. It is around this insoluable paradox that all arguments about "no first use" in Europe, the neutron bomb, and the development of counterforce weapons ultimately revolve.

Because this paradox suggests a sliding scale of differing risks rather than an all-or-nothing logical problem, categorical assertions of the nonutility of nuclear weapons in the narrow military sense are not reassuring. After all, nuclear weapons *have* been used in war, and we know that at times of intense crisis, especially those accompanied by conventional arms clashes, the normal psychological and technical constraints against nuclear use wither very considerably. On a day-to-day basis, the United States and the Soviet Union deter each other excessively—by orders of magnitude. But it is necessarily an open question as to whether deterrence is adequate for that rarest of occasions when we need deterrence most. Given the very morbid consequences of a failure of strategic deterrence, it behooves us to reduce the risks of failure at the margin insofar as we are able. And precisely because nuclear use *is* conceivable at the margin, it is really quite pointless to insist that these weapons have no political ramifications.

PERCEPTIONS AND DETERRENCE

The military use of nuclear weapons is not unthinkable in large part because people have been ineluctably, reluctantly, but persistently thinking about it for forty years. This brings us then to the second point: that nuclear deterrence is an open-ended-problem universe. In other words, human beings affect and change the deterrence relationship by dint of their continually giving thought to the matter, by the exchange or collision of mutual perceptions and assessments of intent about deterrence, and by the consequent dialectic between thought and experience that results. This has always been true, but it is particularly true in the nuclear age, because military strategy under the shadow of the atom has become largely detached from direct human experience. In the past, military preparation generally followed from the lessons and perceptions of recently fought wars. But military strategy in the nuclear age rests more on theoretical abstraction than on personal knowledge. For this reason alone, nuclear strategy has become a logically open-ended enterprise, and the paradoxes of the nuclear age go unsolved because, in the absence of the direct experience that we pray we will never have, they are unsolvable.

Moreover, the relationship between strategic "reality" and our theories about that reality is more complex than first meets the eye. As in most other social situations, we are not discovering reality through our theorizing about it; we are in large part *creating* that reality. How the various relevant actors imagine nuclear reality influences planning for deterrence and war, and this planning in turn shapes how deterrence works—or does not work—and how a nuclear war would be fought if deterrence fails. Social life in general is recursive; that is, it freezes into itself the conceptions we hold of it. Through its material consequences, history reflects back to posterity the melange of judgments, assumptions, prejudices, pathologies, and ideals that human beings bring to its making.

The point is that deterrence cannot be an automatic, a static, or a technologically predetermined relationship; different human minds, operating in different cultural contexts, do not make invariate, automatic judgments from ambiguous information. This is important, because many analysts who ought to know better sometimes talk like technological determinists, as if there is something about the very nature and number of weapons and delivery systems that make deterrence inevitable, or that make it impossible to sustain in the long run. This is the *deus ex machina* fallacy, the fallacy of the ghost in the machine, the fallacy that posits that for all intents and purposes, human values, judgments, cognitive processes, and emotional vicissitudes are irrelevant to the deterrence relationship because *technology itself* has the pride of place that intervenes at the crucial moment either to save us or to destroy us, depending on one's private eschatology of the strategic competition. This is nonsense, of course, if you stop to think about it.

Deterrence is not primarily an engineering problem; it is primarily a psychological problem. The deterrence relationship is different today than it was twenty, ten, five, or even two years ago, not only or mainly because technology has changed, but because the mutual assessment of intentions has changed and continues to change in often subtle but cumulatively substantial ways. The deterrence relationship has changed as profoundly, if not more so, because of the Cuban Missile Crisis, the nonuse of nuclear weapons in Korea and Vietnam, and the arms control process as it has changed because of the development of multiple warhead missiles (MIRVs) or cruise missiles. Nothing is inevitable because of a particular technology—and this, of course, includes the Strategic Defense Initiative.

This is not to say that technology is "neutral." It is not. It does embody social values, and it clearly creates political and policy tendencies, sometimes very strong ones. But if one skips over the human element—the element that both produces the technology and that has to live with its implications—one is desiccating the very soul of political action. One also comes close to casting off responsibility when one posits inevitability. The deterrence relationship, for better or worse, is a malleable one, and we together—ourselves, the Soviets, and others—are responsible both causally and morally for the direction that the relationship takes.

THE DETERRENCE DEBATE

Finally, the third point, also related, is that *because* the deterrence relationship is an open-ended, recursively evolving relationship, we can do ourselves great harm, as analysts and as citizens, by accepting uncritically any prepackaged ensemble of beliefs like those often peddled in the cascade of cacophonous mass-mail solicitations that litter so many mailboxes. Polemical advocacy, political demagoguery, and the willful ignorance that goes along with both, are not yet banished from the debate over deterrence. To paraphrase a well-known remark about a related matter, the deterrence relationship is too important to be left to the public relations firms and those political admen who specialize in raising money and emotions. The full relationship, say, between intercontinental ballistic missile vulnerability, space defense, antisatellite weapons, sea-based counterforce systems, and so on, is *not* obvious, it is *not* unchanging, and it is *not* predetermined by technology alone.

Creative and truly helpful analysis must begin by looking at difficult and novel problems in their unique integrity, and not by relying indolently on stale formulas and worn assumptions that have frequently been poor counsel to us in the past. Here it is worth listening to the voice of the poet, Rainer Maria Rilke:

If we only arrange our life according to that principle which counsels us that we must always hold to the difficult, then that which now seems to us the most alien will become what we most trust and find most faithful.

TRADITIONAL DETERRENCE
Leon Wieseltier

What I would like to do is to present a somewhat coherent outline of the position of what I think is the "radical middle" on the question of the meaning of deterrence—what kind of American posture keeps the peace. Since the question of deterrence at present seems always to be the question of Star Wars—indeed, in Washington just now, every question is the question of Star Wars—Star Wars and the Jewish question, almost—what I would like to do is to distinguish three different possible meanings of Star Wars.

The first, of course, is President Reagan's notion of Star Wars, which he outlined very sincerely and passionately, and with a great deal of ideological and moral intensity. This is the idea of making nuclear weapons impotent, the idea of a perfect defense for the population of the United States, and as he would have it, for the Soviet Union as well. Second, a much more current, and in some ways intellectually much more interesting, notion of Star Wars is the whole variety of euphemisms for an imperfect defense: limited defense and various types of layered defenses, defense of American military installations of various kinds but not a perfect defense of population, and a defense aimed not at ending deterrence but at what is called "enhancing deterrence." The third

Mr. Leon Wieseltier is the Literary Editor of the *New Republic*.

notion of Star Wars, the Pentagon's idea, is the idea of a perfect leak-proof defense against arms control. As I see it, *this* is at least one version of Star Wars that has a very good chance of working perfectly.

REALISM AND IDEALISM

Since the advent of the nuclear age, there has been a debate between what I would call the camp of "nuclear idealism" and the camp of "nuclear realism." Nuclear idealism believes in transformation. Nuclear realism believes in management. By nuclear idealism I mean, for example, all the abolitionisms about nuclear weapons that have accumulated in the past—the abolition of the weapons themselves, the abolition of the arms race, the abolition of war, the abolition of existing sovereign states, the abolition of the evil in man. By nuclear realism, I mean something much more morally and historically ambiguous. I mean the many refinements of strategy, technology, diplomacy, and politics that have been designed over the past four decades simply to prevent the weapons from going off. Idealists will be satisfied only by disarmament. Realists are satisfied by deterrence, and usually by arms control as well.

Now, I would argue at the outset that nuclear idealism and nuclear realism are by no means mutually exclusive. I would think it more sensible to see them as a division of labor. Writing in a different context, Irving Howe makes a distinction between the politics of the near and the politics of the far, and I think that the division between nuclear idealism and nuclear realism is a little bit of that kind. There is nothing the matter with the nuclear idealists—those who search for a final, ultimate release from this terrible fact of our lives—unless they demean or distract attention from the immediate problems of strategic coping.

Similarly, there is nothing the matter with the nuclear realists, with those who carefully calibrate all the balances, stabilities, and instabilities and do the numbers, unless they deny that the danger of mass destruction remains after all, that deterrence is nothing more than the best the realists can accomplish.

Unfortunately, what has been happening recently is that the idealists' argument against the realists is proving much more popular than the realists' argument against the idealists. After all, it is very hard to argue against a vision of the world without nuclear weapons, and it is very hard to be satisfied in your heart with the idea that the greatest danger in human history should be met with ideas taken from textbooks about management. You will not fill the streets with people, people will not march in the tens of thousands, in the name of flexible response, bargaining chips, limited options, and so on.

The big change came with Ronald Reagan's speech. With that speech Ronald Reagan joined the camp of the idealists. And with that long list of abolitionisms I mentioned before, the province of what we call the Left, we must now include Ronald Reagan's idea: perfect ballistic missile defenses. That was the real significance of his Star Wars speech, and the real political brilliance of it. It was the first time that Ronald Reagan signalled that he, too, was afraid of nuclear weapons, and that the American people do indeed have reason to worry.

Now, should we worry, too, about Ronald Reagan's notion of nuclear defenses? No, in the sense that they cannot happen. Yes, in the sense that he is in danger of lulling, deluding, confusing, and even demoralizing the American people. It is hard enough as it is, without this silly idea, to get the American people to accept the fact that we are living in such a dangerous world.

"ENHANCING" DETERRENCE

What about the notion of limited defenses? That, I would say, is another concept of management. Deterrence may or may not be enhanced according to such a scheme of things; it all depends on the mixture of offense and defense in question. But there are a few observations that I would make about even limited defenses and deterrence. First, and this has been a major flaw in the discussion, we must imagine a world not only in which we have defenses, but in which the Soviets have defenses too. We would like to have not only our missiles protected, but theirs also.

I think it may turn out that Star Wars will have the very ironic and surprising consequence of returning the nuclear world to the purest version of MAD, mutual assured destruction, imaginable, because if they have defenses and we have defenses, the only thing you can do in such a world is simply to aim at each other as many missiles as possible and hope that some of them will land. But if you are going to have a counterforce strategy of any kind, which the United States and the Soviet Union do, it seems to me you require some meaningful amount of "open skies." In other words, to pursue a program of precision, accuracy, and "limited" nuclear warfare on the one hand, and defense on the other, is incoherent.

Moreover, while I think that deterrence may be deeply enhanced by some limited form of Star Wars, I exclude from this a program based in space. I know of no strategic problem on earth that will be solved in space, but I can imagine many strategic problems in space that do not exist on earth. I have never understood the passionate argument against defending American missiles in their silos; it seems to me to constitute a very useful extra wrinkle for Soviet planners to contend with; it gives them one less reason for thinking that a first strike might work. Still, as soon as you talk about placing defenses in space, you are talking about introducing a vast new area of vulnerability. Putting these defensive technologies—which, in the case of antisatellite weapons, are offensive technologies—in space, exposes our most advanced, most precarious, and most volatile form of technology in a way that it never was before.

Finally, I would argue that if you are interested in the "enhancement" of deterrence, that is fine, as long as you do not mean by that the controlling of nuclear war. If what is meant by enhancing deterrence is creating an offensive-defensive mix that will give planners the notion that they will be on top of a nuclear war as it is fought, that is a very serious mistake; and then it is not the enhancement of deterrence that we are discussing at all, but the prosecution of a nuclear war.

SDI AND ARMS CONTROL

Two comments about SDI and arms control. First, I would argue that the liberal community in this country—the community of liberal strategists—have, for reasons I do not completely understand, very foolishly made an utter fetish out of arms control. Arms control is the ultimate managerial idea. It accomplishes very little, though I am not sneezing at what it accomplishes, because in a world this dangerous, any lessening of the danger is worth the effort. But a change in kind as opposed to a change in degree is not something that arms control can bring about. Indeed, it may even be argued that arms control has only encouraged unfortunate technological developments. Second, I would argue that if indeed it could be shown either that the population of any country could be successfully defended against nuclear weapons, or that some offensive-defensive mix that involves defenses in space would genuinely enhance deterrence and make the world a safer place, I would think that arms control, and certainly the Anti-Ballistic Missile Treaty (ABM), would be a very small price to pay for that. And I think any kind of dogmatic adherence to this ABM faith is a little forced, if only because of what is happening in science and technology.

On the other hand, the bargaining-chip arguments about Star Wars seem to me to be a very cruel hoax indeed. It seems to me to be essentially a mechanism for neoconservative consultants and pundits to stay in the game without having to agree to a view that they would find embarrassing. Now, Ronald Reagan sincerely believes in his speech; the President is many things, but he is not a liar. And I think that Gorbachev understood quite correctly that by taking the President (or the Pentagon, or whichever obscure, undefinable constellation of senior officials goes about making the bargaining-chip argument) at face value, he has boxed the United States brilliantly into a virtually impossible position in Geneva.

Finally, I would say that the interesting thing about Soviet proposals is that they remind me not only of Reagan's Eureka proposal of a few years ago ("deep cuts"), but also of a proposal that George Kennan made in the *New York Review of Books* a few years ago, according to which both superpowers would cut their strategic nuclear arsenal by half. The point to be made about Kennan's proposal, Reagan's proposal, and Gorbachev's proposal is that the Russians have absolutely no intention of cutting the number of their land-based missiles by half, since these weapons are not just the pride of their military, but the pride of their economy—the only thing that Soviet society has done brilliantly in the past fifty years. But the problem is greater than that. Even if both sides were to cut their arsenals by half, or by even more, the fact remains that the power to blow up the planet, I do not know how many times over, will remain in both their hands. And what that means is that we are left with this hoary idea called deterrence.

Deterrence is not a strategy but the opposite of a strategy. Strategy teaches you how to use weapons; deterrence says do not use them. And we never had MAD as a strategy. At no point, as far as I can tell, in the history of American nuclear war plans, did

a plan exist to begin a nuclear war by destroying Soviet society—
that is a straw man that the right-wing strategic nuclear community has really been a little sleazy about. MAD is, rather, a correct
description of reality. It is the name for our condition. Mutual
assured destruction is what will certainly happen in any form of
nuclear war that anybody with any offensive-defensive mix, or any
kind of nuclear arsenal at all, will start. And in that sense, I think
that the defense of deterrence and the defense of mutual assured
destruction, not as a strategy but simply as the name of our world,
is really the beginning of wisdom on the subject.

THE MILITARY BALANCE

SOVIET MILITARY POWER AND STAR WARS
Andrew Cockburn

The Star Wars folly relies for whatever intellectual coherence it can summon on a number of assumptions, all of them fallacious, about nuclear weapons and Soviet military power. Those assumptions are not new; they have been dredged up and paraded around for most of the Cold War as a means of justifying one or another enormously costly defense boondoggle.

THE WINDOW OF VULNERABILITY

The first assumption is that the Soviets may have the technological capability, and indeed the intent, to launch a preemptive first strike against U.S. land-based missile silos. I am, of course, relying on administration and Strategic Defense Initiative Organization (SDIO) statements qualifying President Reagan's original proclamation of a program to render nuclear weapons obsolete. It now appears to be freely admitted that we are not seeking to erect a leak-proof astrodome over the continental United States, but a more selective defensive system that will protect U.S. missile sites and therefore "enhance deterrence."

Now, we have been through all this before in the debate over the racetrack deployment idea for the MX missile. That program

Mr. Andrew Cockburn is a contributing editor of *Defense Week*.

was also designed to frustrate any Soviet attempt to put a leg over the sill of the "window of vulnerability" by making it impossible for the godless Bolsheviks to destroy our accurate land-based missiles. Many cogent arguments were advanced against this preposterous concept at the time. The decisive opposition, however, came from the Mormon Church and the water lobby in the western states, which goes to show that reason is not enough in these debates. But the concept has a more ancient pedigree. Many people forget that the basis of the famous missile-gap alarm of the 1960 election was not simply that the Russians had more missiles than the United States, but that they had enough missiles to eliminate most of our Strategic Air Command bomber bases and thus to disarm America in a preemptive first strike.

As it turned out, the Soviets did not have enough missiles to do any such thing. In fact, at the time of the debate they had just four intercontinental ballistic missiles, and those were of limited range. Today the debate over the vulnerability of the U.S. deterrent, or at least the land-based portion of it, rests not on numbers of weapons alone, but on more abstruse technological considerations about the accuracy of the guidance systems of Soviet missiles.

The measurement of missile accuracy is a very abstruse art. The Soviets are not obliging enough to paint a large bull's-eye in the middle of their test range so that we can estimate their accuracy like a score on a dart board. The exercise involves a whole series of calculations about the efficiency of the guidance system in flight from which the intelligence analysts extrapolate the miss distance from the intended aim point, wherever that was. Even supposing that the Soviet test firings were going as well as U.S. intelligence claimed, and that is a big if, it is very dishonest for our authorities to claim that this demonstrates a Soviet capability to launch a preemptive strike. To do such a thing, the Soviet leadership would have to assume (1) that their missile designers were telling the truth, (2) that all the missiles being targeted on American silos would work reliably, and (3) that the American President would not simply order the U.S. submarine-based missile forces, which comprise 50 percent of the U.S. strategic nuclear capability, to plaster the hell out of the urban Soviet Union in retaliation.

In considering the first point in making their awesome decision, the men in the Kremlin would doubtless be aware that these missiles have never been tested on an operational trajectory (that is, over the North Pole) and that, according to data from U.S. missile tests, the accuracy of an ICBM is subject to unforeseeable factors, such as the weather over the target area. In considering the second, they would certainly be aware that the reliability of Soviet missiles is not good, less than 50 percent according to knowledgeable authorities. The third calculation is, of course, unresolvable for both the Soviets and us.

One does not need access to classified Soviet missile test data to see that the whole hypothesis is completely absurd, and yet grown men have chosen to take it seriously and expend billions and billions of dollars on the basis of it, and they are proposing to expend further billions on its latest manifestation—Star Wars.

NUCLEAR WAR-FIGHTING

A more fundamental absurdity, of course, is the notion that you can make calculations about the course of a nuclear war just as you can about conventional conflicts, and that nuclear combat can be planned and fought in the same way. Thus the notion that "blunting" a Soviet attack can yield some advantage leading perhaps to victory or, as the former White House national security official Thomas C. Reed said before he was indicted in a stock fraud scandal, allowing us to "prevail with pride." Whenever the real world has obtruded on the nuclear planners, it has been speedily revealed how spurious this whole intellectual discipline actually is. For example, in 1961 the Kennedy administration seriously entertained the idea of launching a preemptive strike on the Soviet Union. The balance of forces was well in America's favor. The Soviet strategic retaliatory capability was minimal. The United States could achieve complete surprise. The Russians would lose, so the planners said, about 100 million people in the attack. But the downside was that, even so devastated, the Soviets might still be able to launch one or two of their primitive bombers or submarine missiles, and this might result in as many as fifteen million American casualties. At the mention of this last figure, the policymakers immediately dismissed the whole plan as a ridiculous fantasy. The world survived.

THE CONVENTIONAL BALANCE

While it is not very hard to dismiss the malign fantasies of the threat inflators as applied to nuclear war-fighting, their assumptions carry an undeserved aura of respectability when it comes to considerations about the conventional balance, which in turn have an important bearing on calculations of the nuclear balance.

For example, it has long been held to be self-evident that it is only the nuclear deterrent that has saved Western Europe from a Soviet conventional onslaught. Ever since the end of World War II, so the theory goes, the Soviets have had such a massive numerical superiority in conventional forces that the Western Alliance has been at a permanent disadvantage at this level. It is worth looking at this assumption in more detail.

On the face of it, it does indeed appear that the United States is faced with a far superior enemy in terms of numbers of men and weapons. The Soviet armed forces comprise upwards of five million men and about 60,000 women, while the United States has just over two million. The Soviet Navy is often quoted as being three times the size of the U.S. Navy, while the Soviet Army is supposed to have five times as many tanks as the U.S. Army. The trouble is that these numbers do not tell you very much when they are taken out of context, as they usually are.

Yes, it is true that the Soviets keep many more people in uniform than does the United States. But who are these Soviet hordes? Well, almost a million of them are what are known as "construction troops." These are draftees who are not trained or intended for any combat role. They are what their name implies, troops used for tasks such as constructing railroads in Siberia or building officers' clubs in Moscow. They are an interesting aspect of the Soviet military system, but they hardly constitute a threat to the United States.

Another 500,000 of these hordes constitute the "Troops of National Air Defense," the men who man the radars, missiles, and guns of the Soviets' antiaircraft defense system. Now, it has been the case since the 1960s that the Soviet Union can be quite satisfactorily obliterated by the ICBMs and submarine-launched ballistic missiles (SLBMs) of the United States and, indeed, its British and French allies, which would seem to make this enormous investment in antibomber defenses somewhat otiose. Its main function appears to be to give employment to a great number of military officials and contractors both in the Soviet Union and in the United States, where "the growing capability of Soviet air defense" serves as a perennial excuse for such costly boondoggles as the B-1 and Stealth bombers. As a matter of fact, these same air defenses, when put to the test, do not reveal themselves to be that capable. The time taken to intercept Korean Airlines Flight 007 in 1982 is one notorious example, but there have been many others.

Soviet manpower is further eaten up by such deployments as the 70,000 men in the Main Political Administration, the political officers whose job it is to pump up the ideological fervor of the troops and report on them to the Party, or the 100,000 civil defense troops entrusted with the formidable task of preserving and repairing the Soviet Union in the event of nuclear holocaust.

Even with combat troops, the numbers are not comparable. The Soviet Union sees fit to keep upwards of 600,000 men on the Chinese frontier because it, unlike the United States, faces potential adversaries on two fronts. And so on. By the time one has eliminated noncomparable categories, like the political officers or the Chinese border force, and taken account of the extra men that the Soviets require to perform an equivalent task—nearly 500,000 for strategic nuclear forces, for example, compared to about 70,000 employed for the same purpose in the United States—it turns out that the numerical disparity between them and us tends to melt away to about two million men on either side.

Faced with such unwelcome intrusions of reality, the standard answer of the threat inflators is to zero in rapidly on the local imbalance of forces in central Europe, where the massed and supposedly cohesive forces of the Warsaw Pact confront the weak and fragmented Western Alliance. The plain fact of the matter is that the Warsaw Pact is by no means cohesive. Careful scrutiny of the deployment, training, and command arrangements of the Pact forces indicates that the prime function of the Soviet armies in Eastern Europe is to ensure the continued loyalty of the Soviet Union's East European allies. Supposedly the Soviets have a comfortable superiority in tanks in this theater, but on closer examination their advantage is small, about 26,000 to 24,000. Much is made of the fact that American reinforcements to be sent to Europe in the event of a crisis would be largely reservists, but this fails to take into account that many of the American reserve units are very good indeed, the Air National Guard for example, while the Soviet reserve forces undergo little or no regular routine training.

The tendentiousness of the orthodox picture is typified by a story once told me by Leonard Firestone, who was the American Ambassador to Belgium in 1975. When he arrived, the NATO Commander, General Goodpaster, arranged a NATO briefing for him on the military balance. Firestone emerged from the briefing feeling rather depressed, since NATO appeared from what he had heard to be hopelessly overmatched by its potential opponent. He told Goodpaster this. The General appeared puzzled by this, and cross-questioned him on what he had been told. "Oh my God," said Goodpaster finally, "they've given you the Congressional briefing!"

SOVIET TECHNOLOGY
AND SOVIET SOLDIERS

Much is made these days of the Soviets' developing their technological capability and thus narrowing the "technology gap" on which the West has long relied to maintain the balance. It is helpful to look at what the Soviets are actually building rather than simply to draw up abstract indices of technological capability. The MiG-23, for example, currently the main frontline Soviet fighter, was hailed as a tremendous improvement over the MiG-21, which it replaced. Yet the MiG-23 is far less maneuverable, far more complex and harder to maintain, and considerably more expensive than the older plane. Israeli pilots who have engaged it in combat are derisive about its capabilities. The BMP armored personnel carrier has likewise had good reviews from the U.S. military, despite the fact that its rear doors double as fuel tanks, thus making life nasty and short for many of the unfortunates who would travel inside during combat. Much is made of the ability of new classes of the Soviet attack submarines to travel deeper and faster than those of the Americans; less is said of the fact that they are extremely noisy—the worst possible attribute for a submarine. Soviet tank gunners may not necessarily appreciate the novel automatic loading mechanism on the T-72 tank, since it has displayed an unwelcome tendency to load the gunner, rather than the shell, into the breech.

Just as Soviet military technology is open to question, so also is the human element. Apart from officers, almost the entire Soviet establishment is made up of draftees serving a two-year term (three in the navy). This severely limits training. There is the additional problem brought about by the racial diversity of the Soviet Union, since many draftees may have only a cursory knowledge of Russian, the language of command. Conditions in the ranks are hardly conducive to high morale and unit cohesion. A vicious form of hazing prevails in the barracks at the expense of the younger draftees, and innumerable firsthand accounts attest to the awesome degree of drunkenness.

A notably facile commentator on the subject of Soviet military power has coined the slogan "drunk they defeated Napoleon, drunk they defeated Hitler, and drunk they will defeat NATO." This ignores, willfully or otherwise, the fact that Napoleon and Hitler invaded Russia, inflicted heavy defeats on the Russians, and were driven out only when an aroused people organized themselves sufficiently to prevail, albeit at terrific cost. Unless NATO plans to invade the Soviet Union, the parallel does not hold true, for a blitzkrieg assault on Western Europe from a standing start inevitably demands a rather higher state of training and sober efficiency than the bloody sacrificial battles of Moscow or Stalingrad.

CONCLUSION

No one suggests that the Soviet Union is powerless militarily. What we are talking about is the degree to which its real capability compares with the inflated claims that have been made, and are being made, on its behalf by interested parties in the military establishments of the West. The main aim of those who interpret and broadcast the minutiae of Soviet military power, and I am talking about the military intelligence community here, is to buttress the case for whatever the American armed services themselves want to procure. Thus the U.S. Navy is currently broadcasting the news that the Soviets have finally launched a "true" aircraft carrier weighing about 65,000 tons and looking just like one of our own carriers. They do this because the navy likes aircraft carriers and wants to have more of them, so it uses the Soviet counterpart as a form of endorsement for their own doctrine. Way down in the small print, however, you may notice that this Soviet carrier has no catapult, which means that it cannot launch planes other than their severely limited vertical takeoff Forger fighter. In other words, the Soviet carrier is not a true aircraft carrier at all.

More generally, the "increasing technological sophistication" of Soviet weaponry is really intended as a form of advertisement for current U.S. procurement doctrine, whether it be in tanks, planes, ships, or the Strategic Defense Initiative. To repeat, the intellectual case for the last, Star Wars, melts away faster than snow on a summer's day once it is closely examined. This may be why its protagonists have to dress up their case with mumbo jumbo about "perceptions" and similar strategic gobbledegook. The bottom line is that we deter the Soviets from attacking us, and they deter us from attacking them. This has long been the case regardless of the numbers and "quality" of nuclear forces deployed on either side, and it will continue to be the case however much treasure we may be tricked into pouring into the pockets of the proponents of Star Wars.

PERCEPTIONS OF POWER
Michael Vlahos

To most Americans, the military "balance" is not simply an abstraction of reality, it is an abstract metaphor. Perhaps even a mystery.

THE MILITARY BALANCE: PAST MEANINGS

In classical usage, the military balance was something you could roll around in your mouth. It was real. It was an equation for use. Military force existed to be used, and the balance of military forces was the working shorthand of strategy.

One example is well known. Between 1907 and 1912, Great Britain and Germany engaged in what is popularly remembered as a "Dreadnought race." Battleships were yesterday's strategic weapons, and they possessed all of the emotional symbolic content that today is associated with membership in the "nuclear club." Britain described its national status in terms of continued naval supremacy. Germany's sense of national identity and purpose was bent on ascending to Britain's level, on achieving *Weltmacht*. Both countries knew how many battleships they needed. The political shibboleth, "We want eight, we won't wait" shows how clearly the "reality" of specific military force levels and national purpose

Dr. Michael Vlahos is an adjunct professor and Co-Director of National Security Studies at the Johns Hopkins School of Advanced International Studies.

was understood throughout the British electorate. It was relatively easy to measure military forces to fit different constructions of national strategy.

Public and diplomatic presentations of the relative balance of military forces between potential enemies have always employed a perceptual mechanism to promote larger national security goals. Simply, the military balance showed who was ahead, who had the *advantage*. In other words, who would win a war. This could be useful political capital indeed. It was the key to the high place in the hierarchy of powers, the stuff of the balance of power, the currency of diplomatic deals, the essence of prestige.

Furthermore, anyone could understand it. National adversaries and interested neutrals all shared its common language and interpretation. In the example of the Anglo-German naval race, there was no misunderstanding each other's actions, and when it became clear that Britain would beggar itself and Germany to keep its dreadnought lead, Germany dropped out.

The anomaly in applying the military balance since 1945 lies in a mutation of American notions about the use of military force. Possessed of nuclear munitions, the utility of force became equated, not with use, but with *deterrence* of use. Deterrence of an adversary through military forces designed *not* to be used is unique in the life of modern society. Traditional arsenals may have deterred through perception of advantage, but instilling the conviction of one's own advantage in an adversary was nonetheless rooted in readiness for use. Use from a position of advantage guaranteed victory. Use in a situation of military parity implied stalemate. This was the least acceptable goal. Anything less implied political subservience.

Granted that a perception of "advantage" was the purpose behind classical calculations of the military balance, is a perception of advantage a useful goal in a deterrent regime? Let us look at America's approach to this question since 1945.

The period from 1945 to 1949 was a time of transformation in American foreign policy. It was then that the United States took on the global commitments and made the alliances it defends today. And the balance between the new adversaries? Simple. The United States had a nuclear monopoly. It was not much in terms of actual weapons; in fact, the United States had just a few, and a questionable delivery system. But America had *advantage*, advantage in Soviet eyes. The United States controlled the perceptual mechanism in defining the military balance. And it was physically safe. The territorial United States was under no threat of attack.

America continued to hold the throttle of perceived advantage during the decade of the Cold War, from 1950 to 1960. Moreover, the United States had no intention of relinquishing control. This nuclear credibility was used to achieve something called "extended deterrence." The threat of a limited Soviet aggression against American allies was to be met with the threat of the full force of nuclear retaliation. The United States became marginally vulnerable to Soviet attack, and yet successful efforts were made to defend the American people. Americans worried about nuclear attack, while the Soviet perception of American advantage continued.

Operation from perceived advantage declined from 1960 to 1965. The Soviet nuclear arsenal was growing, and there was no known defense against their new weapon, the powerful land-based intercontinental missiles, or ICBMs. With the United States open to nuclear attack, the political leverage of the U.S. nuclear advantage was no longer free. No longer able to deter Soviet provocation with the threat of "massive retaliation," deterrence was diversified. Flexible response offered limited tools to meet local Soviet probes in Eurasia without immediate nuclear escalation. At the same time, however, the United States solidified its position of nuclear superiority through a massive missile-building program. It was yet unwilling to forsake the proven benefits of perceived advantage in the nuclear balance. It was difficult to leave it behind for uncharted terrain in mutual perceptions.

THE REJECTION OF ADVANTAGE

Yet forsaken it was. From 1965 to 1976 the United States reversed itself. America suddenly seemed to tire of defining deterrence through nuclear advantage. A new doctrine was substituted, called "mutual assured destruction" (MAD). It fit American cultural yearnings, which were beginning to question the viability, indeed the morality, of employing nuclear forces in a traditional military balance. Domestic political sentiments would no longer accept the initial postwar utility of nuclear weapons as weapons, working within a traditional common language of their political leverage: the military balance. Deterrence of war through advantage was being rejected. Americans were returning to prewar ideas about promoting peace through stability, arms control, and eventual disarmament. Stability in opposing arsenals was the first step, and stability needed a formula.

MAD was the answer: mutual vulnerability of populations, mutual survivability of offensive nuclear delivery systems. In such a construct, it was believed, there would be no Soviet incentive to seek nuclear advantage in the traditional manner.

But they did. From 1976 to 1983 their nuclear effort was the central issue in the debate over American national security. They built and improved, and no number of arms control agreements seemed to stop their anachronistic and seemingly unstoppable quest for advantage in the military balance. The United States was now completely vulnerable to Soviet attack: the price of a working MAD doctrine. Burgeoning Soviet ICBM fields, moreover, were also threatening the survivability of a big slice of the American nuclear force. It was in this period that the perceptions game changed hands. The United States now felt insecure and increasingly imputed the aura of advantage to the Soviet Union. At some point, many argued, MAD would be untenable as a doctrine. It would be superseded by Soviet advantage.

The response to the failure of an experiment did not bring the United States back to a traditional view of the military balance. The last two Carter and the first two Reagan years were marked by an effort merely to regain the stability of stalemate. This involved a program of nuclear force modernization that was no longer fully supported by the American people. Political opposition to a new ICBM created a strategic conundrum. If the electorate accepted neither the force requirements for nuclear stalemate nor the possible consequences of nuclear inferiority, what alternative remained? Reagan's answer—the Strategic Defense Initiative—has more to do with the American belief system forty years after Hiroshima than with the animus of high technology.

Historically, Americans have never accepted the concept of a military balance except at certain critical moments in the national experience when they were faced with imminent attack or had the conviction of an impending threat. Look back beyond the Cold War to the 1920s. Americans saw military force as an onerous burden on the nation. This is an American cultural tradition. Many trendy critics lament the militarization of American society. They should look beyond defense dollar outlays. National sentiment is deeply ambivalent toward positive notions of military utility. In contrast to European traditions that link a nation's military arsenal and image to the international pecking order, Americans can sustain large standing forces only if they believe them to be of necessity.

NUCLEAR STRATEGY, AMERICAN STYLE

American attitudes toward military institutions, the utility of military force, and the interpretation of the military balance are unique. Military forces exist to deter war. With immediate conflict averted, the military balance should be stabilized to encourage an atmosphere of nonaggressiveness that is conducive to arms control. Arms control is the hopeful agency to a future peaceful world.

Two problems have emerged from the American attempt to substitute classical applications of the military balance for a deterrent focus based on equivalent nonadvantage. First, an adroit adversary will recognize the depth of American cultural aversion and court it. It will avoid visible threats to American security and entreat for arms control regimes that will work to its advantage. Treaties are highly favored by Americans as tokens of goodwill: "steps on the road to peace." Superficial cuts in weapons can be exchanged for consolidation of less visible advantages in the military balance. Americans tend to reject the traditional interpretation of the military balance. This makes the task of the adversary easier.

Second, while the United States discarded the classical military balance, the Soviets embraced it. Their premises have never changed. Military forces exist to ensure the security of the state. With the state secure from immediate attack, the military balance should be shaped toward the Soviet advantage. Advantage will create a political climate of influence that will help to achieve long-term objectives. Advantage is the key to these objectives.

There is ample evidence of this atavistic worldview among Soviet leaders. Most Americans, however, reject it for a more hopeful characterization of Soviet strategic values. Americans tend to project their own native patterns of thought and behavior on the Soviet leadership. Without cultural projection, MAD could never have been sustained in the face of glacial Soviet classicism.

Advantage in the nuclear balance is transcendental. Who can quantify it? In contrast to traditional calculations based on a body of war experience, on continual, even comfortable, use, nuclear advantage cannot be tested. Yet it exists, and it is tested in the political arena every day. The era of U.S. "nuclear superiority" may have been notorious for its translation of advantage into tactical victory. Today, however, it holds a kind of nostalgia for many who feel the cold wind of incipient Soviet advantage.

And then there are the Soviets. They have spent the past four decades lusting for that ticket to advantage in the military balance. Do they have it now? No. Will they abandon its pursuit? No.

THE DANGER OF MISPERCEPTIONS

More important to Americans than Soviet advantage is the dangerous gap between Soviet and American strategic worldviews. In the early 1940s, a profound separation of American and Japanese worldviews led to war. Both the United States and Japan had specific though divergent calculations of the naval forces necessary to achieve their respective notions of national security. The failure of the United States to keep pace with Japanese naval building eventually led to a sense of false security in Japan based on American naval inactivity and an uninterested electorate. When the United States suddenly started a crash program in shipbuilding, the prospect for Japan of naval inferiority replacing hard-won superiority in the western Pacific was unacceptable. This shock helped to promote the decision for war.

War came neither from Japanese "militarism" nor from an American naval arms buildup *in themselves.* War was the product of mutually insensitive cultural projections. The Japanese erected a strategy based on American patterns of political passivity toward the military balance. Americans assumed that Japan would never dare challenge the United States directly.

Advantage is in the eye of the beholder. It is waiting political capital, and it is to be sought along diplomatic lines as well as in the military production line. Arms control, in the Soviet worldview, is potentially as effective a means of securing advantage in the military balance as a nuclear building program. If the adversary appears to be on the verge of gaining a military advantage, arms control diplomacy is both cost-saving and critical. Just ask the Soviets why they came to Geneva.

The Soviets believe that a nuclear advantage is the key to their future. There is no way in which the United States, through arms control offers, can dissuade them from seeking it. It is also important to recognize that the Soviets do not yet believe that they have achieved a working advantage. Their behavior, it might be argued, has remained relatively restrained in proportion to their precise calculations of the nuclear balance. To concede advantage to the Soviet Union according to its definition would be a mistake. It would encourage a conviction in the Kremlin that creating a general perception of Soviet advantage equates to real political leverage.

In a world where the Politburo believed it could act as it wished, the United States and its allies would be helpless to restrain Soviet behavior. In an atmosphere tinged with politico-military coercion, Americans would be forced once again to embark on an arms-building program—to "right" a disadvantage in the balance.

Even in the American cultural cosmos, where the nuclear balance is thought to describe a calculus of force that cannot be used, advantage rules. Advantage is perceived mutually, no matter how we position cultural blinders. Advantage is the basis of strategic behavior. In crisis, it is the final consultation.

Thirty years of "arms control" have shown that the United States cannot reform the Soviet strategic worldview through diplomacy, and the obvious alternative, political accommodation to Soviet objectives, is still unacceptable to most Americans.

But there is another option. The United States can try to destroy the utility of nuclear weapons within the Soviet belief system, and the Strategic Defense Initiative provides just such a conceptual tool. SDI is not simply another strategic weapons program, it exists to outflank Soviet military efforts to gain advantage in the military balance. It has already undermined Soviet perceptions of strategic advantage by jeopardizing the political utility of nuclear weapons. SDI has forever altered Soviet expectations of the future military balance by shifting the boundary posts of the Soviet strategic worldview.

PART THREE

NUCLEAR FUTURES: THE STAR WARS DEBATE

THE VISION OF STRATEGIC DEFENSE
Caspar Weinberger

I would like to describe how we in the administration see our research into defensive technology fitting into our overall strategy for peace and stability, why we consider it such a bright hope for mankind, and why we cannot regard SDI as a bargaining chip to be negotiated away.

THE ORIGINS OF SDI

My goal is to correct a fundamental deficiency in the debate over SDI—a deficiency shared by expert and layman alike. And that is the lack of strategic perspective that is brought to bear on this complex issue. Too frequently, critics isolate SDI from the international environment and the threats we face. They fail to look at strategic defense research as a part of America's overarching strategic design. This strategic tunnel vision is born of the simplistic idea that there is really no substantial difference between the doctrines and capabilities of the United States and the Soviet Union. Indeed, if you read only domestic critics and Soviet propaganda, you would think that SDI emerged full-blown from our minds without reference to Soviet capabilities or strategic history.

The Honorable Caspar W. Weinberger is Secretary of Defense of the United States.

In fact, our research into the possibility of a defense against nuclear attack results from this administration's broad reassessment of our foreign and defense policies, which asked the question: What must we do after a decade of neglect of our forces?

SDI expresses the President's belief that we should seek to transcend the policy that rests all our hopes and lives on deterrence based on the threat of mutual annihilation. We see great hope in SDI, and so we are determined to continue vigorous research until we can know which defensive concepts are feasible. We do this, not only because the Soviets are doing it, but because it is right, morally and militarily.

Our critics must understand that any successful strategic design must take into account not only the threats we face in the world, but also the character and requirements of our own political system.

When President Reagan took office, one component of our strategy was in particular need of attention—nuclear doctrine and capability. Our broad examination of the strategic nuclear context led to a very troubling conclusion: the Soviet Union had rejected the notion of deterrence through agreed mutual vulnerability. In fact, the Soviets had been modernizing and increasing their offensive arsenal and simultaneously stepping up their defensive programs—all with the clear aim of gaining a first-strike capability.

No responsible leader could ignore this threat. Indeed, we joined the previous administration, with whom we had some notable differences, in demanding modernization of our strategic arsenal to reverse the increasing vulnerability of our nuclear forces and the consequent erosion of our deterrent capabilities.

Since strategy cannot be isolated from the threat, we had to consider both the Soviets' doctrine on nuclear war and their capabilities. And although a great many people joined us in this assessment, a good many stayed behind. A host of analysts persisted in calling for strategies and forces based on the amazing premise that the United States was largely responsible for the arms race, that it was America that threatened the peace, and that it was we who sought to destabilize the delicate balance of deterrence.

Strategy must also take into account our political system. As a democratic and peaceful nation, we cannot rest easily with a deterrent policy that depends exclusively on the threat of mass destruction or mutual suicide. President Reagan clearly under-stands this problem, and that is why strategic defense is one of his highest priorities. Thus, our strategic defense initiative has as its goal a new, more effective, and more moral basis for the deter-rence of war—a policy completely consistent with democratic values.

In the face of a persistent effort on the part of our critics to put blinders on strategy, this administration is fulfilling the require-ments of leadership, not to mention common sense. We have subjected the strategic nuclear capabilities that came down to us from the 1960s to a very realistic and hard-headed reexamination. Our reassessment led us to believe that a research program into all forms of strategic defense is an absolute necessity for the long-range peace and security of America and our allies. Let me explain why we concluded that security and peace require a vigorous SDI program.

THE SOVIET OFFENSIVE AND DEFENSIVE BUILDUP

Though many Western analysts believe that offensive technology will forever dominate defensive efforts, that is not the case in Soviet military doctrine. Adopting a rather traditional view of warfare in the nuclear age, the Soviets did not let their massive buildup of superior offensive forces—like those now facing our allies in Europe and Asia—preclude them from seeking the advan-tages of purely defensive systems. They did both. And this is right in line with their doctrine.

Since history and technology do not stand still, the Russians believe a defense against intercontinental ballistic missiles, though difficult to contemplate today, will be a reality in the future. Consequently, they have not locked their forces into an offense-only strategy. Given this Soviet doctrine, it would be, at the very least, a dangerous and possibly fatal folly to ignore the capabilities they continue to build to implement their doctrine.

So, what *have* the Soviets been doing? For many people, the signing of the SALT I agreement and the Anti-Ballistic Missile Treaty in 1972 signalled the inauguration of an "era of good feeling," or detente, between the United States and the Soviets. However, the Kremlin made clear that detente neither altered its intention to achieve a more favorable correlation of forces nor ended the ideological struggle between democracy and communism. Yet the hope in the West for an end to the Cold War was pervasive and comforting. Unfortunately, this hope was based on illusion.

The arms limitation agreement proved little more than a fleeting record of the existing balance of forces. The Soviets continued to modernize and add to their nuclear arsenal with so many weapons with such accuracy and throwweight that they threatened our retaliatory force. Since 1971 they have deployed at least four new types of ICBMs and nine improved versions of their existing ICBM and submarine missile forces, and we will soon see their new intercontinental bomber. The lifting power, number of warheads, and accuracy of Soviet missile forces make it impossible to view them as a second-strike force consistent with the strategy of agreed mutual vulnerability.

This Soviet buildup flew in the face of what many had expected to happen after SALT I. In what can only be described as supreme arrogance, some policymakers thought they had educated the Soviets on the realities of nuclear deterrence. Defense against a missile attack, we were told, was impossible, and the only real deterrence was the threat of mutual annihilation or mutual suicide. But if the Soviets had agreed, they would not have engaged in this massive and costly buildup and at the same time spent roughly as much on strategic defense systems as on their enormously expensive offensive strategic systems.

Along with SALT I, we signed a treaty limiting a whole range of activities in the area of strategic defense. This treaty strictly limited our nationwide defenses, and it is a treaty with which we remain in total compliance.

The agreement was seen by some as a capstone—as the assurance that our notions about deterrence were shared by Moscow. Indeed, one of the basic assumptions of SALT I and the ABM Treaty was that they would be the first step toward dramatic reductions in offensive forces. Recalcitrant students though they were, the Soviets had finally seen the light—or so it was argued at the time. But the anticipated reduction in offensive arms never happened, although thirteen years have passed since the ABM Treaty was signed.

In fact, the treaty did not foreclose the possibility of strategic defense. The architects of this treaty saw that at some future time technology might make defense possible, and so it permits research into defensive systems. It also provides for future negotiations between the signatories.

Had the ABM Treaty signified Kremlin acceptance of mutual vulnerability, their actions would have been roughly similar to our own. We abandoned our single ABM site, reduced expenditures on defense-related research, and virtually gave up our efforts on defensive systems of any kind.

We expected and bargained for one thing, but we got quite another. Far from abandoning the ABM site allowed under the treaty, as we did, the Soviets continued to improve it. Today they have the world's only operational ABM system—a system that is even now being upgraded.

In clear violation of that treaty, they are constructing a missile detection and tracking radar in Krasnoyarsk. The ABM Treaty limits such radars to the periphery of the nation, pointing outward to operate only as an early-warning radar. The Krasnoyarsk radar, however, is located 750 kilometers from the nearest Soviet border and looks across 4,000 kilometers of Russian territory. This radar closes an important gap in Soviet defense radars. However, the Soviets deny what we know to be true about the Krasnoyarsk radar. As Lincoln said, "If someone says the tail of a dog is actually a leg, the dog still has only four legs."

The Soviet Union has also developed rapidly deployable ABM engagement radars and interceptor missiles. They have probably tested surface-to-air missiles, normally used against bombers, to intercept ballistic missiles. All of this threatens a very rapid Soviet "breakout" from the ABM Treaty.

Additionally, Soviet research into advanced strategic defense technology—such as particle-beam weapons, radio-frequency weapons, kinetic-energy weapons, and high-energy lasers—has been extensive. More than 10,000 of their scientists and engineers are involved in this effort and, in some cases, they have made great progress well beyond the research stage. For example, the Soviets now have ground-based lasers that could interfere with our satellites. By the late 1980s, they could have prototypes of ground-based lasers able to hit ballistic missiles.

What the Soviets are doing is certainly clear, and why they are doing it is spelled out in their doctrine. But the question remains: What should *we* do to ensure that we can still deter them from starting a nuclear war? The President faced and answered that most fundamental of all strategic questions. He made a radical decision that if the research program into strategic defense that he has ordered shows it is feasible, we could change our strategy. And it is a decision that stands alone as the right, and indeed the only, thing to do—to remove the threat of mutual destruction, regardless of Soviet activities.

THE STRATEGIC DEFENSE INITIATIVE

What we do in foreign and defense policy is closely connected with who we are and what we value. Naturally, we desire a realistic and moral deterrence policy that is responsive to the threat and reflects our democratic values. Our uneasiness with the strategic doctrine and programs developed in the 1960s is therefore perfectly consistent with our goals and principles. And with the Soviets clearly rejecting the concept of agreed mutual vulnerability, there is only one prudent course of action: change our own doctrine and programs. We must seek and secure a defensive capability that could ultimately lead to the end of nuclear missiles. This is not only prudent, it is far more in keeping with our democratic ideals than a mutual suicide pact.

In acknowledging the need to study the feasibility of a defense against Soviet missiles, we took a course radically different from that of the Soviet Union—we actually told the world what we are doing, and we invited the world to help us to achieve such a defense. We even briefed the Soviets on SDI in Geneva so they could understand our program and join us in discussing how we might fashion a stable transition away from deterrence based on offensive threats, if defensive technologies prove feasible.

In fact, we have explained to everyone our long-term goal, which is simply to study the potential of a transformation of the strategic order so that the threat of nuclear offensive forces and nuclear mass destruction can be drastically reduced—and eventually eliminated. We have learned that the dogma of agreed mutual vulnerability, over the long term, is not a safe guarantee against nuclear war, particularly when the Soviets do not accept it. Nor can it offer the world any hope of halting the ever-mounting stockpile of offensive arms. History has proven this.

But as we go forward with the needed transformation to a strategic order based on defense, we cannot, nor do we intend to, neglect our triad of deterrent offensive systems. Rather, for some time to come we must maintain and, indeed, modernize our deterrent forces and their communications systems. We do not yet know whether a thoroughly capable defense system can be established, so prudence demands that we not allow the dangerous gap between our triad and the growing Soviet nuclear force to widen. Nor do we wish to condemn ourselves to a future in which, as Churchill said, safety is "the sturdy child of terror." The survival of civilization must be built on a firmer foundation than the prospect of mutual terror.

We all recognized from the outset that if the research bears fruit, a complete system for strategic defenses could not be deployed overnight. We seek a stable transitional period when some defenses would be deployed and operating before others. Some have argued that this transition would be particularly dangerous, that it would upset the present deterrent system without putting an adequate substitute in its place.

The opposite is the case. If properly planned and phased, the transitional capabilities would actually strengthen our present deterrent capability. In fact, they could make a major contribution to the prevention of nuclear war, even before a fully effective system is deployed.

If the Soviet leaders ever contemplated initiating a nuclear attack, their purpose would be to destroy U.S. or Allied retaliatory capability and the military forces that would blunt Soviet aggression. Even partially effective defenses that could deny Soviet missiles their military objectives, or shake the Soviets' confidence in their ability to achieve such dire objectives, would discourage them from considering such an attack and would thus be a highly effective deterrent.

Recognition that a fully effective defensive system could not be deployed overnight must not dilute our efforts toward finding a thoroughly reliable, layered defense that would destroy Soviet missiles outside the Earth's atmosphere and at all phases of their flight. And let me stress that the choice is not between protecting military forces and protecting cities. The goal of our strategic defense research program, the vision and hope of the President, is to stop Soviet missiles *before* they could destroy *any* targets, be they in the United States or anywhere else. The goal is noble and straightforward: to destroy weapons that kill people.

Thus, based on a realistic view of Soviet military planning, the transition to strategic defense would not be destabilizing. In fact, any initial defensive capabilities would offer many benefits. They would contribute to deterrence by denying Soviet attack goals, and should deterrence ever fail, they would save lives by reducing the scope of the destruction that would result from a Soviet attack. The more effective the defenses, the more effective this deterrence would be. This objective is far more idealistic, moral, and practical than the position taken by those who still embrace the mutual assured destruction (MAD) theory that defenses must be totally abandoned.

I know that some of our allies fear that our pursuit of the defense initiative would tend to "decouple" America from them. This is quite wrong. The security of the United States is inseparable from the security of our allies. In addition to strengthening our nuclear deterrent, such defenses would also enhance Europe's ability to deter Soviet aggression by reducing the ability of Soviet intermediate-range ballistic missiles—both conventional and nuclear—to put at risk either our allies or those facilities essential to conventional defense such as airfields, ports, depots, and communications networks. The same is true with respect to Japan and Korea. An effective defense against ballistic missiles would create great uncertainty in the mind of the aggressor, reduce the likelihood of a conventional attack on Western Europe, and thereby reduce the chance that the Soviet Union would contemplate such an attack in the first place.

If such a system can be developed, it will offer the Soviets a strong incentive to reduce their investment in offensive forces, and this is precisely what President Reagan is seeking. Even now we are asking the Soviets to join us in deep reductions in offensive weapons. But if we stop our work on strategic defense and give it away at the negotiating table, we will forever lose one of history's best chances to end the shadow and the fear of nuclear weapons.

CONCLUSION

Today we have but one choice if, by accident or design, deterrence fails—and that is retaliation with our offensive systems. Of course, we all hope deterrence will never fail. That is why all our efforts are designed to persuade any enemy that the cost of their aggression is too high.

The President's proposal at last offers us the first real opportunity to transform and enhance deterrence—the opportunity for us to make a major contribution to strengthening peace and preserving our liberty. But this hope exists only if we, in this generation, seize this matchless opportunity that is now given to us. We are, indeed, in Lincoln's words, "the last best hope of mankind." Let us then try the only hope we have of leading mankind away from the constant threat of nuclear holocaust.

THE STRATEGIC DEFENSE PROJECT
James Abrahamson

What is the Strategic Defense Initiative? I would like to offer an overview. Let me begin by highlighting the obvious—that large national programs take much time, energy, and sweat. We have all been very busy in the Strategic Defense Initiative Organization (SDIO), and I am pleased to report that our progress to date has been excellent and that the evidence suggests the same for the future.

But, of course, the various elements within SDI have much longer histories than the two and a half years the SDIO has been in existence as an agency within the Defense Department. In fact, many SDI program elements have the considerable benefit of long years of highly productive research by dedicated scientific laboratories and the military services. The SDI program is actually built on the efforts of others, reaching back in some cases to the 1960s. This is one reason we feel so confident about our future prospects. Another reason is our faith in the technological competence of the American scientific and industrial community, and in their ingenuity and ability to overcome obstacles. Only the misinformed would fail to appreciate this nation's great scientific and technical prowess.

Lt. Gen. James A. Abrahamson is the Director of the Strategic Defense Initiative Organization of the Department of Defense.

SDI is a research effort, and clearly within the letter and intent of the ABM Treaty. However, the research program is building the infrastructure and industrial capability so that we can quickly go into a development and deployment phase when that decision is made—despite the chorus of critics who have been working overtime against this program. The main source of strength for SDI has been, in fact, the American people, for they have shown both the common sense and courage to recognize the potential importance of active defenses for our nation and to lend their strong support to the President's program.

As I travel and speak on behalf of SDI, I can sense throughout America that our citizens really believe this to be an idea whose time has come. They want to see this concept fully explored. And they are as confident as I that, if our research bears fruit, this nation will—after taking appropriate diplomatic steps—have an active strategic defense to protect ourselves and our allies. There is simply nothing I can say that I feel to be more important.

THE PROGRAM ELEMENTS

We have now completed review of the various "systems architecture" and key trade-off studies by our "horserace" contractors. The results are very encouraging. The contractors have worked hard to carefully define all aspects of architectural analysis. We have seen innovative approaches to survivability and battle management that show real promise. Discrimination, for example, is a very difficult problem, and the contractors are struggling to identify successful approaches in that area.

The goal of our innovative science and technology program is to establish scientific feasibility and engineering validation of revolutionary concepts, concepts with potential for full SDI technological development. This forward-looking office has a broad research charter that focusses on advanced directed-energy concepts such as gamma-ray lasers, on novel sensing and data preprocessing techniques, on advanced materials for space applications, on innovations in spacepower, and on emerging space-science applications and ultra-high-speed supercomputing. Interest in such exotic areas of science and technology clearly illustrates that SDI has greatly facilitated the mobilization of our nation's scientific community.

In the spring of 1985, this office sponsored a review conference for universities. Over 150 academic institutions representing forty-seven states attended. Subject areas included composite materials, rocket fuels, electronic materials, systolic-array processing, software development, optical computing, and space science. Since that review, we have received thousands of creative and interesting proposals for this program from around the country. Perhaps this is the best response I can give to those stories in the media concerning academics and university scientists who choose not to work on SDI—and somehow expect headlines for such a decision.

Three of the criteria for judging whether SDI is feasible will be system effectiveness, cost, and survivability. Analyses have shown that survivability will be a critical element in determining the feasibility of strategic defenses. Potential defensive systems must be capable of operating in a potentially hostile environment, and this applies to land-, air-, and space-based systems. In recognition of the importance of survivability, I have established a separate survivability project to manage these efforts centrally.

I am greatly encouraged that SDI architecture contractors have been considering survivability as an integral part of potential designs, because we will judge any potential defensive system desirable only if it is survivable and cost-effective at the margin. We intend, in fact, that potential SDI system designs should consider survivability on an equal basis with mission performance.

Elsewhere in the SDI program the news is also good. During the past year, the surveillance/acquisition, tracking, and kill assessment program has seen broad technological progress. It has initiated efforts to define the requirements and has addressed some key problems, such as discriminating reentry vehicles from decoys. For key sensor elements, it has identified a need for advanced focal-plane materials, cryogenic coolers to maintain operating temperatures, and signal processing capability.

In the directed-energy program, we continue to make excellent progress. Of particular note are the very encouraging test results of the large chemical laser (MIRACL) at White Sands Missile Range. The beam quality has been significantly improved as a result of tilting the modules slightly and thereby eliminating problems with the uniformity of the flowing laser gas caused by strut wakes. This advance gives us greater confidence in our ability to focus the laser beam into a small spot at long range.

The kinetic-energy program at SDI has as its foundation the successful efforts by the military services and the Defense Advanced Research Projects Agency in the technologies upon which the concepts of kinetic-energy weapons for strategic defense application can be built. An excellent example is the Army's June 1984 Homing Overlay Experiment (HOE), which conclusively proved that ground-launched exo-atmospheric hit-to-kill intercept of a reentry vehicle was feasible. The payoff for chemically propelled interceptors is being studied in terminal, midcourse, and boost phases, with uncertainties remaining primarily in the area of terminal accuracy and cost. Electromagnetic and other novel launchers which can propel interceptors to significantly higher velocities than rockets are also being studied.

Finally, we are planning to conduct a major program of space experiments to demonstrate target tracking with the precision necessary for a number of missions, including support of kinetic-energy weapons and surveillance sensors, as well as directed-energy weapons. This series of experiments is being conducted aboard the space shuttle.

THE SDI DEBATE

For over two years I have listened to well-intentioned people speak with sincerity and concern against the Strategic Defense Initiative. They say it will not work, it can be easily overcome, it is too expensive, it is destabilizing and dangerous, and it threatens peace. Some even assert that SDI severely damages the prospects for arms control.

I wonder, does SDI's *research* into strategic defense actually threaten peace? Does it damage the legitimate search for nuclear-arms reductions? Or does common sense tell us that SDI, which threatens no one and is designed only to research the possibility of physically defending America and its allies against the devastation of nuclear ballistic missiles, is indeed a principal reason that negotiations are again underway between the superpowers? Perhaps we might ask whether the evidence suggests that SDI *promotes* rather than threatens peace and stability. We might recognize the possibility that SDI can deliver mankind from the need to base deterrence only on retaliation, that it can help to strengthen deterrence, and that there may be no other alternative available that can potentially deliver such benefits. Those who have taken the time to consult the facts on SDI have generally favored research, and have seen the hope in President Reagan's vision.

But there is yet another body of facts which I believe are worth studying in light of the propaganda campaign mounted by the Soviet Union to identify the President's Strategic Defense Initiative as the mortal enemy of world peace and arms control, as not hopeful but threatening. And perhaps we should all note carefully that, while the Soviets are eager to discuss *our* research on active strategic defenses, they are extremely reluctant to discuss their own expansive efforts in these same areas.

What of those Soviet programs? What are the facts? Experts have concluded that since the Anti-Ballistic Missile Treaty of 1972, the Soviet Union has spent about as much on strategic defenses as on their enormous buildup in offensive strategic nuclear missiles. Their air defenses are the densest and most sophisticated in the world. They have made civil defense preparations for much of their population and all of their leadership. Around Moscow they have constructed and continue to modernize the world's only operational ABM defense system, and they have used this system to upgrade, test, and gain operational ABM experience. They also possess the world's only operational antisatellite system.

In addition, the Soviets have invested very heavily for more than two decades in other forms of antiballistic missile defense, including *precisely* those technologies encompassed by our own SDI research program. Given these facts, does it not seem hypocritical that the Soviets would excoriate the U.S. SDI program in tones of outrage and moral indignation? Is it not hypocritical that they are now constructing a radar in central Siberia which blatantly violates the very ABM Treaty they claim to want stringently enforced? And is it not also the height of hypocrisy that the very scientists in charge of developing Soviet nuclear strategic offenses, strategic defenses, and chemical-biological warfare programs would publish and sign a *Pravda* statement deploring our SDI as a threat to world peace? I would note, parenthetically, that the U.S. SDI program is being conducted in full compliance with the ABM Treaty.

These kinds of facts are not generally provided to the public by those who malign SDI. Nor do they admit that our research results, though incomplete, have generally shown strong evidence that an effective strategic defense is possible and that SDI research provides a prudent hedge against a Soviet breakout from the ABM Treaty.

If we are to provide some future president and Congress with a solid body of information on the feasibility of active defenses, we must closely adhere to this President's objectives, milestones, and sense of priority. But even as the program is borne steadily forward by the tremendous efforts of American science and industry and by those in government responsible for research and management, I would be remiss to suggest that *all* the news is good.

In each of our budget years thus far, Congress has determined that major reductions were necessary in an SDI budget request based precisely on President Reagan's March 23, 1983 mandate for strategic defense research. We have attempted through innovative management and just plain hard work to overcome these shortfalls, and we will keep working with the Congress to keep the program intact.

It is essential that the President's program receive adequate support so that ultimately we will be able to provide the sound basis for an informed decision on the future development and deployment of active defenses when it is needed. It is for this reason above all—and in view of the concerted Soviet attempts both to achieve offensive superiority and defensive monopoly at the strategic level, and also to work actively to undermine public and Allied support for our SDI research program—that it is so urgently important for the great majority of Americans, those who wisely understand the need for our nation to protect itself adequately, to see the importance of this research program.

I believe that most Americans now recognize the critical importance of SDI. They know that SDI is the key element of President Reagan's vision to keep the world free of nuclear conflict—and to make this a first step in rendering nuclear ballistic missiles impotent and obsolete. They know that while deterrence will remain at least partly based on offensive systems and a doctrine of retaliation well into the future, the enormous buildup of nuclear offensive missiles by the Soviets could increasingly call into question our own deterrent capability, our doctrine, and ultimately our national safety. They know that SDI may be the key to reversing the buildup in offensive arms, to strengthening deterrence, and to building greater stability and security. And they support the President's clearheaded thinking about SDI and arms control. He has repeatedly stated that the SDI program is not a "bargaining chip" because it is far too important to America and its allies. That was true wisdom speaking.

Americans are intuitively wise people. They know that SDI is an idea important to their nation and to the human race. They see through those who have sought for their own purposes to portray SDI as a political debate, as an ideological argument, or as a strategic commonplace. They have also come to understand that SDI critics offer no positive alternative for strengthening strategic stability. Instead, Americans see the idea of the Strategic Defense Initiative—our President's own idea—as the possible key to the future peace and freedom of mankind. Thank God that we do.

CAUTION ON STAR WARS
James Schlesinger

Churchill might have said about this subject of strategic defense, "never in the course of human history has so much been said by so many about something so speculative and long-run." In the SDI area, the rhetoric has indeed gotten out of hand, and it is a purpose of mine to help bring it back to earth.

In the search for truth in the strategic defense area, I have been guided by the counsel of that very wise American Mr. Yogi Berra, who has stated that "one can observe a lot by just watching." So I have been watching the defense scene for a number of years, and I start with three observations.

THE HISTORICAL SETTING

First, we should not forget that the United States deployed a strategic defense system in the 1950s, largely in Canada. It was advertised as capable of stopping all Soviet bombers attempting to move toward the United States. Components of that system were given great fanfare. The only problem was that it did not work very well, and it has since been largely dismantled. If we proceed with Star Wars, we will need to deploy another air defense system, again mainly in Canada.

The Honorable James R. Schlesinger is a former Secretary of Defense.

The second point to bear in mind is that the United States started to deploy its first antiballistic missile capabilities, the Safeguard system, in 1970. That was vastly better than anything the Soviets had at the time, and the Soviets knew it, but it too had a major weakness in that it did not work very well. And after the Anti-Ballistic Missile Treaty was signed, we dismantled it.

The third gleam of historical light emerges from the fact that prior to 1983 the Department of Defense, under pressure to move ahead in the ABM area, openly scoffed at those who advocated space-based defense capabilities. It insisted that these systems would not work. That was, of course, before the Department had seen the light. And the light changed suddenly in the form of a presidential speech in March 1983. For the Department of Defense, which rapidly wheeled around and became—to a greater or lesser extent, depending upon the individual involved—true believers, that event was like a flash of light on the road to Damascus.

The President's speech in March 1983 came as a total surprise. Indeed, it came as a surprise to all but a few advisors in the government and a few outside the government. It led to inconsistencies in the United States' peacekeeping philosophy that are being exploited today in Soviet propaganda on Star Wars. Many members of the federal establishment were unpleasantly surprised by this speech, but they were obliged by circumstances to repress whatever dissatisfaction they might have felt. There had been no prior consultation with our allies, all of whom believed in the deterrent system already in place. There had been no prior indications to our rival, the Soviet Union. There had been no consultation within the federal government. It came as a surprise to the Departments of State and Defense. Indeed, the Under Secretary of Defense for Research and Engineering learned about the details of the President's speech only the day before it was given. This means that there was not a full governmental review.

The surprise was disturbing because there has been an acknowledgment by the superpowers since 1972, for better or worse, of their mutual strategic vulnerability. That has long been the cornerstone of strategic arms control discussions. It may not be a comfortable cornerstone, but it has been the accepted one, and it has worked. Moreover, our British and French allies have depended upon both superpowers, and most notably the Russians, to refrain from deployment of strategic defenses that might vitiate their investments in their own independent nuclear capabilities.

RHETORIC VERSUS REALITY

Since all discussions of strategic arms reduction have been premised on the presumed infeasibility of strategic defense, it is understandable that there was consternation at the time of the President's speech. The biggest problem with the strategic defense initiative is that the rhetoric has gotten out of hand. Though the strategic and force-structure implications of SDI are still in the research phase, the rhetoric has implied that the United States may become invulnerable to the Soviet Union's threat. The compelling question is, Can it be done? But the answer depends on a more basic question: What is it?

There are two versions of strategic defense. The President said in his speech that this defense would render nuclear weapons "impotent and obsolete." He was presumably thinking of ballistic missiles rather than aircraft or cruise missiles, but he implied that it would render all nuclear weapons impotent and obsolete. That is a very demanding task, to say the least. It would require the establishment of an "astrodome" over the United States.

There are those associated with what is known as the "high frontier" who believe that that capability is here today, that it is an off-the-shelf capability, and that we should get on with the task. Indeed, technology has moved along. We are better able to deal with the ballistic missile defense issue today than in 1969. There is a possibility of layers of defense. I underscore a *possibility*. We have in recent months heard more and more about the three layers of strategic defense—boost phase, midcourse, and terminal intercept—and that each of these layers would intercept some proportion of Soviet missiles. One can watch this on television in those splendid cartoons put out by the media in which you see objects in space being zapped out. They show a mirror placed up at 23,000 miles and a laser that moves up from a site on a mountain in the United States. The laser is reflected back to another satellite that promptly zaps a Soviet reentry body. In sober truth, we are no where near that. We do not have that kind of technology.

The President's vision of Star Wars, of eliminating the possibility of attack by ballistic missiles, assumes that space defense will work perfectly. There can be no leakage through the three layers of defense. It must work perfectly the first time, because it can never be tested. I do not ask you to dismiss the possibility that this can be done, but just to take some of what you may hear about it, where we are going and how rapidly we are getting there, with a grain of salt. Mr. Reagan's vision is mutual assured *survival*, not dependent upon Soviet restraint, but on the hardness under real attack of an American nuclear defense astrodome.

THE TECHNICAL PROBLEM

The President's vision by and large drives public opinion, but it is scarcely credible. It will not be achieved, in part because of the immense technical difficulties of intercepting 50,000 objects in space the first time with a system that has never been tested. Most weapons do not work perfectly the first time. We had to abandon the Sergeant York ground-to-air system against low-flying helicopters because it proved ineffective. If we cannot manage that relatively simple task, how can we have confidence in our ability to intercept warheads descending from outer space?

SOVIET RESPONSES

We must deal with the certainty that any success we approach in ballistic missile defense will encounter Soviet countermeasures. The Soviet Union will not stand idly by while its capacity to strike at American targets is being eroded. It will seek to develop fast-burn missiles, more deception, more decoys, more penetration aids, more throwweight, and more lifting ability in their rockets to deliver such hardware. But more important, there are ways of attacking the United States that are not dependent upon ballistic missiles. There is still what the jargon of the military establishment has referred to as the "air-breathing threat"—bombers and cruise missiles. We are building the B-1 bomber and researching Stealth systems precisely because we believe they can penetrate the sophisticated Soviet air defense screen. Our air defenses, as I have mentioned, are in disarray. How are we supposed to cope with these alternative nuclear delivery systems?

There may be no perfect air defense. A few years ago, a Cuban pilot defected with an advanced MiG from Cuba and we did not know about it until the plane was sitting on the runway in Miami.

The Soviets can easily expand their fleets of bombers and submarines with a cruise missile delivery capability. There is also the possibility of what is known as depressed trajectories for weapons fired from submarines. That technology would permit submarine-launched ballistic missiles to penetrate all three SDI defense layers, including the ground-based layer. The inescapable fact is that we are not going to have the perfect defense that the President has talked about and that lies behind much of the political support for SDI.

COSTS

Then there is the question of cost. A credible ballistic missile defense system based on foreseeable technology will likely cost a trillion dollars at 1985 prices. If one is thinking of hundreds, if not thousands, of space stations for purposes of surveillance as well as attack, the cost could escalate astronomically. Where will that kind of money come from? The national political will for big defense budgets is faltering. To carve 80–120 billion dollars a year out of that budget to make room for SDI, and the vital air defense system needed to supplement it, would dangerously truncate the United States' conventional capabilities on which we depend to keep peace in Europe and the Third World.

CONCLUSION

So what should we do? I mentioned that there is another version of strategic defense. That version is being pushed within the Pentagon by revisionists. The line of argument is that if we cannot protect our people we can at least protect our missile fields. That is certainly a more credible objective. The rationale is that by protecting our missiles we would be protecting our deterrent and thus enhancing stability. It is a plausible argument but quite different from the President's. The President has said that we are going to protect people and not weapons. But what the revisionists in the Pentagon want to do is to protect weapons and not people. This alternative could enhance stability, but it is a long way from the political magic that the President initially evoked when he suggested to the public that at some future date they might become invulnerable to a nuclear holocaust.

These two versions of the SDI mission have led to a certain ambiguity about what is meant when we talk about strategic defense. There are some who cherish and seek to preserve that ambiguity. So if you want to go for strategic defense, recognize that what you will get, if anything, will not be that astrodome over the nation that will make us invulnerable to Soviet attack.

What should we do? As I mentioned earlier, the rhetoric seems to me to be getting out of hand. We are engaged in examining the strategic and force-structure implications of something that no one has designed yet. That seems to me to be premature. This is basically a research program and should remain so, at least for the foreseeable future. And in a research program we normally allow for the technical uncertainties to be resolved before we draw conclusions about strategy and force structure. In this case, the sequence has been turned on its head. We are drawing conclusions about a new posture of mixed offense and defense at a time when the research stage is still an amorphous embryo.

Should we deploy a limited defense to protect our missile fields? Possibly. But before we do that, we must think it through with great care. It means the end of the ABM Treaty, certainly if it is not negotiated with the Soviets. We will be creating incentives for the Soviets to expand their offensive forces in order to overwhelm a defensive shield that may never materialize. And we should, above all, think long and hard before we actually deploy components of the system that may work on the assumption that the rest will come along later. It probably will not, and certainly not in the next forty years. In a world that relies on an exquisite strategic balance to forestall the holocaust, it would be the worst of blunders to jolt the tightrope when the safety net is tied at only one end.

DEFENSE AGAINST NUCLEAR WEAPONS: ASSESSMENT IN THE FACE OF UNCERTAINTY
Franklin Long

The 1983 Star Wars proposal of President Reagan to develop a fully effective defense against nuclear weapons—which was followed by the prompt establishment of a major research project, the Strategic Defense Initiative (SDI), to seek some of the required new weapons—initiated a debate that is remarkable for its complexity, for the acrimony it has generated, and for the level of uncertainty that surrounds it. Much of the uncertainty was inevitable, given the sweeping character of the Reagan proposal, which was to replace the deterrence of nuclear war by the threat of nuclear retaliation with the development and deployment of an impregnable defense. The obvious questions were: Is such a defense feasible? What would be the character and effectiveness of Soviet responses? What would be the impact on our NATO and other allies? Would U.S. security be enhanced if the goal were attained?

In considering a major new military program like this, the usual situation is that the largest uncertainties and the most complex debates relate to the political, diplomatic, and economic aspects of the proposal. The technologies for the new military systems are normally well understood. This is not the situation in the Star Wars debate. The needed technologies are not in hand,

Dr. Franklin A. Long is Professor Emeritus of Chemistry and of Science and Society at Cornell University's program on Science, Technology and Society.

and the objective of the Strategic Defense Initiative is to search for those needed for defense against nuclear-armed ballistic missiles. Opponents of the program are arguing vigorously on technical grounds that the goal is unobtainable for the foreseeable future. This basic controversy impacts sharply on the other areas of uncertainty—the political, economic, and military. The result is a thoroughly confusing debate in which people make various assumptions on technology and postulate differing goals for defense. When to these uncertainties are added the inevitable imponderables of Soviet and Allied responses, the complexity becomes almost unbounded.

An important sharpening of the debate was presented by Paul Nitze in a speech given before the World Affairs Council of Philadelphia in February 1985. In the speech—which, given Nitze's official position within the government, quite certainly had been formally approved—he emphasized the need for evolution of the "U.S.-Soviet strategic relationship" and suggested joint discussions "as to how we might together make a transition to a more stable and reliable relationship based on an increasing mix of defensive systems." This goes well beyond the notion, implicit in the President's Star Wars speech, that the United States is considering only a unilateral development of defenses. Nitze noted that a decade or more will be involved in beginning to move away from our current position of deterrence by retaliation, and pointed out that during this decade, "we will seek to reverse the erosion that has occurred in the Anti-Ballistic Missile (ABM) Treaty regime," and "we will be pursuing the SDI research program—in full compliance with the ABM Treaty." And he added, "Should new defensive technologies prove feasible, we would want at some future date to begin . . . a transition, during which we would place greater reliance on defensive systems for our protection and that of our allies."

Nitze then pointed to two criteria by which the feasibility of new technologies will be judged: "the technologies must produce defensive systems that are survivable" and the "new defensive systems must also be cost-effective at the margin." Further, "if the new technologies cannot meet these standards, we are not about to deploy them." These criteria, and the proposal of parallel U.S. and Soviet approaches, are important clarifications that help focus the debate. There are, however, many remaining problem areas, so the debate still rages.

OBJECTIVES

The ultimate goal that President Reagan identified in his 1983 speech was "eliminating the threat posed by strategic nuclear missiles," which, of course, would in turn eliminate the necessity for the United States to maintain nuclear weapons for deterrence by retaliation. As if to emphasize this, the President spoke of being able to "intercept and destroy strategic ballistic missiles before they reached our own soil or that of our allies." Given the immense destructiveness of nuclear weapons, this goal clearly calls for a perfect defense. This is a daunting challenge, since in addition to developing the requisite technologies and deploying them in an effective overall system in the face of Soviet countermeasures, the system must be good enough so that there is *high confidence* that the defense is indeed perfect. In subsequent discussions and speeches, the President and his then science advisor, George Keyworth, have reiterated this goal of a total defense.

A less demanding and technically far more feasible objective is a "very good defense," a defense that with high probability could destroy between 90 and 99 percent of attacking Soviet weapons. The distinction between the utility of this defense and that of the perfect defense is very marked. The essential point of a perfect defense is that it would give protection not only to our military forces, but also to our population and industry. However, a very good defense, capable of intercepting 95 percent of the current Soviet arsenal of 10,000 strategic nuclear warheads would still leave 500 of them to impact on U.S. targets, a quite intolerable number if they were directed at U.S. cities. Hence, a very good defense would surely *not* permit abandonment by the United States of deterrence by threat of nuclear retaliation.

A third and still less demanding objective would be to develop partial defenses against nuclear weapons. This might suggest an effectiveness of anywhere from 25 to 75 percent interception of attacking nuclear warheads. Those who favor striving first for this limited objective argue for it as a means of strengthening deterrence by threat of retaliation. The emphasis of a partial defensive system would then be on preferential defense of high-value military targets, and in particular on defending silo-based missile fields, and command and control centers.

There are major differences in technologies between a perfect or very good defense and a partial defense that focuses on strengthening deterrence by threat of retaliation. For the latter, the preservation of U.S. nuclear forces and command and control is a high priority, and this in turn argues for extensive dependence on terminal defense of missile silos and command centers. In contrast, to attain a very good or perfect defense, there is a consensus in the technical community that Soviet missiles must be attacked and destroyed in their initial boost phase, that is, as they are launched from silos well within the Soviet Union. To accomplish this, there seems to be no alternative to attack from space by directed-energy weapons or high-velocity projectiles. Technologies for terminal defense have been extensively studied by both the United States and the Soviet Union. However, the space-based technologies required for attack on launch have only recently been considered seriously, and the technical challenge to develop effective weapons and then to ensure their survivability in space is formidable.

COSTS

Some of the uncertainties about the feasible goal for a U.S. defensive system, assuming the research program is successful, arise from attempts to estimate costs. The same applies to the question of cost-effectiveness, which will be discussed somewhat later. The most reasonable case to start with is the President's explicit goal of a fully effective defense with reliance on space-based defenses for attacking the Soviet missiles as they launch. However, this is also the case where the technologies are most uncertain, and this means that costs are unavoidably speculative. That the costs of a full defense will be very large is foreshadowed by the current expectation of the Defense Department that about $90 billion will be spent in the research program before the decision to go ahead is made. This is an amount that would look large for a fully-deployed weapons system in ordinary times.

In spite of the speculative character of a complete defense, a number of people have made rough estimates of costs by using analogies with other systems and using costs of launching materials into space. Cost estimates vary somewhat, but all are high. Ex-Secretaries of Defense Harold Brown and James Schlesinger have estimated that the full system would cost on the order of a trillion dollars. George Field of Harvard estimated a similar amount for just a satellite laser system. Estimates by Hans Bethe, based particularly on the cost of putting materials into orbit, come out to roughly the same figure. Note, however, that this trillion-dollar estimate is just for a system to counteract warheads delivered by ballistic missiles. The complete defensive system must also be able to offer a fully effective defense against all other modes of delivery of nuclear explosives, cruise missiles and strategic bombers in particular. The magnitude of the defensive system that the Soviet Union has deployed against U.S. strategic bombers suggests a U.S. cost of a few hundred billion dollars for systems to counter these other delivery modes. The resulting complex system would need to be on full operational alert at all times, and operational costs will be very large, probably on the order of tens of billions of dollars per year. More detailed analyses can be made of the costs of a terminal defense system to protect silo-based missiles and command and control centers. The estimated costs here should be much less than for the space-based systems, but they nevertheless could be on the order of tens of billions of dollars.

All of the uncertainties discussed for estimating the costs of these systems apply equally strongly to estimates of cost-effectiveness, where one must compare these costs with those of the countermeasures that the Soviet Union might take against U.S. defensive systems. Some fairly detailed analyses of cost-effectiveness were made in the late 1960s on the request of then-Secretary of Defense McNamara. These calculations were for ground-based U.S. defensive systems, with the Soviets responding by deploying more ballistic missiles. The general conclusion was that under a variety of conditions and levels of defense, the defensive systems were not cost-effective relative to the cost to the Soviet Union of overcoming them. In the twenty years since these studies were made, there have been major improvements in the effectiveness of offensive missiles and also in the effectiveness of defenses against them. Hence these early analyses can only serve as a warning that even partial defenses may not be cost-effective.

General considerations strongly suggest that defense systems are likely to be most cost-effective for partial defenses of missile silos and least cost-effective for the final deployments of a perfect defense system. One part of the argument is that a perfect defense depends strongly on the use of space-based systems, and space is inherently a very expensive medium in which to operate. A rather different argument concerns the fact that for the initial deployment of defenses of missiles in silos, a system can be developed that relies on preferential defense, whereas at the extreme other end, a nearly perfect defense, it is equally straightforward for the offense to develop a posture that relies on preferential offense.

To illustrate these arguments, consider first the problem of a partial defense of missiles in silos. Note that the aim of the defense need not be to ensure that all of our missiles survive. Consider a field of one hundred missiles in silos and a strong attack by the opponent. If twenty of the missiles survive, they will constitute a potent retaliatory force—against cities, for example. Assume next that each of the weapons for the defense can be used to attack any incoming warhead, that is, that it can cover the entire missile field. The defenders can then choose to defend strongly a random selection of, say, twenty-five missiles and ignore defending the other seventy-five. By this tactic, the missile field can survive a heavy attack by the offense and still have perhaps twenty of its silo-based missiles survive.

At the other extreme, consider a near-perfect defense designed to defend the population and industry, as well as the military targets, of an entire nation. Assume that at a given time the offensive and defensive systems are just balanced, that is, that there are precisely enough defensive weapons to take care of all offensive weapons. Now, suppose the offense deploys one additional weapon with a single warhead. Since this can be aimed at any of a hundred cities, the defense will need to bolster the defense installation around each of these cities by one more defending unit. Clearly the cost effectiveness of defense at this point is exceedingly low. With the kinds of defensive systems now envisaged, one can thus contemplate a situation in which defense is relatively cost-effective for initial deployments of defense and yet lacking in cost-effectiveness by a large factor for the development of a near-perfect defense.

SOVIET RESPONSES

It seems inevitable that the deployment of defensive systems against nuclear weapons by either the United States or the Soviet

Union will lead to responses by the other, and hence to an extension and acceleration of the arms race between them. If the United States goes ahead with the deployment of defenses that are now being searched for in the Strategic Defense Initiative, the Soviets can respond in three different ways, or in mixtures of them. The most obvious response would be for them to increase the number of nuclear-armed weapons that are aimed at the United States. For attack by intercontinental missiles, they could do this by increasing either the number of missiles or the number of nuclear warheads carried by each missile. They could also enhance the survivability of their missiles and warheads by decreasing the launch time of the missiles, which would make them more difficult targets for space-based defensive systems, they could develop and deploy decoys for their missiles during their midcourse travel, or they could complicate terminal defense by using nuclear warheads with terminal guidance.

Another alternative for the Soviets would be to develop other modes of delivering nuclear warheads. They could increase their force of cruise missiles for delivering such warheads, and these could be air-, land-, or sea-launched. They could develop a fleet of intercontinental bombers, which would force the United States to develop an air defense system.

Finally, the Soviets could develop countermeasures against space-based assets of U.S. defensive systems. The Soviets could, for example, announce that they would not permit the travel over their territory of orbiting battle stations designed to destroy their missiles at launch, and they could then back this up by deploying ground-based antisatellite weapons (ASATs). Alternatively, they could deploy space-based ASAT systems designed to intercept orbiting satellites of the U.S. defense system. These could operate against space-based sensors and command and control units, as well as against defensive battle stations.

The technologies for these various Soviet countermeasures are relatively straightforward, and many of them are in some measure already known to the Soviet Union; hence Soviet countermeasures could be deployed relatively rapidly and with modest cost compared to that for the U.S. defensive system. The United States, of course, could attempt to develop counter-countermeasures.

The Soviets could also extend the offensive-defensive arms race by developing and deploying defensive systems of their own

designed to counter U.S. offensive systems. From a cost-effectiveness point of view, however, it would seem more sensible for
the Soviets to focus on countermeasures against U.S. defenses.

It was noted earlier that for the United States to decrease
sharply its dependence on deterrence by threat of retaliation, it
will need an impregnable defense in which confidence is high. An
area where it may be particularly difficult to develop high confidence is the command and control of a large multitiered defensive
system. Given the immense complexities of a major offensive-
defensive engagement, the command and control system will necessarily rely almost completely on computers to analyze the data
from sensors and to direct the firing of defensive weapons. Developing adequate and error-free computer software for this battle-
management task will be a problem of formidable magnitude, and
one where confidence will be difficult to attain. Many U.S. experts
are persuaded that the software problem for the computer systems
will be the most difficult problem of all. When this and other
technical uncertainties are added to the uncertainties about Soviet
responses, it is hard to envisage a situation where the United
States will find it possible to move away from reliance on deterrence by threat of retaliation, that is, to be able to eliminate a
strong dependence on its own offensive nuclear forces. A major
goal of the Strategic Defense Initiative is to attain a situation
where the U.S.-Soviet military confrontation is much more stable
than it is now. It does not, however, appear feasible to reach this
stability by a unilateral U.S. deployment of defensive weapons
systems.

THE IMPACT ON NATO ALLIES

The new U.S. objective, as outlined in President Reagan's 1983
speech, "to counter the awesome Soviet military threat with
measures that are defensive," came as a total surprise to the
decision-makers of the NATO countries. Probably in anticipation
of their concern, the President responded directly to it. He said:

As we pursue our goal of defensive technologies, we recognize that our
allies rely upon our strategic offensive power to deter attacks against
them. Their vital interests and ours are inextricably linked. Their safety
and ours are one. And no change in technology can or will alter that
reality. We must and shall continue to honor our commitments.

Considerable attention has since been given by the leaders of the NATO nations to the implications of the new U.S. initiative toward strategic defenses. In the main, however, official European responses have been cautious. This is not surprising, since in the absence of knowing what the technologies are and what kind of defensive system may emerge, the level of uncertainty is, again, inevitably high. The United States has offered participation by European countries in the SDI research programs, but the specifics of this seem not to have been developed. In the meantime, however, there has been some skepticism about the attainability of the President's objectives, and considerable concern about their implication for the European countries.

Two military concerns are paramount. One is the concern within France and the United Kingdom that a major U.S. defensive system will lead to Soviet development of a comparable system, and this in turn will greatly decrease the deterrent capability of the nuclear weapons of France and Britain.

The other concern is far more general. It is whether the United States, in its drive toward a defensive system, will move toward a "fortress America" stance, with less concern about the security of Western Europe. This shift in emphasis need not occur on the basis of a direct policy decision. It could equally well take place because of the enormous costs for a Star Wars defensive system which, if given top priority, could diminish U.S. expenditures for the defense of Europe.

Finally, the Europeans have always seen reasonable working relations between the United States and the Soviet Union as a requisite for stability in Europe. From this point of view, one of the most worrisome aspects of SDI in European eyes is that it foreshadows a time of great uncertainty and tension in U.S.-Soviet relations, with new types of armaments being developed and with a reopening of the whole question of how to deter nuclear war. The Europeans are understandably skeptical whether in such an atmosphere significant arms control treaties can be negotiated, and they worry that even the modest existing arms control arrangements may become undone.

The two concepts that are most frequently discussed in these considerations of new weapons systems and changing relations between the United States and the Soviet Union, as well as between the United States and its European allies, are security and stability. The U.S. emphasis has tended to be on security, and in the main we have sought security in the military arena. Security is the obvious objective of those who believe that freedom from concern about nuclear weapons can be gained by a perfect defense. Even those in the United States who argue for partial defenses do so primarily in the name of military security, arguing that they will enhance deterrence by threat of retaliation. Most Europeans doubt that their security will be enhanced by the military moves and countermoves of the United States and the Soviet Union— hence their strong tendency to seek stability under the quite reasonable assumption that substantial instability is the most likely cause of war on the European front. These different perceptions of where security is to be found lead many Europeans to believe that the U.S. Star Wars program constitutes a threat to the NATO Alliance. Since it will be some years before firm assessments can be made of the technologies for nuclear defense, one can look forward to an extended period of uncertainty and consequent unease. In this connection, the Nitze comment that "we would see the transition period as a cooperative endeavor with the Soviets" is of critical importance. If, on the contrary, the two nations continue for several years on competitive unilateral programs, the instabilities could become large, and perhaps in some measure irreversible.

REDUCING THE RISK OF NUCLEAR WAR: IS STAR WARS THE ANSWER?
Robert McNamara

Messrs. McGeorge Bundy, George Kennan, Gerard Smith, and I published an article in the December 1984 issue of *Foreign Affairs* magazine entitled "The President's Choice: Star Wars or Arms Control." In it we said, "We believe the President's initiative to be a classic case of good intentions that will have bad results because they do not respect reality."

THE PRESENT STRATEGIC SITUATION

The arsenals of the United States and the Soviet Union hold, in total, some 50,000 nuclear warheads. Each weapon, on average, is far more destructive than the bomb that obliterated Hiroshima. Just one of our thirty-six strategic submarines has more firepower than man has shot against man throughout history. Thousands of nuclear warheads are ready for immediate use, but just a few hundred of them could utterly demolish any nation.

To deter war, each side seeks to convince the other that it is ready and able to wage a nuclear conflict—having the military objectives of a bygone age. What is known of Soviet nuclear war plans is open to various interpretations, but they appear to rely on tactics derived from Russia's prenuclear military experience. And

The Honorable Robert S. McNamara is a former Secretary of Defense.

our own current defense policy similarly calls for nuclear forces that are sufficient to support a "controlled and protracted" nuclear war; forces that could eliminate the Soviet leadership and that would even permit the United States to "prevail."

The nuclear war-fighting notions of each side lead to enormous target lists and huge forces. Our 11,000 strategic warheads are directed against some 5,00u targets! And NATO Alliance war plans are based on early first use of some 6,000 tactical nuclear weapons in response to a Soviet conventional attack. Both NATO and the Warsaw Pact routinely train their forces for nuclear operations. The war-fighting doctrines create a desire for increasingly sophisticated nuclear weapons. Today both sides are committed to weapons programs that will threaten a growing portion of the adversary's vital military assets with increasingly swift destruction.

These armories and war plans are more than symbols for bolstering self-confidence. Moscow and Washington both presume that nuclear weapons are likely to be used should hostilities break out, but neither knows how to control the escalation that would almost certainly follow. No one can tell in advance what response any nuclear attack might bring. No one knows who will still be able to communicate with whom, or what there will be left to say, or whether it could possibly be believed. Surely it is reckless to stake a nation's survival on detailed plans for something about which no one has any idea.

It would be vastly more reckless to attempt a disarming first strike. Nevertheless, the arms race is driven by deep-seated fears, held by each side, that the other has or is seeking the ability to execute just such a strike.

Those U.S. leaders who believe the Soviets possess a first-strike capability envisage the following scenario: The large force of increasingly accurate Soviet missiles would, at one stroke, eliminate most of our Minuteman intercontinental ballistic missiles; our surviving submarines and bombers would only be able to retaliate against Soviet cities, but we would not do so because of our fear of a Soviet counterattack on our urban population, and thus we would have no choice but to yield to all Soviet demands. Those who accept this first-strike scenario view the Soviet ICBMs and the men who command them as decoupled from the real world. They assume that Soviet leaders would be confident that these highly complex systems, which have only been tested individually in a quiet environment, would perform their tasks in perfect harmony during the most cataclysmic battle in history; that our electronic eavesdropping satellites would detect no hint of the intricate preparations that such a strike would require; that we would not launch our missiles when the attack is detected; that the thousands of submarine-based and airborne warheads that would surely survive would not be used against a wide array of vulnerable Soviet military targets; and finally that we would not use those vast surviving forces to retaliate against the Soviet population, even though tens of millions of Americans would be killed by the Soviet attack on our silos. Only madmen would contemplate such a gamble. Whatever else they may be, I do not believe the Soviet leaders are madmen.

That a first strike is not a rational Soviet option has also been stated by the Scowcroft Commission. It found that no combination of attack from Soviet submarines and land-based ICBMs could catch our bombers on the ground as well as our Minutemen in their silos. And it believed our submarines at sea, which carry a substantial percentage of our strategic warheads, are invulnerable.

Despite all such facts, I believe the majority of experts in Washington—including, for example, Messrs. Weinberger, Nitze, Kampleman, and Brzezinski—believe that the Soviets have, or are seeking to achieve, a first-strike capability.

The Soviets appear to hold similar views about us. Americans often find this incredible. They cannot understand how the Soviets could suspect us of such monstrous intentions, especially as we did not attack them when we enjoyed overwhelming nuclear superiority in the 1950s, 1960s, and 1970s. In 1960, for example, we had 6,300 strategic nuclear warheads to the Soviets' 300 and as recently as 1975 we had 8,500 to their 2,800. Nevertheless, the Russians distrust us deeply. They know that a first strike was not always excluded from U.S. strategic thinking, and they have never forgotten Hitler's surprise attack.

The war-fighting mania and the fear of a first strike are eroding confidence in deterrence. Though both sides are aware that a nuclear war which engaged even a small fraction of their arsenals would be an unmitigated disaster, each is vigorously deploying and developing new weapons systems that it will view as highly threatening when the opponent also acquires them. Thus our newest submarines will soon carry missiles accurate enough to destroy Soviet missile silos. When the Soviets follow suit, as they always do, their offshore submarines will, for the first time, pose a simultaneous threat to our command centers, our bomber bases, and our Minuteman ICBMs.

The President has said repeatedly, "A nuclear war cannot be won and must never be fought." However, the absurd struggle to improve the capacity to wage the war that must never be fought has shaken confidence in the ability to avert that war. The conviction that we must change course is shared by groups and individuals as diverse as the freeze movement, the President, the Catholic bishops, the bulk of the nation's scientists, and the President's chief arms control negotiator. All are saying, directly or by implication, that nuclear warheads serve no military purpose whatsoever. They are not weapons. They are totally useless, except to deter one's opponent from using them. But that being said, the consensus dissolves, for the changes of direction being advocated follow from very different diagnoses of our predicament.

VERSIONS OF STAR WARS

The President's approach has been to launch the Strategic Defense Initiative—the creation of an impenetrable shield that would protect the entire nation against a missile attack and would therefore permit the destruction of all offensive nuclear weapons. The President and the Secretary of Defense appear to remain convinced that this strategic revolution is attainable.

Virtually everyone else associated with SDI now recognizes that such a leak-proof defense, should it ever prove feasible, is so far in the future that it offers no solution to our present dilemma. They therefore advocate other forms of ballistic missile defense. These alternative systems range from defense of "hardened" targets (missile silos or command centers, for example) to partial protection of our population.

For the sake of clarity, I shall call these alternative programs Star Wars II to distinguish them from the President's original proposal, which I shall label Star Wars I. It is essential to understand that these two versions of Star Wars have diametrically opposing objectives. The President's program, Star Wars I, would substitute defensive for offensive forces. In contrast, all Star Wars

II systems have one characteristic in common: they would require that we continue with offensive forces but add the defensive systems to them.

And that is what causes the problem. President Reagan, in a little-remembered sentence in the speech in which he announced his Strategic Defense Initiative on March 23, 1983, said, "If paired with offensive systems, [defensive systems] can be viewed as fostering an aggressive policy, and no one wants that." The President was concerned that the Soviets would regard a decision to supplement our offensive forces with defenses as an attempt to achieve a first-strike capability. That is exactly how they are interpreting our program. That is why they say there will be no agreement on offensive weapons if we continue to pursue Star Wars in a way which will place them at a strategic disadvantage if we abrogate the Anti-Ballistic Missile Treaty unilaterally.

In sum, neither Star Wars I nor Star Wars II, in whatever form one considers them, is an effective response to the public's intuitive awareness of the unacceptable risk posed by our present nuclear strategy. Our security demands that we replace our nuclear war-fighting doctrine with a policy that is in firm touch with nuclear reality. Hans Bethe, the Nobel laureate who was one of the designers of the first atomic bomb, and I put forward such a plan in the July 1985 issue of the *Atlantic Monthly*. We state it in the form of a goal to be achieved, perhaps a quarter of a century from now. Let me first summarize it for you and then I will turn to the question: Can the negotiations in Geneva be shaped to be a step toward that goal?

AN ALTERNATIVE FOR SECURITY

The risk of the catastrophic escalation of nuclear operations, and the futility of defense, lead us to base our proposal on the axiom that any initiation of nuclear warfare against a similarly armed opponent would be an irrational act. Hence, as I have said, nuclear warheads have only one purpose—that of preventing their use. They must not do less; they cannot do more. Therefore, a restructuring of nuclear forces, designed to reduce the risk of nuclear war, must be our goal. All policies, every existing program, and each new initiative must be judged in that light.

Post-Hiroshima history has taught us three lessons that shape our proposal. First, all our technological genius and economic prowess cannot make us secure if it leaves the Soviet Union insecure; we can either have mutual security or mutual insecurity. Second, while profound differences and severe competition will surely continue to mark U.S.-Soviet relations, the nuclear arms race is a burden to both sides, and it is in their mutual interest to rid themselves of its menace. And third, no realistic scheme that would rid us of all nuclear weapons has ever been formulated.

Our ultimate goal, therefore, should be a state of mutual deterrence at the lowest force levels consistent with stability. That requires invulnerable forces that could, without question, respond to any attack and inflict unacceptable damage. If those forces are to remain limited, it is equally essential that they do not threaten the opponent's deterrent. These factors would combine to produce a stable equilibrium in which the risk of nuclear war would be very remote.

This kind of deterrence posture should not be confused with the current status of U.S. and Soviet nuclear forces. The 25,000 warheads each nation possesses today did not come about through any plan. They simply descended on the world as a consequence of continuing technical innovations and the persistent failure to recognize that nuclear explosives are not weapons in any traditional sense.

The forces we propose could include a mix of submarines, bombers, and ICBMs. Two considerations would determine the ultimate size of the force: that it could deter attack with confidence, and that any undetected or sudden violation of arms control treaties would not imperil this deterrence. We believe that, ultimately, strategic forces having as few as 10 percent of the currently deployed warheads would meet these criteria, and tactical nuclear forces could be eliminated entirely. In short, the present inventory of 50,000 warheads could be cut to perhaps 2,000.

The proposed changes in U.S. and Soviet strategic and tactical nuclear forces would require, as would the President's SDI, complementary changes in NATO and Warsaw Pact conventional forces, or appropriate increases in NATO's conventional power. If the latter were necessary, it could be achieved at a fraction of the cost we will incur if we continue on our present course.

Now, having identified our long-term goal, can Geneva be a step toward it? I believe so.

PROSPECTS FOR ARMS CONTROL

Paul Nitze, the administration's senior arms control advisor, faced the problem squarely in a remarkable speech to the World Affairs Council of Philadelphia on February 20, 1985. In speaking on strategic defense systems, which appear to be the stumbling block in Geneva, he said any such system must meet three criteria before its deployment can be justified: it must be effective, survivable, and cost-effective at the margin. He went on to say that no such system would meet these tests soon. Therefore, as far as the arms talks are concerned, Nitze foresaw them dealing with three periods. The first phase, which would last at least ten years, would be one in which no defensive systems would be deployed and we would "reverse the erosion in the ABM Treaty." The second phase would be a transition period in which some form of Star Wars II might be deployed alongside our offensive weapons. The second phase would last for at least several decades. It might ultimately be followed by a third phase, if Star Wars I proved practical.

Why did Mr. Nitze place such emphasis on adherence to the ABM Treaty during the first phase? Because the treaty formalizes the insight that not only the deployment, but even the development of strategic defenses would stimulate an offensive buildup. Were the treaty to collapse, we could not move toward our goal of reducing the offensive threat.

The treaty severely restricts the testing of components of ABM systems. But within the near future the United States almost certainly will be violating these restrictions if we place our research program on the time schedule implied by recent statements of SDI Director Gen. James Abrahamson. He has said that a "reasonably confident decision" on whether to deploy Star Wars could be made by the end of the decade or in the early 1990s. If we are unwilling to refrain from the tests associated with such a schedule, the Soviets will, with good reason, assume that we are preparing to deploy defenses. They will assiduously develop their response, and the prospect for offensive arms agreements at Geneva will evaporate. The treaty's central purpose is to give each nation confidence that the other is not readying a sudden deployment of defenses. We must demonstrate that we will adhere to it in that spirit.

The ABM Treaty does not forbid antisatellite weapons, and unless that loophole is closed we shall have an arms race in space long before we have any further understanding of what, if anything, space defense could accomplish. Hence a ban on the testing of antisatellite weapons, which is verifiable, should become a part of the ABM Treaty regime. Because we are much more dependent on satellites than are the Soviets, such a ban would be very much in our interest.

When Mr. Nitze discussed the second phase of what could be a new arms control regime—a phase in which a defensive system would be deployed alongside the offensive systems—he acknowledged that the problems of how to write an arms control agreement which, during that transition period, would limit offensive arms but permit defensive arms, had not been solved. He said to write such an agreement "would be tricky." But, by implication, he was saying that this was an issue for the future and need not prevent progress at Geneva.

Nitze did not address the issue of offensive arms limitations. This will prove to be a very complex problem. As I have emphasized, each side fears the other has, or seeks to attain, a first-strike capability. At present, deterrence is unstable because of these fears. The great danger is that in a period of high tension one side or the other would be tempted to launch a preemptive attack.

The primary objective of offensive arms negotiations, therefore, must be to increase the stability of deterrence by eliminating the perception of a first-strike threat. Because of the asymmetry of forces, this will be very difficult to accomplish. It will require that each side reduce the ratio of the number of its warheads to the number of the other side's vulnerable missile launchers. In other words, what is needed are deep cuts—on the order of 50 percent—in the number of nuclear strategic warheads, but cuts shaped to eliminate first-strike fears.

It would be reasonable, for example, for the United States to insist on large reductions in the number of Soviet ICBM warheads, but in the bargaining we would have to be ready to make substantial cuts in our counterpart forces, including, for example, the yet-to-be-deployed, highly accurate submarine-based D-5 missile. Deep cuts, shaped to eliminate the fear of disarming strikes, are feasible. They could be negotiated. Will they be? I can only hope so.

We should all recognize that the arms negotiations in Geneva do represent an historic opportunity. We are facing a plus sum game! It is a game from which both sides can emerge as winners. It is an opportunity to lay the foundation for entering the twenty-first century with a totally different nuclear strategy, one of stable deterrence instead of war-fighting; with vastly smaller nuclear forces, perhaps 2,000 weapons in place of 50,000; and with a dramatically lower risk that our civilization will be destroyed by nuclear war.

Several themes should govern our attitudes and policies as we move through those negotiations toward our long-term objectives. Each side must recognize that neither will permit the other to achieve a meaningful superiority—attempts to gain such an advantage are dangerous as well as futile. The forces pushing both sides in the direction of first-strike postures, at least from the standpoint of the adversary, must be reversed. A stable balance at the lowest possible level should be the goal.

We must not forget Churchill's warning that "the Stone Age may return on the gleaming wings of science," and we should learn to shed the fatalistic belief that new technologies, no matter how threatening, cannot be stopped. While laboratory research cannot be constrained by verifiable agreement, technology itself provides increasingly powerful tools that can be used to impede development and to stop deployment.

We must allay the fears that each side legitimately holds: the Soviet fear of our technology, and our fear of their obsessive secrecy. These apprehensions provide an opportunity for a bargain: Soviet acceptance of more intrusive verification in return for American constraints on technological innovation. The penetration of Soviet secrecy is to our mutual advantage, even if the Kremlin does not yet understand that. So is technological restraint, even though it runs against the American grain.

CONCLUSION

We have reached our absurd confrontation by a long series of steps, many of which seemed to be rational in their time. Step by step we can undo much of the damage. The program Dr. Bethe and I have put forward would initiate that process. It would steadily reduce the risks we now face, and it would rekindle confidence in the future. It does not pretend to rid us totally of the nuclear menace, but it does address our first duty and obligation: to assure the survival of our civilization. Our descendants could then grapple with the problem that no one yet knows how to attack.

A EUROPEAN VIEW
Francis Pym

It has been more than three years since President Reagan announced the Strategic Defense Initiative. It was a very important decision with far-reaching implications. There are many opinions about it, and there is no disguising its controversialism or its significance. But I want to say at the outset that my attitude toward it is a positive one: to make the most of it, whatever "it" may turn out to be. To make the most of it toward the preservation of peace and the prevention of war to the benefit of mankind.

DETERRENCE

Neither the believers in strategic defense nor the skeptics can yet *know* whether the theoretical possibilities will prove to be feasible in practical terms. Nobody knows. Therefore, it is unwise to come to concrete conclusions at this stage. The idea behind the initiative has obvious attractions. No one likes the concept of mutual assured destruction, which has been the basis of peace, at least in Europe, since World War II. The President recently referred to the MAD approach to security as being in some ways immoral. It would be very nice if there were a better form of deterrence. But we do not

The Right Honourable Francis Pym is former Secretary of State of Great Britain for Foreign and Commonwealth Affairs.

know yet whether a better form exists. Paul Nitze, whose views are well respected in Europe, has stated that it will be at least ten years and probably much longer during which we will have to continue with mutual assured destruction for world peace. It seems unwise, therefore, to call its morality into question.

The idea of building secure defenses to destroy Soviet missiles before they arrive has an attractive simplicity about it, a very popular appeal. Obviously the principle of physically assured invulnerability is, if achievable, preferable to retaliation. But the first point to be made is that very few people believe that nearly perfect defense is possible. And to be effective, such defense would have to be nearly perfect, not only against intercontinental ballistic missiles, but also against cruise missiles launched from submarines or aircraft with comparatively short flight times. Hardly anybody in the scientific world thinks that such a system is devisable, at least for a very long time. But if not all the missiles can be intercepted, then the need to retaliate remains.

The protagonists of SDI proclaim that the initiative creates a real opportunity to stop the arms race, because the proliferation of missiles would no longer be a useful way of threatening another country. They say it will eliminate any idea of a successful first strike. But these arguments depend for their validity upon the feasibility of a perfect or nearly perfect defense, and that is thought to be unattainable.

VULNERABILITY

In any case, the Soviet Union will see to it that Western defense is not impenetrable. They have the will to see to that, and the ability. They have been in the space business for a long time; in fact, they were the first in it. The Soviet Union could devise a direct attack on the Star Wars system. Any system which envisages parking satellites and other devices in space is itself highly vulnerable. In addition, the weapons devised to destroy missiles could also be capable of destroying the defending satellites. It has even been suggested that two adversaries could place exploding satellites beside each other's defensive satellites and destroy the other's "shield" just prior to an offensive attack. This indicates that there is a danger, a possibility—and I put it no higher—that research into defenses in space by both superpowers could lead to the opposite result to that which we want. It could lead to an extension of the arms race into space. That would be the worst of all worlds. Mankind would not find room for any forgiveness if the nuclear powers allowed that to happen.

COSTS

At present, of course, the SDI program is research only. That research is bound to produce benefits and spin-offs. This always happens with new research, and it will do so especially in this case because of its gigantic scale. Sixty billion dollars over ten years! And that is just for R & D. Nothing on this scale has ever been attempted before. And Europeans wonder if the United States can afford it. We know how rich you Americans are, but we still wonder whether you can afford it. We wonder whether too many resources will be diverted from other defense purposes—for example, from maintaining adequate conventional forces. Indeed, if the Strategic Defense Initiative were to reduce the military utility of nuclear weapons, would not the need for strong conventional forces be all the greater? And they are far more expensive. So the cost is a potent consideration. Now, if deployment were ever contemplated, the cost would be so great that it is beyond anybody's estimation or imagination. Quite certainly deployment, if ever contemplated, would have to be negotiated, unless the ABM Treaty were to be abrogated. The U.S. administration clearly acknowledges this.

EUROPEAN ANXIETIES

It is clear, therefore, that the concept of SDI contains many possibilities, but also many uncertainties. What is more, the concept itself, together with its uncertainties, relates to the heart of East-West relations, to arms control negotiations, and to the preservation of peace. So we all have an interest in it, not just the United States, but all its allies, indeed the whole world. The initiative is intended to determine whether a drastic change in the whole basis of our security efforts can be brought about. It is all the more surprising, then, that there was no warning of the President's announcement. It was a unilateral decision. On a major issue of this kind, the handling of it is no less important than its substance. Events may prove both the decision and the handling to be right, and I very much hope so, but let me explain the background to some of the European anxieties.

Our central objective is international security at a lower level of armaments. Enormous efforts have been made over the years to achieve this, with remarkably little success. Yes, we have had the Test Ban Treaty, the Non-Proliferation Treaty, and the Strategic Arms Limitation (SALT) agreements. All are important and all have applied constraints on the buildup of forces and armaments, but on the main issue of first limiting and then reducing the level of forces there has been spectacular failure. What we witness are more and more weapons being created—nuclear and conventional. No wonder people protest. It is only human. The overwhelming need is to stop the escalation, and that means that agreements have got to be reached. And they have to be reached with people who have very different values and priorities from our own, and very different interests and objectives.

How is that going to be done? Recent experience is not very encouraging. It may or may not be changed by the new Soviet leadership. That remains to be seen. The restraint shown by the Western Alliance in the 1970s was not reflected in the Soviet Union. They indulged, as we know, in a sustained military buildup of 3 to 5 percent per year, year after year. At first there was no Western response, but in due course the growing imbalance had to be corrected. Otherwise, our deterrent would become ineffective. From the European point of view, the most visible expression of that response was the deployment of the Pershing IIs and cruise missiles, a deployment which was stimulated to a considerable degree by the earlier deployment of the SS-20s by the Soviet Union. The Soviet Union mounted a massive campaign to prevent the U.S. allies from making that deployment, but that campaign failed, to the lasting credit of the allies. When it did fail the Soviet Union walked out of both the theater (INF) and strategic arms control (START) talks.

Now, in the light of that and the invasion of Afghanistan, it was understandable that the United States had some harsh things to say about the Soviet Union. We heard a mounting rhetoric of abuse and recrimination exchanged between Moscow and Washington. That seemed to be acceptable to the United States—up to a point, even popular—and it was accepted in Europe for a time. But after a year or so it caused deepening concern in Europe. Not because the Europeans were unaware of the Soviet buildup. How could we be? The Soviet forces are on our doorstep. Nor because the Europeans had become soft, as some people like to believe. We became alarmed by this megaphone diplomacy, as it came to be called, because of its futility. We could not understand how two peoples could ever reach an agreement on anything if they continued to shout abuse at each other in that way. And then came a change—a very welcome change. Only in 1984 did the President begin speaking about the need for dialogue and for meaningful talks.

This, in brief outline, is the landscape onto which the Strategic Defense Initiative was pitched—unpromising terrain to say the least. Any attempt to reach negotiated agreements in such circumstances or against such a background is difficult to imagine. In my view, there are four prerequisites for such an agreement. First, the maintenance at all times of an adequate deterrent commensurate with the perceived threat. Second, the development of better practical working relations with the Soviet Union so that there can be some kind of modus vivendi in which it is possible for the two disagreeing sides to come to some agreements. Third, close cooperation among all the allies, including the United States. And fourth, arms control proposals that are equitable to both sides and that take account of the different interests of both sides.

This is where the complexity really begins, because the forces of the two superpowers are structured quite differently. They are different in size, in their characteristics, and in the geography of their deployment. Each side's forces serve distinctive political and military purposes. Thus, any arms control proposal will have quite different effects on the two sides, and the challenge is to find proposals that take account of these differences yet are equitable in practical terms. Now if you accept that criterion, it is difficult to say that SDI falls within it; the Soviet Union was bound to reject it.

My view is that the concept of the Strategic Defense Initiative would have been better pursued *with* the Russians rather than against them. I note that Paul Nitze has said that this kind of cooperation is envisaged at a later stage and that the sooner that can be begun, the better. It may not be practical immediately, but the concept is totally right, because neither side wants an arms race in space. Both sides have strong incentives to "do a good deal" in their own interests.

PUBLIC OPINION

There is a final point I want to make. The bedrock of our security is the positive acceptance by our peoples of an effective strategy for both defense and disarmament. To obtain that acceptance and support is among the top priorities for all politicians and statesmen in the West. What is required is a continuous process of presentation and explanation of what the issues are—presentations that analyze the problems fully, frankly, and fairly, and that expose the options available. It is not a question of "selling" SDI; it is a question of taking people into your confidence. What will be appreciated in Europe is a totally genuine, frank, and continuous explanation of the SDI program as it develops. Hard choices will have to be made. The United States must involve its allies in this initiative, for we all share the same objectives: the preservation of peace and the prevention of war. We all want to work toward a calmer, more stable, more peaceful world. The test for the SDI program will be the extent to which it contributes to that goal.

PART FOUR

CAN "IT" BE DONE?

BECOMING A REALITY
Simon P. Worden

On March 23, 1983 President Ronald Reagan told the nation:

I call upon the scientific community in our country, those who gave us nuclear weapons, to turn their great talents now to the cause of mankind and world peace, to give us the means of rendering these nuclear weapons impotent and obsolete.

With these words, President Reagan launched one of the most intense scientific debates of the century. Following his historic speech, the President directed that a sweeping study be undertaken to answer whether the vision he outlined was indeed technically within our grasp and to provide a road map for pursuing that vision. Based on this study, now known as the Defensive Technologies, or Fletcher, Study, the President mandated the formation of the Strategic Defense Initiative (SDI) research program in January 1984. During this same period an intense, and often heated and acrimonious, debate has been conducted within the U.S. technical, strategic, and arms control communities. While this debate is by no means over, remarkable agreement is beginning to emerge, at least with respect to the criteria which must be met in order for the President's hope to become a reality.

Lt. Col. Simon P. Worden is the Special Assistant to the Director of the Strategic Defense Initiative Organization of the Department of Defense.

REALISTIC GOALS

Before addressing whether "it" can be done, the "it" must be defined. President Reagan's speech dealt only with ballistic missiles. However, if his famous words "impotent and obsolete" are taken to mean that nuclear weapons will become incapable of causing harm, then both the technical requirements and the type of defenses and arms control which must be pursued are much different from what has been primarily discussed in the debate about SDI.

The answer to the question of what objectives strategic defenses should have lies in consideration of the meaning of deterrence and the role of arms control in preventing a nuclear war. Deterrence exists, and is stable, if a potential aggressor assesses that the results of an attack will not justify the gains. The results can either be a retaliatory strike or a defensive capability good enough to deny the objectives of the strike. Thus, defenses enhance deterrence if they can deny an effective first strike.

There are several thousand military targets—storage depots, bases, missile silos, and communication nodes, for example—in the United States. An effective Soviet first strike must be able to destroy most of these. Today, the Soviet Union has more than 90 percent of its offensive forces in the form of ballistic missiles. The 6,000 accurate warheads on the Soviet SS-17, SS-18, and SS-19 intercontinental ballistic missiles (ICBMs) are sufficient to place two to three warheads on each U.S. military target in a first strike. Deterrence exists when the Soviet Union recognizes that a devastating retaliation would occur in response to the first strike, or when the success of the first strike in destroying most of the targets is in question. We rely mostly on retaliation for deterrence today but also have an element of denial in that some U.S. military assets, such as command and control centers, are mobile or hardened. Because Soviet bombers and cruise missiles are relatively slow, they are not credible first-strike weapons. For this reason, efforts to render nuclear weapons obsolete—as first-strike weapons—concentrate on ballistic threats.

A deterrent strategy based primarily on denial is clearly possible and would go far in making nuclear weapons obsolete in the military sense of the word. If the Soviet Union were faced with an effective multilayered U.S. missile defense, they would truly recognize the futility of a first strike. A three-layer system with each layer having a modest 80 percent effectiveness would reduce the Soviet 6,000-warhead first-strike force to military impotence, capable of destroying only a handful of the U.S. military targets; manifestly not an effective first strike.

DEFENSE AND STABILITY

In order truly to render nuclear weapons impotent and obsolete, however, strategic defenses must also be "arms control stable;" that is, they must have three technical characteristics which ensure that the introduction of defenses would not lead to an offense-defense arms race. Effective defenses must encourage arms control which will reduce and ultimately eliminate nuclear weapons as instruments of international policy, in this way making them truly impotent and obsolete.

The stabilizing defenses must, first, be cost-effective at the margin and affordable. The basic cost of a future defensive deterrent must, of course, be affordable to our nation. But, more important, it must be clear to any potential aggressor that an attempt to overwhelm the defenses in question by simply building more offensive forces can be countered in turn by far less costly further enhancement of the defensive system. Second, the defenses must be survivable in the sense that they themselves do not represent first-strike targets to an aggressor. If defenses are vulnerable, they can actually encourage a first strike during a crisis. Third, the defenses must be robust. This means that new developments in offensive armaments can be met with a less costly enhancement or improvement of the defenses.

CAN IT BE DONE?

Technical arguments have centered on whether these three criteria can be met today or in the future. Discussion of this issue is, unfortunately, premature. Today SDI is primarily a research program, and no final system concepts exist. However, many ideas exist, and a representative scenario can be advanced which can provide a basis for discussing the critical stability criteria.

One rapidly maturing technology identified by the Fletcher Study is the class of kinetic-energy weapons (KEW), which are simply based on the concept of an interceptor and which are sophisticated enough to home in on and destroy their targets by crashing into them. At the speed of many thousands of kilometers per hour of a ballistic missile or warhead in flight, such a collision is nearly always lethal.

There are several concepts for kinetic-energy weapons systems which could be incorporated into systems deployable during the 1990s. A conventional kinetic-energy system has a homing interceptor projectile. Our goal at SDIO is to develop such a device weighing a few kilograms or less. This projectile would be launched toward its target on a small chemical rocket. The rocket launcher could be a spacecraft or a ground-based launcher.

Two recent demonstrations have proven that this technology is workable. In the Army's successful Homing Overlay Experiment (HOE) of June 1984, a mock warhead was fired from Vandenberg Air Force Base in California to the Kwajalein Missile Range thousands of kilometers away in the Pacific Ocean. When radar sensors at Kwajalein detected the incoming warhead, a missile was fired on which was mounted a nonnuclear homing interceptor. After leaving the atmosphere, an infrared (heat-seeking) sensor which detected the incoming warhead opened up. A computer controlled a rocket engine on the interceptor in order to maneuver it into the direct path of the warhead, executing a collision over 100 miles up in space. The HOE weighed about 1,000 kilograms. A dramatic demonstration of the progress being made in the homing interceptor area occurred in September 1985, when the Air Force's Miniature Vehicle (MV) antisatellite weapon (ASAT), based on technology similar to the HOE, intercepted a satellite. The MV ASAT interceptor weighed about twenty kilograms, an improvement of a factor of fifty in a few short years!

SYSTEM DESIGN

A defensive system for the 1990s, based on kinetic-energy weapons and capable of defeating the current Soviet strategic missile force as well as the intermediate-range ballistic missile threat to Europe, might be divided into three phases, with associated battle-management systems. For the boost-phase defense—designed to intercept attacking missiles while their main booster rockets are still burning—thousands of rocket-powered homing interceptors are carried on several hundred satellite carriers, each holding dozens of interceptors. An interceptor missile and warhead capable of diverting from its course sufficiently to intercept all missiles within its range might together weigh in the range of 100 kilograms. These interceptors cannot operate inside the atmosphere and therefore have no potential against ground targets. A boost-phase surveillance and tracking system deep in space would provide attack warning and booster tracking information. These same systems could also operate for the multiple-warhead systems in the postboost phase, during which the multiple warheads are deployed.

A space-based kinetic-energy system has at least one additional intercept opportunity during the midcourse phase, when the warheads are travelling on a ballistic trajectory above the earth's atmosphere. However, there are two complicating factors during this phase. First, the interceptor must attack a "cold" warhead target rather than the "hot" booster. Since infrared sensors "see" the heat of the target, cold objects are much harder to detect and track than hot ones. In order to intercept such cold objects, the interceptor must be guided fairly near to the target in order for its heat-seeking sensor to take over and perform the final homing in on the target. Second, decoys may be present in large numbers during midcourse. These decoys can be constructed so that they look very much like the warhead targets and could confuse and exhaust the defense's interceptors. For these reasons, a network of infrared sensor platforms is needed in addition to those sensors which would detect the boosters during the boost phase. These sensors would be able to locate potentially threatening objects precisely, to discriminate decoys from warheads, and to track potential targets.

Midcourse provides additional opportunities for both warhead interception and discrimination of warheads from decoys. Ground-based kinetic-energy interceptors can be committed to attack a target based on accurate tracks and target identification while potential targets are still in early midcourse flight. A first wave of intercepts would thus occur while the warheads are still thousands of kilometers from their targets. After the first midcourse intercept attempt, midcourse sensors can assess the outcome and commit another wave of interceptors for those cases where the first intercept failed. Since each ground-based interceptor site can defend an area of several thousand kilometers in diameter, a handful of sites would be sufficient for either Europe or the United States. Each site would contain several hundred interceptors. Since ground-based interceptors weighing about 1,000 kilograms or less appear feasible (due in large part to the much smaller sizes possible for nonnuclear interceptors), each interceptor missile could be relatively inexpensive to deploy.

The terminal phase provides an additional intercept layer as warheads reenter the atmosphere at altitudes between ten and thirty kilometers. At these high altitudes, even attacking warheads which have been salvage fused to detonate when intercepted, will be unable to damage unhardened sites on the ground, such as cities or large military bases. Intercept inside the atmosphere, or "endo-atmospheric" intercept, has the advantage that entering the atmosphere serves to strip away lightweight decoys. Two different sensor concepts exist for this phase. In the first, a set of "optical" subsystems consisting of various infrared and laser ranging sensors would be carried on an airborne platform to perform tracking and discrimination functions. Such "airborne optical systems" might ultimately be carried on high-altitude unmanned aircraft. Each airborne sensor system could perform the required sensor function for an area of 1,000 kilometers in diameter or more. Consequently, only a few would be needed for all of Western Europe or the United States. The second sensor option, which may ultimately be used in conjunction with the first, might be a series of ground-based terminal imaging radars. These radars would begin discriminating warheads from decoys outside the atmosphere by forming an image of a potentially threatening object. The ground-based radars may be small enough to be mobile, thus enhancing their survivability. Each radar could cover a circle several hundred kilometers across. The small "footprint" of coverage for the radars makes them best suited for defense of high-value areas, such as military staging areas, battle areas, or densely populated civilian targets.

Terminal interceptor missiles would be distributed over many sites, with only a few missiles per site. This distribution, and the possible mobility of the sensors and interceptors, could make terminal systems highly survivable. Nonnuclear terminal interceptors guided to their targets by a combination of external commands and onboard infrared homing sensors are the current focus of the SDI investigation. The interceptor is guided to within a few meters of the target, which is then destroyed by a small pellet cloud explosively launched from the interceptor.

AFFORDABILITY AND COST-EFFECTIVENESS

No one knows the cost of future defensive systems. However, we can estimate the cost of maintaining an offensive deterrent comparable to the present one. The United States is currently developing a concept for 500 small mobile missiles (the Midgetman). This 500-warhead force is estimated to cost slightly less than $50 billion, or about $100 million per warhead. The current U.S. deterrent consists of about 10,000 warheads. If this deterrent were replaced and upgraded over the next twenty years, as it obviously will be, the estimated cost would be close to $1 trillion. This estimate is consistent with the current percentage of the U.S. defense budget devoted to strategic, mostly offensive, forces, which is 15 percent, or about $50 billion per year. Very rough cost estimates for multilayered defense systems of the type discussed here are in the range of tens to hundreds of billions of dollars. It certainly appears that, in the context of a shift to a defense-reliant deterrent strategy, defensive systems offer the promise of an affordable deterrent.

More important than the basic system costs are the costs at the margin to enhance the defensive system in response to proliferating offensive threats. It is reasonable to assume that the Soviet offensive forces cost an amount comparable to U.S. forces. Even highly MIRVed systems (that is, multiple-warhead systems) like MX cost about $20 to $30 million per warhead. In the face of a three-layer system of moderate effectiveness (80 percent per layer), the Soviets must add hundreds of thousands of warheads at an equivalent of trillions of dollars to preserve their present ability to destroy several thousand U.S. military targets in a first strike. The additional cost of defensive KEW interceptors is unknown, but the SDI goal is less than $1 million per interceptor missile, whether space- or ground-based. Since each missile is comparable in size and complexity to current surface-to-air or air-to-air missiles, which cost about $100,000 per missile, the SDI goal certainly appears reasonable. It therefore seems unlikely that a future defensive system could be overwhelmed by a simple proliferation of current offensive missile systems.

SURVIVABILITY

The Fletcher Study identified survivability as critical, particularly that of the defensive system elements which might require prepositioning in space. To achieve the required level of survivability, the defensive system does not need to be invulnerable, but it must be able to maintain a sufficient degree of effectiveness to fulfill its mission, even in the face of determined attacks against it. As with cost-effectiveness at the margin against an offensive system, the cost of making the defensive systems survivable must be less than the cost of the defense suppression measures an opponent might use against them.

Three types of threats to space-based elements might exist: kinetic-energy ASATs, nuclear-explosive ASATs, and directed-energy threats, such as space-based particle beams or ground-based lasers. It appears that satellites may be hardened against nuclear attack to a degree that essentially a direct nuclear hit would be needed to destroy it. Shielding appears feasible against lasers and particle beams. Such shielding appears effective against even advanced directed-energy threats which might not exist for many decades. Both nuclear and nonnuclear ASATs may be countered through a combination of maneuvering and the enforcement of a "keep out" zone using the same kinetic-energy interceptors envisioned for missile defense weapons as self-defense weapons. A similar cost exchange advantage as would exist against ballistic missiles should exist for ground-based ASAT attackers, since a ground-launched ASAT might require nearly as heavy and sophisticated booster or launch systems as a nuclear warhead. Sensor satellites with vulnerable optical elements may be placed at sufficiently high altitudes that they would be both difficult to detect and difficult to attack. Moreover, these sensor satellites could also be defended by escort kinetic-energy interceptors. A very exciting new development offers a particularly potent cost exchange advantage to a prepositioned space-based defense.

A new technology, supersonic combustion ramjet (scramjet) engines, appears to make possible an aircraft which can literally fly into orbit and deliver mass into space at two orders of magnitude less cost than today's $3,000 per kilogram. Analysis has shown that, if it is cheaper to preposition mass in space than to boost it suddenly from the ground on a rocket, then all methods of survivability (maneuver, deception, armoring, and self-defense) favor the defense with the prepositioned defensive element. The scramjet technology breakthrough, if realized, thus seems to promise even more strongly that cost-effective and survivable defensive systems can be constructed and maintained.

The survivability of ground- and air-based systems is also essential. The mobility of air-based and possibly ground-based sensors makes it very difficult to locate and destroy these elements. The dispersal and possible mobility of interceptors similarly enhances their survival. Since a multilayered defensive system has boost-phase and midcourse defensive layers, it would be difficult for an aggressor to calculate the force levels necessary to destroy those ground-based defensive elements which lie behind the first defensive layers. The fact that a successful preemptive attack must first destroy each layer of a defensive system also greatly decreases the aggressor's confidence in a successful attack. Deterrence is thereby enhanced greatly by the very existence of multilayered defensive systems.

ROBUSTNESS

To ensure long-term stability, a defensive system must evolve to counter new types of offensive threats specifically designed to defeat an initial system. Two general types of countermeasures have been discussed. One is a redesigned, possibly hardened, booster rocket. The booster would be designed to burn out quickly, possibly while still within the atmosphere, to minimize its vulnerability to boost-phase weapons. A second class of countermeasures is the development of large numbers of credible decoys, perhaps thousands of balloon shrouds, a few of which would enclose the real warheads. Faced with perhaps hundreds of thousands of similar targets, a space-based defense might be unable cost-effectively to destroy both decoys and decoyed warheads. The addition of advanced directed-energy devices, lasers, and particle beams, however, offers effective responses to these countermeasures.

It appears that moderate-power lasers or particle beams may be available in the 1990s to aid in actively discriminating decoys from warheads. This all but eliminates the utility of decoys. For example, moderate-power laser pulses can strike a potentially threatening object, causing it to recoil. Heavy objects, presumably warheads, would recoil only slightly compared to a lightweight decoy, thereby identifying the heavy warhead as a threatening object.

The assumption that fast-burn boosters can defeat a defensive system ignores the fact that it is not the boost-phase defense alone which makes an effective defense feasible; rather, it is the ability to have multiple independent layers which is key. If boost-phase intercept proves difficult, yet there are several independent layers starting with the postboost phase, the same overall system effectiveness can be maintained. Analyses have shown that if the decoy problem is solved, midcourse defenses alone can perform the boost-phase function.

Within fifteen to twenty years, it appears likely that directed-energy technology will have advanced sufficiently so that lasers and particle beams will be powerful enough to serve as primary defensive weapons. High-energy lasers can reach deep within the atmosphere to attack even boosters with very short burn times. Thus, an opponent seeking to defeat a boost-phase defense by developing fast-burn boosters which burn out while still within the atmosphere would achieve little from this development. Lasers and particle beams with effective ranges of many thousands of kilometers and retarget times of a small fraction of a second appear feasible. Space-based directed-energy weapons or directed-energy weapons with space-based elements thus could counter even an extremely large number of threats. The numbers and performance of space-based lasers needed to counter advanced ballistic missile threats has been hotly debated in the scientific community. Some groups of scientific critics have stated that thousands of lasers would be needed to counter an equivalent number of boosters. However, both SDI critics and supporters are now in fundamental agreement about the calculation of these numbers. Using these calculations, it is clear that about 100 space-based lasers with suitably advanced performance could very effectively counter thousands of advanced ballistic missiles.

Thus, while the SDI research program still has a number of years to go before the answers are in, results to date are already very promising. If SDI research programs are successful, multilayered defenses which are cost-effective and robust can begin, in the next decade, to give us a safer and better basis for deterrence.

COUNTERMEASURES AND COSTS
Richard Garwin

Can General Abrahamson, the Director of the Pentagon's Strategic Defense Initiative Organization, successfully accomplish his goal? If his goal is to learn whether a strategic defense system is feasible, yes, he can. Will this achieve the goal of President Reagan's famous Star Wars speech? No, it will not, if that goal is to be able to give up our nuclear weapons for deterrence against Soviet nuclear weapons and instead be secure by defense so that we could neither be destroyed nor coerced. As former Secretary of Defense James Schlesinger has emphasized, it is entirely premature to declare, as have Secretary of Defense Weinberger and Under Secretary Fred Ikle, that henceforth and immediately strategic defense will be the centerpiece of our security. This is inconsistent; it is nonsense.

The question is not whether the Strategic Defense Initiative program can be done. Of course it can be done. In fact, the defense community knew before the SDIO was created that we could cost-effectively and survivably deploy *some* kinds of strategic defenses. What are we waiting for then, and why are we planning ten to twenty years of R & D in the face of an imminent threat before doing this? It is because, when we consider these

Dr. Richard L. Garwin is an IBM Fellow at the Thomas J. Watson Research Center, Yorktown Heights, New York.

options, we have decided that they are not worth doing; there are costs other than the monetary cost.

But can SDI as defined by Paul Nitze be done? Can it be made survivable and cost-effective and still do a useful job? Can we defend society, not just the missiles? The President would not be satisfied with the kind of strategic defense that just defends missiles and hence enshrines deterrence by the threat of retaliation. The Scowcroft Commission, appointed by President Reagan in 1983 and which studied our total strategic posture, has pointed out that the defense of missiles is only one among many approaches to a survivable retaliatory force.

The chief problem with the defense of our intercontinental ballistic missile (ICBM) silos is that we cannot at the same time abide by the commitments of the Anti-Ballistic Missile (ABM) Treaty of 1972, by which we have agreed not to deploy or lay the basis for a nationwide ballistic missile defense, or even to deploy more than 100 interceptors. And continued *Soviet* compliance with a healthy ABM Treaty is very much in the U.S. interest.

Dr. Schlesinger has said that we do not even know whether we can build an effective defense. That is correct. If we spend a very long time, and the Soviets cooperate in our disarming them (as has been demanded by the Fletcher Committee in its analysis), then we *might* eventually be able to do this. I leave it to you to assess the probability of that happening. The question in the real world is whether we can have a defense which precludes Soviet destruction of U.S. society when they do not *want* to be so disarmed.

THE GOALS OF SDI

Three possible goals of the Strategic Defense Initiative have been offered. First, the President's goal: assured survivability, with defense *replacing* deterrence. Second is the deterrence of nuclear attack by persuading the Soviets that they will not be able to count on the success of some militarily important attack. And the third is the defense of the strategic retaliatory forces, the sort of thing which was implied earlier, against a Soviet first strike or preemptive strike.

But, in fact, there has been a progression through these possible goals. President Reagan had in mind city survival and throwing away the retaliatory forces because they are "immoral." Then there was a phase of "denying military goals," and now we are back to the "window of vulnerability" and the bargaining chip— "If you had not had the President's announcement, the Soviets would not have come back to the bargaining table"—and now jobs. But, in any case, "replacing deterrence" has become "strengthening deterrence," with support for the SDI happily coexisting with a strengthening of the strategic missile force the SDI was created to supplant.

THE TECHNOLOGY

Some of the tools of a strategic defense against nuclear-armed missiles have been mentioned—ballistic missile defense in the boost phase, where you have only a thousand or a few thousand missiles, which are very visible. To attack missiles in their boost phase deep within the Soviet Union, one can hope to use space-based lasers, space-based mirrors with ground-based lasers, X-ray lasers, or neutral-particle beams. In midcourse, these weapons would face tens of thousands of nuclear warheads and perhaps a million decoy warheads. For midcourse intercept, General Abrahamson has said that the current multi-thousand-pound Army interceptor and the 50-pound Air Force interceptor would be replaced by homing-kill vehicles weighing less than ten pounds.

COUNTERMEASURES

But what of the countermeasures? In the midcourse phase, the micro-homing-kill vehicles, if we ever get them, and I think we will eventually, are totally frustrated by balloons attached to the reentry vehicles. Even a very smart rock will strike one of those. An ordinary moderately intelligent rock will go just halfway between them. There is also the countermeasure of space mines— small nuclear- or nonnuclear-armed satellites costing only a few million dollars each, which proceed always within kill radius of the billion-dollar defensive satellites. (This is not my number for the cost of a defensive satellite, but that of leading strategic defense proponent Robert Jastrow in his testimony to the House Republican Caucus. He estimated their cost at several billion dollars each.)

Another problem is antisatellite weapons. There is a whole panoply of ASAT possibilities, things that can destroy the satellites on which we will base our defense. There are some countermeasures to ASATs, but not to protect very costly satellites, so that will drive a strategic defense based in space to many thousands of satellites—not a few hundred or a few dozen effective high-cost satellites.

In fact, all of the technologies for boost-phase and early midcourse defense require satellites in orbit. General Abrahamson was pleased with the success of the Army's June 1984 Homing Overlay Experiment—hitting a bullet with a bullet—and with the ASAT tests a few weeks ago. But he should have looked at the dark side of those experiments: they show that satellites in orbit are very vulnerable. They travel on predictable courses, and to preserve an offensive capability, you only have to destroy a small fraction of the satellites—those that are in a position to counter the offense at the time.

Belief in the progress of technology is not enough to allow you to believe that the defense can succeed, because technology can be used *against* the defense. Not only can the existing countermeasures that we know all about be so used, but also the technologies that we will find out about in the SDI program itself and in a concerted program to discover countermeasures.

Take the X-ray laser. The prominent physicist Edward Teller, a strong supporter of strategic defense, has considerable confidence that such a thing can be built. But it should be noted that Edward Teller has been very vocal in all his congressional testimony, interviews, and writings in saying that we cannot base our defense in space, because satellites in space are terribly costly and vulnerable. They can be destroyed in advance of an attack. So he favors, for instance, X-ray lasers which can be "popped up" on rockets launched from U.S. submarines as close as possible to Soviet silos. Unfortunately, X-ray lasers can serve even better to destroy the X-ray lasers of the defense.

COSTS

System costs, of course, we do not know. Secretary Schlesinger says a trillion dollars, but that is for a system to defend us all, which will not work. Major Worden of SDIO says, a "couple hundred billion dollars" for a system which will not do that but is devised to defend some "two to four thousand military targets." When I was on the Scientific Advisory Group of the Joint Strategic

Target Planning Staff, we did not think there were only two to four thousand military targets in the Soviet Union. We thought there were a lot more.

Major Worden claims that additional Soviet missile warheads will cost $20 to $30 million each, and can be destroyed at a lower cost. A high cost for Soviet warheads would make it easier to have a defense that costs less to augment than to overwhelm. What are the facts?

Just a few years ago, the Air Force testified formally in Congress to a committee chaired by the Honorable John F. Seiberling that the Soviets could add warheads at $2 million per warhead. The $20 to $30 million per warhead estimate is derived from the enormous costs projected for new U.S. offensive systems and has little relation to actual Soviet efforts.

General Abrahamson said that we would need at least a factor of ten reduction in the cost of launch to orbit. Major Worden has said that the charge to orbit is $1,500 per pound. Let me remind you what the promise of the NASA Space Shuttle Program was—the program that Dr. James C. Fletcher initiated and that General Abrahamson brought to fruition. The promise of the Space Shuttle Program in 1970 was $50 per pound to low earth orbit—not $1,500. On that promise, we modified our national security planning, we made ourselves vulnerable, and we increased the cost of launching military satellites to orbit. We must beware of these projections. Two to three dollars per pound to low earth orbit would be just wonderful, but do not hold your breath. Indeed, a November 1985 article in *Discover* by Alex Roland, a former NASA historian, documents early NASA claims of $5 per pound to orbit for the space shuttle itself.

The SDI is not the only government program which follows this set of milestones: a sincere program statement, an avoidance of critical assessment, a confusion of program goals, and a denial of alternatives. (If the task is to defend the strategic retaliatory force, there are many ways to do that, but the President's Science Advisor, Dr. George Keyworth, claims that successful defense of silos by close-in systems is unacceptable because it would not move us along the particular path chosen by the President.)

The astonishment that anybody would think of countering the SDI system instead of agreeing with it has led to the exaggeration of the competitive (not the counteractive) threat. In his March

1983 speech in which he launched SDI, the President said nothing about the Soviets being ahead, about deterrence not working, and yet, that is what you hear now—the "strategic defense response," because we have to catch up with the Soviets. In fact, technical testimony from then Under Secretary of Defense for Research and Engineering Richard DeLauer shows that we are far ahead in every one of the important technologies in strategic defense.

There is also the vilification of critics—if you cannot answer the arguments, attack the arguers. In addition, the program manager always tries to have the "too early to cancel" and the "too late to cancel" overlap, so there is no time at which the program can be judged. When I testified in May 1984 to the House Armed Services Committee, the members were complaining that the long-wave chemical laser program had gotten enough money so that it was politically impossible to cancel it, whereas in the previous year it was "just a research program—too early to judge" and could not then be cancelled.

I have had a major role in a lot of military space activities and have dealt with many weapons, both defensive and offensive. The bureaucracy does not prize people who try to help the Congress and the American people make up their minds by providing technical facts insofar as possible. I did that recently in a *Nature* article of May 23, 1985, titled: "How Many Orbiting Lasers for Boost Phase Intercept?" On the same date, Ed Gerry (a member of the Fletcher Committee and an SDI contractor) and I published fifteen publicly agreed propositions at Dartmouth.

One of them was that my *Nature* calculations provide a reasonable estimate of the number of laser battle stations required to counter boosters of assumed hardness and numbers. Those numbers, in fact, depend on the brightness assumed for the lasers, the laser mirror (optically perfect and just about the size of a large room), twenty-five megawatts of laser light (ten times as much average power as we have been able to make so far and of a perfection not thus far achieved), and boosters of very moderate hardness—only twenty kilojoules per square centimeter. On this last point, the press has reported testimony by Dr. Robert S. Cooper about "laser armor" which is 100 times as effective as anything that we have thought of so far, but apparently we are not allowed to think about putting that armor on boosters, only on satellites. But the Soviets might put it on boosters!

In fact, if the Soviets harden their boosters, without new technology, to twenty kilojoules per square centimeter hardness, which is easy to do, and simply double the number of nuclear weapons they have in their strategic offensive force from 10,000 to 20,000, with the new warheads on fast-burn boosters, which would cost some $11 million per delivered warhead (according to McDonnell Douglas and Martin-Marietta), every three fast-burn boosters would take one laser battle station. Since the total cost for the three boosters is some $30 to $40 million, compared to $3 billion per laser battle station (according to these unreliable numbers), that is *not* cost-effective at the margin.

CONCLUSION

We have not worried about the Soviets toying with SDI-like research over the last twenty years, because we know that we can *counter* that. Not by mimicking their work, however; our response is countermeasures. The Soviets do not like our SDI, but that does not mean that we should. They do not like it because they will have to respond. They will not mimic it; they will counter it. Just as former Secretary McNamara said to his audience at the conference on strategic defense held by the World Affairs Council of Philadelphia in October 1985, seeing a nascent Soviet ballistic missile defense in the 1960s, he would have built 50,000 offensive warheads (at a time when we had 1,000) to counter the 5,000 expected nuclear-armed interceptors of the Soviet ABM system. The Soviets have in fact deployed 32 interceptors, although since the 1972 ABM Treaty they are allowed 100 in their modification of the Moscow ABM system. They will no doubt have 100. But those who claim that the ABM Treaty has not changed Soviet behavior from what it would have been in the absence of the treaty should assume the burden of explaining why the Soviets do not have the 5,000 ABM interceptors nationwide which we expected them to have.

We should not imperil the security provided us by the ABM Treaty by driving the Soviets to abandon the treaty. This will happen if we threaten the Soviet Union to the extent that they must react both by building their offensive forces and by building the kind of ballistic missile defense that they can now. By being excessively optimistic about the prospect of nationwide defense, which cannot occur for twenty, thirty, or forty years, we can create, right now, totally new ways for nuclear war to erupt. We should think first, declaim later.

There is nothing we can do about the March 23, 1983 speech, but we can be careful about what we say in the future. We should roll back SDI. If it is a research program, that is all it is, and it cannot be used as a centerpiece of our security now. There is nothing wrong with this research. Indeed, I have contributed to it. What is wrong is the magnitude of the research, the suppression of alternatives, the exaggeration of Soviet efforts and of our own success, and the seizing of SDI as a tool to destroy the valuable mutual security tool of arms control.

We have to look at countermeasures. We have to counter the Soviet defense program, if it should emerge, with countermeasures, and not by mimicking it.

People who live in glass houses, as we live in the glass house of deterrence by threat of retaliation, should not throw stones. They should also not teach other people how to throw stones. There is a big difference between a research program designed to see how much stone throwing the adversary is learning how to do and one which perfects novel ways of throwing stones to destroy the glass house which keeps out the rain and the nuclear warheads.

A MODERATE VIEW
Robert Cooper

The answer to the technical question about strategic defense which asks, Can "it" be done? is a simple one. No one can say at this time whether the answer is yes or no from a purely technical point of view. Whether or not a reliable defense against ballistic nuclear missiles can be conceived must await an extended period of research and development which is now underway in the Western Alliance and in the Soviet Union.

The policy decision to substantially increase the level of research funding related to strategic defense was taken by President Reagan in March 1983. That decision was ratified by the Congress in two successive years through increases in the strategic defense research budget totalling over 200 percent. Public opinion has generally supported these high research expenditures despite many confusing and ill-informed public pronouncements from the scientific and engineering community. In my view, it is time for the technical community to cease the political rhetoric about strategic defense aimed at the lay public and begin the purposeful examination of the ongoing U.S. research program to ensure its scientific and engineering integrity.

Dr. Robert S. Cooper is the President of Pollard Road, Inc. and former Director of the Defense Advanced Research Projects Agency (DARPA).

TWO TECHNICAL VIEWS

In the past two years, the public has been exposed to two diverse and highly political points of view on the technical efficacy of strategic defense. The view from the right wing of the political spectrum is that a reliable strategic defense system can assuredly be built. In general, they base their arguments on "silver bullet" technology which is variously claimed to be "on the shelf" or perhaps more conservatively "in the lab." Some of the "bullets" claimed are conventional rocket technology, space-based lasers or particle-beam weapons, and ground-based lasers or nuclear-pumped X-ray lasers. Even "smart rocks" have been invoked by some. In any case, the development time needed to begin fielding systems based on silver bullet technology is claimed to be five years or less.

On the political left the assessments are entirely different. Assertions range from the flat statement that it is patently ridiculous to believe that strategic defense is technically feasible to the milder assertion that the prospect for strategic defense is *so* remote that it should not be made the basis for public policy.

Neither of these views is well-founded. We do not know how to build a fully effective strategic defense system today, nor can we say with assurance that a satisfactory technical solution is or is not possible in the future. We do know that strategic defense is a very difficult problem which will require the successful resolution of a myriad of technical problems before the engineering development and deployment of a system can proceed.

Meanwhile, the best strategy for the lay public is to take a moderate "show me" attitude about strategic defense systems. We should all take an interest in the research programs proposed by the administration and insist that they be of high quality, that they be efficiently managed, and that they yield a high technological return on the public funds invested. Those of us in the scientific community who are best qualified should provide constructive criticism of the programs and projects at a scientific and engineering level. Otherwise, the democratic process of consensus building around *any* position regarding technical feasibility in the future will break down, and the public interest will not be served.

GOALS, POLICIES, AND THREATS

The goal of a future strategic defense system would be to completely thwart a ballistic nuclear missile attack on the continental United States or any other country in the Western Alliance. Prior to March 1983, the U.S. ballistic missile defense (BMD) research goals were (1) to continue at a modest level of expenditure ($500 million per year) to develop conventional weapon and sensor technology largely aimed at the defense of the Minuteman intercontinental ballistic missile silos, and (2) to pursue advanced technology (at a level of $400 million per year) which might hold a promise of comprehensive defense against ballistic missiles in the future.

Subsequently, the President has reordered the priorities of ballistic missile defense research. He has placed the latter goal first, largely de-emphasized silo defense, and increased the research budget by a factor of three. The U.S. policy is now to vigorously pursue advanced strategic defense technology. This course is viewed by the administration as opening up a future alternative to the current complete reliance on the threat of retaliation by U.S. strategic offensive forces to deter a Soviet strategic missile attack on this country or its allies. Meanwhile, the United States will continue to rely on its retaliatory forces as the principal means of deterrence in the foreseeable future.

One major reason why the future prospects for strategic defense are so uncertain is that we do not know what countermeasures the Soviet Union may take in their attempt to assure penetration of a future high-technology defense system. Defense researchers must take account of possible Soviet reactions in developing new technical options for defense. They must seek technical solutions which are resistant—or, better still, immune— to any countermeasures. Not only must they anticipate solutions to today's ballistic missile threat, but they must foresee all reasonable Soviet responses and assure the effectiveness of a future defense system against a future reactive threat as well.

Including all missiles which threaten the United States and its allies today, we face nearly 3,000 launchers capable of placing more than 10,000 warheads on targets in the free world. This force is being modernized and replaced at the rate of 10 percent per year, with small increases in the total number of warheads resulting from multiple-warhead upgrades to the force. From these facts we can infer that, without significantly increasing missile and warhead production, the Soviet Union could double the number of missiles and somewhat more than double the warhead count in their force in the next ten years. The facilities and operational costs to deploy these units, however, would be an enormous drain on the Soviet economy.

Even in the face of this formidable force, or the potential future proliferation of the Soviet force, one cannot say with certainty that all is lost. New technologies do hold promise for dealing with such massive threats. At present, the Strategic Defense Initiative Organization (SDIO), charged with the responsibility of managing the U.S. research program, is conducting large-scale studies of advanced systems which could potentially deal with the present and projected threat. These system studies should be thought of as aids in revealing general system design goals rather than as credible potential systems for deployment. Analyses of the theoretical performance of the systems conceived should point out fruitful directions for research and provide a context within which research investment strategies can be formulated. Researchers have made informed guesses about potential Soviet reactions as an aid in setting realistic goals for the performance of a future system.

If research continues at today's pace, we should know within ten years if the goal of a reliable ballistic missile defense is feasible. Only then will actual system design and development be possible. With current knowledge of the Soviet ballistic missile force and the advanced technologies being investigated to counter it, it is likely that a workable and affordable future system will involve concepts, techniques, and technologies not currently conceived. Fortunately, within the structure of the current research program there is ample room for innovation and new concepts to be developed and exploited.

STAR WARS SYSTEMS AND TECHNOLOGIES

Although we cannot say precisely what a strategic defense system will look like or what specific technologies will be involved, we can say a good deal about its functions and its functional elements.

The functions or tasks which any system must successfully perform are:

1. To unequivocally detect and broadcast the nature of a nuclear ballistic missile attack.
2. To locate, discriminate, track, and target booster rockets, MIRV buses, and individual reentry vehicles armed with nuclear weapons.
3. To assign weapons to attack and destroy each target.
4. To assess the effectiveness of each attack.
5. To retarget threatening objects and continue the attack throughout the entire flight regime until the desired result is assuredly achieved.

Retargeting and selective reengagement are crucial to achieving the needed high degree of reliability (that is, a low leakage rate). Keep in mind that all of these functions must be accomplished while maintaining positive human control over the operation of the system, even in the face of likely attacks on the system itself.

The system elements which will be necessary to achieve these five functions might be characterized as follows:

1. Boost-phase surveillance and assessment system.
2. Target acquisition and discrimination system.
3. Target tracking and weapons assignment system.
4. Space- and ground-based weapons system.
5. Kill assessment and retargeting system.
6. Communication system.
7. Command and control system.

An overall system with these functional elements must be thought of as a system of systems. Estimates of the number and complexity of the equipment to be deployed in order to realize these system functional elements against today's threat based on today's technology have often caused the fainthearted to claim proof of infeasibility at this point. However, advanced technology may hold the key to simplification which will make system building a manageable engineering task.

What are the promising technologies being advanced to support design and future development of these system functional elements? There is no short answer to this question. If the present pace of research continues, between $20 and $30 billion will be invested in strategic defense research programs over the next ten years. Moreover, an additional $5 to $10 billion worth of related research—not specifically charged to strategic defense but with potential application to future system designs—will be accomplished by the military departments and agencies for other military missions. At the high end, this level of funding would support approximately 200,000 man-years of scientific and engineering effort over that ten-year period. This level of effort corresponds to an organization the size of NASA working full-time for ten years.

The men and women involved will be among the most talented technical people in the nation. Therefore it is readily apparent why we should all be concerned that the programs be well formulated and well directed. It should also be apparent why a comprehensive summary of the research to be pursued by all of these people is not possible.

Nevertheless, there are some key technologies which in my view will be crucial to a successful outcome of the SDI research program. The news media have focused on the possibly exotic weapons needed to destroy ballistic missiles. They have also been preoccupied by the fact that intercepting attacking missiles early in their boost phase will require that many, if not most, of the system elements may be deployed in space, thus opening up a new era which they have characterized as "the militarization of space." In so doing, the media have focused on space technologies, often confusing the issue of antisatellite technology with strategic defense technology.

PROBLEMS FOR STAR WARS SYSTEMS

There are a number of really knotty problems for any strategic ballistic missile defense system. What follows is a list of such problems in the order of their importance.

SYSTEM COMPLEXITY

A system capable of dealing with 3,000 to 6,000 launchers and 10,000 to 25,000 reentry vehicles will be incredibly complex. It will be necessary for the system to deal with a constantly changing attack which involves a great many uncertainties. No system, except perhaps the U.S. telephone system, has ever been engineered with this level of complexity or uncertainty in mind. Key technical issues for such a system are:

- its architecture;
- the information flow within the system;
- the concept for information storage and management;
- the concept for semiautonomous battle management.

DISCRIMINATION OF POSSIBLE TARGETS

A likely Soviet countermeasure will be the use of decoys, radar chaff, and other techniques for rendering the real targets undetectable and untrackable, but techniques and technologies to provide unequivocal discrimination of targets in the exo-atmosphere do not exist and must be invented. More than any other issue, discrimination may be the one which prevents a successful search for an effective strategic defense concept.

KILL ASSESSMENT

Some weapons, though capable of disabling a targeted reentry vehicle or MIRV bus, do not leave an unequivocal confirmation that they have killed their target, so technologies and concepts for kill assessment must be found in order to avoid exhaustive reengagement of already disabled targets.

SURVIVABILITY OR RESISTANCE TO ATTACK

Both tactics and doctrine will be the key to the survival of space-, air-, and ground-based assets of any future systems. However, technologies to harden and protect system elements against both nuclear and conventional weapons attacks will be needed.

COST OF SPACE DEPLOYMENT

Large-scale deployment of strategic defense system elements in space may be required. Hundreds of thousands, or perhaps millions, of tons may require lifting to low earth orbit. Currently, the space shuttle is the primary American means for space lift, but each trip can lift no more than 30 metric tons and a volume of about 380 cubic meters into low earth orbit, and the cost for lifting one pound is about $4,000. The cost to lift mass into low earth orbit must therefore be reduced to less than $100 per pound to make space-based elements of a strategic defense system affordable. Technology to accomplish this cost reduction is the key to the potential space elements of a strategic defense system.

Note that lasers, particle-beam weapons, railguns, smart rocks, and other exotic weapons are not the key issue. It is my view that effective weapons, which perform only one of the vital functions of a strategic defense system, will be developed in due course. However, there are many other, knottier problems to be solved, and which have much greater technical risk associated with them, before system feasibility will be proven. Fortunately, substantial funding to attack these problems is currently allocated within the Strategic Defense Initiative research program.

THE COST OF THE SYSTEM

Questions are inevitably raised about how much a possible future system might cost. This question cannot, of course, be answered, because no one knows either the structure of a system which would meet the SDI goals or any of the essential elements of cost from which an estimate might be made.

In response to a query at a House Armed Services Committee hearing, Dr. Richard D. DeLauer, then Under Secretary of Defense for Research and Engineering, answered this question by pointing out that one might expect a future ballistic missile defense system to cost as much as the development and deployment of our strategic *offensive* forces. To calibrate that number for the public, the record shows that since World War II the United States has allocated about $7.7 trillion (in 1985-equivalent dollars) to defense appropriations. Last year, 16 percent of the defense budget was allocated to the strategic forces account. If that proportion applied throughout the past forty years, then $1.2 trillion has been allocated for strategic offensive forces. Some interesting current numbers to keep in mind in this respect are that the annual gross national product of the United States is $4 trillion, the total national debt is $2 trillion, the annual federal budget is $1 trillion, and the annual defense budget is $0.3 trillion.

Someday, perhaps ten years hence, if the strategic defense research program is fully successful, the public may be faced with the question of how much strategic defense is worth. Only then, certainly not now, will engineers be able to estimate within reasonable bounds of error (perhaps 20 percent) what the cost of a reliable strategic defense system would be.

RECAPITULATION

I wish to stress the following points:

- We have not yet determined the feasibility or infeasibility of a reliable strategic defense system, and it will be ten years before the issue is settled.
- The long-term goal of a comprehensive strategic defense against ballistic missiles *is* conceivable, though very, very difficult to achieve. Advanced technology is our only hope of achieving it.
- The public should insist on the most for its money in the ongoing research program.
- It is premature to discuss any specific system design, although system functions and functional elements are fair game for discussion to guide research.
- Many advanced technologies may contribute to a future strategic defense system, probably the least of which are the weapons technologies.
- No one can estimate the cost of a future strategic defense system at this time.

If our national public debate on strategic defense is to be constructive, these current uncertainties must be kept in mind.

PART FIVE

SHOULD "IT" BE DONE?

DETERRENCE AND STRATEGIC DEFENSE: A POSITIVE VIEW
Colin Gray

The basic U.S. purpose in its national security policy is to preserve or restore peace *with security;* it is not, and cannot be, simply to prevent war. The victim of aggression usually can prevent war and maintain peace, with high assurance, if it declines to resist an aggressor.

An important reason why there is a seemingly endless and indeterminate debate in U.S. domestic politics over the subjects of which strategic policy to adopt and how many and what kinds of weapons to acquire is that all parties to the ongoing debate are compelled to guess in the face of some irreducible uncertainties. The United States has to make decisions today about the quality— and even, in some respects, the quantity—of its strategic arsenal ten to twenty years from now. No one can "demonstrate" beyond reasonable doubt in the mid-1980s just how much, or how little, strategic power assuredly will be "enough" for 2000 or 2005.

The background to the debate over deterrence, the Strategic Defense Initiative (SDI) and related topics, should include public recognition that it is our purpose to be able to deter a currently unknown Soviet leader, or leaders, from taking currently unidentifiable hostile action in pursuit of objectives that we cannot

Dr. Colin S. Gray is the President and founder of the National Institute for Public Policy.

predict precisely today and at a time that is also unknown. Hence the great difficulty in designing defense policy and the problem of replying responsibly to domestic critics who charge the administration of the day with the sins of overarming or underarming.

The day-to-day domestic U.S. debate over policy for deterrence tends overwhelmingly both to be conducted at a very general level of high abstraction and to treat strategic nuclear issues in isolation. But the real world of statecraft is about the particular, not the general. One cannot sensibly debate the abstract adequacy of the chosen deterrent posture. Instead, one has to examine its adequacy to deter particular people from doing particular things at a particular time. U.S. strategic forces may enjoy an overabundance of leverage with reference to the deterrence of a Soviet assault on American cities yet be grossly inadequate to extend deterrent coverage over the territory of some far-distant friend.

While long-range nuclear weapons cast a menacing shadow over crisis diplomacy and over military operations employing weapons of a much lesser scale of destructiveness, the problem of war and peace—and hence of deterrence—cannot be reduced simply and exclusively to the issues pertaining to the Great Deterrent to a possible apocalypse. Even with narrow reference to the prospects for the occurrence of a so-called "central" (that is to say, homeland-to-homeland) war between the superpowers, it is close to a certainty that such a war would evolve from, or erupt out of, campaigns on the ground and at sea. Little sense of the unity of force and the interrelationships among conflict on land, at sea, in the air, and in space pervades the perennial U.S. debate over the need, or lack of need, for this or that intercontinental ballistic missile (ICBM) or bomber.

The passion for quantification endemic to an American defense community that is vastly underpopulated with historians, anthropologists, and psychologists promotes the idea that anything important can be counted, and if it cannot be counted, it is not important. Quantities of military power, relative and absolute, are very significant. But it is well to recall Napoleon's maxim that the moral is to the material as three is to one. In practice, political will, a reputation for courage, a record of self-sacrifice, and historic political ties should, or certainly may, count far more heavily in the balance of competing deterrent effects than do the quantity or quality of missiles.

THE MISSION OF THE U.S. STRATEGIC FORCES

Members of the Congress complain frequently, and often with excellent reason, that they are asked to vote large sums of money for weapons programs whose strategic rationales are at best obscure. In the absence of a plain and plausible strategic story, the suspicion is fed that a service wants the "Widgetman" weapon system for no better purpose than to buy the latest hardware, to keep the defense industrial base working, or to enhance the relative power and prestige of the organization. In short, what tends to be lacking in both the official briefings and testimony on asserted need and in the media debate is a strategy perspective. How would "Widgetman" promote the national security?

On close examination, it transpires not infrequently that rival debaters over a particular weapon system lack almost entirely a common frame of theoretical and policy reference for their arguments. Common sense suggests that unless one can articulate what a particular weapon should accomplish for policy, one cannot possibly provide a rationale for acquisition that has integrity. Similarly, if rival debaters either have different missions in mind for a strategic weapon or disagree over what is required to accomplish a mission, they are bound to offer contrasting recommendations on what to buy.

At some risk of being overelaborate, the following comprise the current missions of the U.S. strategic forces, presented in ascending order of difficulty of accomplishment:

1. To deter a large-scale attack on urban-industrial America.
2. To provide a suitably impressive latent threat behind day-to-day diplomacy.
3. To deter a large-scale countermilitary attack on the United States intended to disarm U.S. forces and/or to paralyze U.S. command arrangements.
4. To deter *relatively* light coercive attacks on urban America in order to influence the U.S. will, rather than its capacity, to fight/retaliate.
5. To deter large-scale counterpopulation attacks upon U.S. allies.
6. To deter coercive attacks on U.S. allies.
7. To deter large-scale (nuclear) countermilitary attacks on U.S. and U.S.-allied forces abroad.

8. To help to deter the use of theater nuclear weapons by an enemy.

9. To help to deter large-scale conventional attacks on U.S. and U.S.-allied forces abroad.

Opinions differ, as opinions will, as to just what it might take to accomplish any one or all of the above, but it is important that the public understand the true extent of the deterrent burden placed upon the strategic forces, both offensive and defensive. In somewhat different perspective, it is accurate to claim that the United States charges its strategic forces with the support of peacetime diplomacy, the discouragement of deliberate crisis initiation, the denial to an adversary of attractive military breakout options from a crisis, the provision of the United States with the means to control a war that erupts out of a crisis, the denial of an enemy's objectives, and the ability to restore peace on terms compatible with vital U.S. security interests.

THEORIES OF DETERRENCE

There are two principal theories of deterrence, with many variants of each occupying intermediate positions. First, there is the theory which advises that deterrence can best, and should, be effected by the threat to punish an enemy's society. Second, there is the theory that deterrence prospers most reliably when an enemy can, in his estimation, be denied military, and hence political, success. The punishment theory of nuclear deterrence is often characterized as mutual assured destruction (MAD); the denial theory frequently is described as a war-fighting perspective. These pejorative labels, MAD and war-fighting, have great potential for misleading the unwary. Adherents to a MAD approach to deterrence do not want actually to destroy anything, while advocates of a war-fighting deterrence are profoundly desirous of the United States avoiding a need actually to fight. Both of these theories are theories of deterrence. The public should be alert no less to unscrupulous liberal demagogues who purport to identify a "choice" between the prevention of war and the waging of war than to overexcited conservatives prone to paint their debating rivals as advocates of Armageddon.

Bearing in mind the persisting uncertainties as to what might be needed to assure deterrence of particular hostile acts by a particular Soviet leader at a particular time and place, I am a proponent of the denial/defense, or so-called war-fighting, approach to deterrence. A wide array of theoretical arguments can be woven for and against a war-fighting deterrent, but five points rise above all others to compel respect for the denial theory.

First, only credible threats are likely to deter. Threats to destroy Soviet cities as the deliberate intent of action policy are thoroughly incredible.

Second, for good or ill it is a matter of public record that the present and each of the past five U.S. presidents have insisted that they have available preplanned choices in nuclear strategy that extend far beyond the ability just to create a near-instant holocaust in the urban Soviet Union. Whatever the objective merits of assured destruction, or society punishment, as an all-purpose deterrent threat, subjectively no recent president has been prepared to live with such a restriction on his options.

Third, there is very widespread agreement among Western scholars of Russian and Soviet history and of the contemporary Soviet political system that a direct threat to the Soviet state—to its truly essential assets, including its instruments of foreign and domestic coercion—is superior as a deterrent to a far more generalized threat to wreak radioactive havoc upon Soviet society at large.

Fourth, it is plausible to predict that in the event that prewar deterrence should fail, the U.S. government would be far more interested in saving U.S. and U.S.-allied lives than it would be in killing Russians. The defense or war-fighting theory of deterrence holds out some, albeit very uncertain, promise that a major war might be terminated short of a general holocaust and short of its triggering a "nuclear winter."

Finally, it is a religious, ethical, and legal principle of very long standing that states should both intend and effect as little harm to "innocent civilians" as is consistent with military necessity. The war-fighting deterrent, by intent, does not threaten civilians at large, and it is oriented more or less strictly to the prospectively efficient application of military power against legitimate military targets. (This is not to deny that a nuclear war could not help but wreak enormous damage upon civilian "bystanders.")

Understandably enough, those who debate strategic policy choices in the relative calm of a noncrisis time have major difficulty leaping over the "imagination barrier" to think realistically about what may be needed to deter truly desperate Soviet leaders. The Soviet Union portrayed, or caricatured, by many American public commentators is a Soviet Union that is suspiciously easy to deter.

A U.S. strategic deterrent appropriate in quantity and quality for that one occasion in perhaps thirty or more years when a Soviet leader asks himself, "Am I deterred?" necessarily will provide a deterrent effect that is heroically excessive for the needs of day in and day out, even year in and year out, diplomacy. Unfortunately, the United States cannot rent a sufficiently awesome strategic deterrent just for the very rare occasion of unmistakable need like renting a tuxedo for a formal dinner.

SOME GENERAL POINTS ON STRATEGIC DEFENSE

The process of public debate has a way of driving positions farther apart and of directing attention to areas of disagreement rather than to common ground. In fact, there is a great deal less to the current debate over strategic defense than meets the eye immediately. It is important that people should recognize what the debate today is *not* about. It is not about the respective and allegedly relative merits of defense as opposed to deterrence, because defense is a way to deter. Furthermore, it is not about the value or otherwise of the United States spending tens or hundreds of billions of dollars to deploy strategic defenses. Rather, it is about the pros and cons of a research program—SDI—that may or may not yield effective, survivable, and affordable protection. Such questions as: How best should the United States deter the Soviet Union? and, What would be the implications for international security of U.S. (and presumably Soviet) deployment of a very competent defense? are indeed interesting and are discussed here. But President Reagan's SDI, today, is not about to transform the terms of deterrence in short order.

The supercharged negative rhetoric on SDI that is the stock-in-trade of many domestic and foreign critics needs to be cooled by reference to some pertinent contextual facts, not opinions.

First, the superpower arms control process was proclaimed by both liberal and conservative commentators to be in a state of deep crisis—a crisis of relevance as well as a crisis of negotiability—long before President Reagan introduced his idea of an SDI in 1983. There is no disagreement worthy of much note among expert observers that the U.S. Anti-Ballistic Missile (ABM) program, Safeguard, was in its day a critically important source of American leverage for negotiating the first offensive arms control agreement, SALT I. Similarly, there is near universal agreement that the introduction of SDI in 1983 and the creation of an SDI program office (SDIO) in 1984 provided the Soviet Union with a necessary and sufficient motive to reenter a process of negotiation and to produce the most radical proposal for force-level reductions in the entire history of arms control.

Second, the idea of defending the homeland, toward which SDI only aspires today, was U.S. policy until the early 1960s (recall the air defense plans of the 1950s), and is Soviet policy today. The notion that it is desirable, as opposed to being simply unavoidable, for homelands to be totally vulnerable, is a "tradition" of scarcely more than twenty years' standing.

Third, the Soviet Union has a much larger and much better funded strategic defense program than does the United States. The Soviet Union is well down the road in pursuing the very same technologies that are under investigation in the U.S. SDI. With sublime hypocrisy, the leading Soviet scientific critic of the U.S. SDI, Dr. Y. P. Velikhov, is the "father" of the Soviet military laser program. (For details on Soviet activities, see U.S. Departments of Defense and State, *Soviet Strategic Defense Programs*, GPO, October 1985.)

Fourth, while it would be difficult to exaggerate the importance of the political commitment by the President to seeing the research program through to the point where informed decisions can be made for or against actual deployment, it is a fact that the United States always has believed in conducting research into the technologies of defense. There is no disagreement between proponents and critics of the SDI over the necessity for the conduct of such research.

Fifth, difficult though it seems to be for some people to grasp the point, there is no functional difference between protecting U.S. military power by the familiar means of mobility, concrete and steel, or the proliferation of numbers and protecting it by active defense. Strategic defense may be thought of as "silos in the sky."

Finally, some critics of the SDI have chosen to purvey some very bad military history with frequent references to an American Maginot Line. SDI, if weaponized, most likely will provide not a single "line" of defense, but instead will defend sequentially throughout the course of 8,000 miles of defensive space for engagement—some "line"! Furthermore, if we seek inspiration in military history, critics of the SDI should be asked to explain away, if they can, the enormous value to Germany of the Siegfried Line in the winter of 1944–45. Truly impregnable defenses are a theoretical impossibility—one can always invent, on paper, a weapon that penetrates them, or grant the attacker the one additional unit of attack that runs the defender out of ammunition— but history is replete with cases of defenses that "worked."

Intellectual arrogance inclines the "certified expert" to believe that if he or she does not know how to do something, then that something cannot be done. Thus it was with heavier-than-air flight, with atomic fission, and with intercontinental ballistic missiles—before they were, in fact, "done."

A major source of confusion in the debate about SDI today is that both pro and con expert witnesses frequently neglect to specify just what it is that they are claiming can or cannot be done, both on the technological feasibility and affordability of effective defenses. The point was made earlier that deterrence is a convenient catchall concept, but to say meaningful things about it one needs to specify who is to be deterred from doing what to whom over what issues and in which locations. Similarly, strategic defense is not an either-or subject, no matter what excited debaters may assert or appear to believe. To return to the point about common ground, everyone knowledgeable about strategic defense technologies agrees that defense is feasible and affordable for *some* specific purposes.

POSSIBLE MISSIONS FOR STRATEGIC DEFENSE

There are as yet no officially approved missions for ballistic missile defense. The range of possible missions is illustrated in the following list:

1. Protect strategic offensive forces.
2. Protect the National Command Authorities (NCA) and strategic command, control, and communications (C3).
3. Protect U.S. and allied theater nuclear and general-purpose forces and their logistic infrastructure (ports, airfields, bridges, depots, and crossroad choke points).
4. Protect U.S. and allied cities against light coercive attacks, "stray" warheads, and careless countermilitary strikes.
5. Protect those U.S. and allied economic and administrative assets that are essential for recovery.
6. Protect against an accidental or unauthorized missile launch.
7. Protect against nuclear blackmail by "crazy states".
8. Protect U.S. and allied societies against heavy attacks.

These missions call for different kinds of defenses, and the difficulties and cost of fulfilling them are substantially distinctive. It is worth noting that the critics of SDI typically choose to focus upon the problems of mission 8, the defense of cities against many thousands of warheads. The debate is not over the technological feasibility and affordability of a literally "leak-proof" defense. Perfection can only be a human goal.

Proponents of SDI argue that less than perfect, even very much less than perfect, defenses would be suitable for most prospective missions, that nearly perfect performance should be attainable with respect to protection against light attacks (whatever their targets), and that even an admittedly "leaky" defense of cities still could have very important positive consequences for the prospects for national survival. The defense of cities would be far more difficult than the defense of military forces (where protection of only 50 or 60 percent may be "good enough"), but it is well to remember that the destruction of most U.S. cities would not advance Soviet war-fighting objectives. It follows that the quality of Soviet motivation actually to assault the urban United States cannot be high.

Finally, the absence today of approved missions for strategic defense does not reflect indecision or muddled thinking on the part of the Reagan administration; rather, it reflects the fact that the SDIO is still exploring what should be feasible, survivable, and affordable. Some critics of SDI have charged the administration with inconsistency because it has discussed defense with reference both to the protection of the whole country and to missions much more limited in scope. There is no inconsistency. Most of the technologies applicable to the less burdensome missions would be vital elements in a comprehensive architecture of defense for the protection of cities.

THE CASE FOR STRATEGIC DEFENSE

To recognize that there would be costs and difficulties of different kinds associated with the deployment of defenses (depending upon the missions to be performed) is not to say anything very profound. There are no free lunches in the defense realm any more than there are in any other field of endeavor. Those of us who are strongly supportive of SDI and who see great merit in proceeding to deploy defenses—technology and dollar costs permitting—are fully aware of the problems that would attend such deployment. Whether or not the SDI-supportive camp will one day be judged correct at the bar of history, it is a matter of record that, thus far at least, pro-SDI debaters and discussants have tended to be far more respectful of, and knowledgeable concerning, criticisms of their position than have their opponents. Ironically, perhaps some of the more troubling difficulties that would or could attend new defensive deployments actually were first identified and thought through by supporters of the President's program.

It is my belief that, on careful reflection, there are no policy "showstoppers" for SDI or for actual defensive deployments. However, there are difficulties, as one would expect, and there are many problems that need to be treated constructively as opportunities.

Each person will frame and weigh the questions and issues pertaining to strategic defense in a somewhat individual manner. What follows is *not* an attempt to persuade readers to favor strategic defense, but rather an attempt to share with readers some of the reasons why this commentator favors the President's course on SDI.

First, there is a plain absence of feasible alternative paths to a much safer world. Ideas for strategic stability, and even for a vast scale of truly balanced reduction in nuclear armaments, are easy to design. The problem is that they have a distressing tendency to require, as a precondition for success, a revolutionary change in the character and purposes of the Soviet Union. The real alternative to defensive deployment is a United States confined to competing with new offensive weapons. It should not be forgotten that the primary motive behind SDI is President Reagan's profound unhappiness with the social and psychological costs, as well as the risks, of an offense-offense arms competition.

Second, strategic defenses would enhance stability for deterrence. A multilayered defensive screen that could take out 40, 50, or 60 percent of Soviet warheads would not offer much protection for American society, but it would subvert utterly any military sense that there might otherwise be in the Soviet strategic war plan. Soviet planners could not predict which of their weapons would be able to penetrate and which would not. In such a situation, the Soviet Union would never choose to attack.

Third, the defense of military assets in Western Europe and of U.S. strategic forces at home would greatly strengthen the security of the allies. Protection in Europe, and of the logistical train from North America to Europe, would have to facilitate the nonnuclear defense of allied territory. By protecting U.S. retaliatory forces, strategic defenses would serve to dampen the prospects for an explosive escalation process. The U.S. strategic nuclear "extended deterrent" would be defended against the possibility of preemptive attack.

Fourth, strategic defenses would save lives. Quite aside from the strategic value for U.S. deterrence of being able to deny Soviet nuclear weapons access to most of the American people, it is an essentially moral point that the U.S. government has an obligation to protect Americans physically. If people can be defended, they should be. Since neither side wants to attack the civilian population of its enemy, even a relatively light area defense should have a marked effect in depressing potential casualty rates. It must be emphasized that the United States and its allies need not pay a price in an enhanced risk of war—that is to say, in a reduced quality of prewar deterrence—for the admittedly imperfect physical protection secured for society.

Fifth, SDI is essential if the Soviet Union is to be denied the possibility of securing a major military advantage through the exploitation of its research on defensive technologies. "SDIskiy" is real, large, and—the current Soviet formal position in Geneva notwithstanding—not negotiable in its vital elements. The United

States has no responsible alternative other than to discover for itself what the Soviet defense establishment knows and might find out about defenses.

Sixth, in the absence of strategic defensive deployments, arms control and disarmament agreements worthy of the name will not be negotiable. Long and, for some, disillusioning experience with SALTs I and II and then with START has demonstrated as plainly as can be that the United States cannot negotiate stability-enhancing strategic arms agreements when the focus is exclusively upon the regulation of offensive weapons. Competition in the deployment of ballistic missile defense was switched off in 1972 by the ABM Treaty, since which time the Soviet strategic offensive arsenal has climbed from 1,900 to approximately 10,000 warheads. Meaningful nuclear disarmament will be possible (it certainly will not be guaranteed) only if Soviet leaders believe that their long-range nuclear weapons systems lack military utility and if a very radical disarmament regime can be "policed" against rapid breakout or cheating by active defenses.

Seventh, and finally, SDI is the only path for U.S. policy that could offer a high-confidence solution to the possibility of "nuclear winter" in the event of a failure of prewar deterrence. SDI may or may not one day be translated into several layers of deployed defenses capable of destroying all but a tiny fraction of the Soviet missile warhead arsenal. What is certain is that if strategic defenses cannot remove the danger of nuclear winter, nothing else can.

THE TRANSITION TO DEFENSE DOMINANCE

The problems of managing an orderly defensive transition have been greatly exaggerated by people who either have very limited skills in strategy or who are not highly motivated to think constructively of such a transition as an opportunity. It is firm U.S. policy that before new defensive deployments are begun there would be extensive discussions with both our allies and the Soviet Union.

The key to maintaining stability through a transition is a continued U.S. commitment to maintaining its strategic offensive arsenal at an appropriately deterring level. Those offensive forces would "guard" a defensive transition and, in turn, be guarded by the newly deployed defenses in a benign synergism. While President Reagan affirms and reaffirms his determination that the research program of SDI is not negotiable, the pace of the actual deployment of defenses and retirement of offensive forces would be very negotiable indeed. One need not have a Ph.D. in strategic studies in order to understand that a cooperatively managed defensive transition would be very much in the U.S. interest. No less important, in the face of an increasingly competent U.S. defense and a still-formidable U.S. offense, the Soviet Union should be strongly motivated by self-interest to participate in such a venture.

Critics of strategic defense assert that no one knows how to design and implement a defensive transition that could be effected in safety. It is difficult to avoid the suspicion that those critics must be either incompetent or insincere. Allegedly, crisis instability would be fueled by a transition. But since deployed defenses— even on a rather modest scale—would undermine the military confidence of a potential attacker, why would he be motivated to strike first with an assault that could not preclude a fatal level and quality of retaliation? If the Soviet Union should come to fear a possible U.S. first strike, with a U.S. president supposedly confident in the ability of U.S. defenses to defeat the Soviet survivors in their retaliatory mode, it still would not make sense for them to strike first. In the face of U.S. defenses, a first strike would *guarantee* catastrophe for the Soviet Union. However, U.S. policy has a very convincing answer to this nonproblem. Specifically, the United States would be very willing to negotiate a scale of offensive force reductions such that there could be no U.S. first-strike threat, even in the minds of very conservative Soviet defense planners.

In conclusion, one should never forget that the Soviet Union has, as its first and overriding priority, the protection of the political system of Soviet power. A cooperative defensive transition would enable the Soviets to do exactly that, with great assurance, vis-à-vis U.S. and U.S.-allied nuclear threats. This writer has challenged Soviet analysts to explain why a cooperative defensive transition would not be very much in the Soviet interest and has yet to receive a convincing reply.

FINAL CONSIDERATIONS

Public debate tends to encourage people to dramatize that which really is most unlikely to be attended by any drama. History tells us that governments are capable of making terrible mistakes, as well as that the expertise of "experts" is easily exaggerated and extended to cover predictions that fall far outside their professional competence. The American public may come to notice that the front rank of critics of SDI, though undoubtedly all honorable people, by and large is composed of theoretical scientists who are typically remote from the practical engineering of the SDI program and who lack specialist credentials in what may be termed "strategic history."

Should the United States decide to proceed from the SDI program of the 1980s into actual defensive deployments, those deployments would occur over a period of many years—indeed, possibly over several decades. Transition problems would neither erupt by surprise nor would they need to be resolved in the course of a frantic weekend.

Phoney issues are attracting far too much attention. The U.S. public is advised by Soviet propagandists—functionally aided and abetted by some well-meaning Americans—to worry about "the militarization of space," as if outer space has not been used for military purposes by both superpowers for the better part of twenty years already; "space strike arms," neglecting to mention that the U.S. SDI has to be very interested in defenses that can operate in space for the elementary reason that the principal Soviet military threat to the United States would come through and from space; "crisis instability," as if either country would choose to launch an attack that must be militarily futile; and "acceleration of the arms race," as if the Soviet Union is not modernizing its *entire* strategic offensive arsenal already today in the quest for "destabilizing" military advantage.

It would be a tragedy of historic proportions if the United States and its allies were to take counsel of unreasonable fears and deny themselves the only possible route both to a benign transformation in the terms of deterrence and to physical protection from the worst that could happen in this permanently nuclear age.

NO TO STAR WARS
Robert Bowman

If there is one thing on which I agree with the proponents of space weapons, it is that the debate over the Strategic Defense Initiative (SDI), more popularly known as "Star Wars," should not be engaged on the level of technological feasibility but on the level of strategic suitability. The important question is not, *Can* we deploy a Star Wars system? but, *Should* we? The answer to that question depends upon the effect such a deployment would have on our national security. There are many of us in the military, both active and retired, who believe that the effect of a Star Wars system would be to *destroy* our national security by:

1. Greatly increasing the likelihood of nuclear war.
2. Causing such a war to be even more destructive.
3. Complicating, rather than enabling, a transition to a less threatening future.

Our answer to the question, Should we? is a resounding NO!

THE QUESTION OF PERFECTION

No Star Wars system could be perfect—on this, too, both sides agree. What we disagree about is the degree of imperfection we

Dr. Robert M. Bowman is the President of the Institute for Space and Security Studies.

should expect. The proponents blithely promise the American people a 95 percent perfect system, while I confidently predict that the actual effectiveness would lie between zero and 10 percent, even if it worked.

Let us assume that all the enormous technological advances required to build a Star Wars system were actually achieved. What would we have when we deployed this five-layer system of chemical laser battle stations, electromagnetic railguns, particle beams, nuclear-weapons-generated X-rays, orbiting mirrors, and other weapons? We would have a complex organism consisting of many fists (kill mechanisms) and arms (pointing systems), a few eyes (sensors) and ears (discriminators), a brain (a battle-management computer) and a central nervous system (a communications network). This system could be rendered totally useless by disabling any one critical element among the many that are inherently extremely vulnerable, particularly those based in space. It could be penetrated with ease by employing any of several countermeasures already available. And, like any Maginot Line, it could be gone around with delivery systems which do not go through space. In short, what we would have would be a system which (if everything worked correctly) might stop 10 percent of the nuclear missiles directed against us. But then again, if something in this enormously complex organism malfunctioned or was damaged by natural phenomena, space junk, or enemy action, we could have a trillion or so dollars worth of useless junk unable to stop anything.

Let me be perfectly plain. Even if the claim of 95 percent effectiveness were credible, I still would not want the system. There is no more a legitimate military objective for a 95 percent effective system than there is for a 10 percent effective system.

STAR WARS AND MILITARY OBJECTIVES

The objectives laid out in the President's Star Wars speech of March 23, 1983, were to make nuclear weapons impotent and obsolete, to do away with mutual assured destruction (MAD), to do away with deterrence by threat of retaliation, to enable us to discard our offensive weapons, and to "save lives rather than avenge them." These are admirable objectives. To achieve them, however, would require an absolutely perfect system. For the past two years, almost everyone in or out of government has given the

President the message that such a system is not attainable. And neither are his objectives.

Star Wars is now being justified by an entirely different set of objectives. We are now being told that even an imperfect system would be militarily useful in denying an enemy success in a first strike and therefore would enhance deterrence. Let us translate that into understandable terms. What kind of success is an enemy seeking in a first strike, and how would the prospect of failure deter him from the attempt? Of course, what an enemy would be attempting in a first strike would be to disarm us. The prospect of failure would deter him because it would lead us to retaliate with the weapons remaining. Thus it becomes clear that this new Star Wars justification is diametrically opposed to the President's original objectives.

The President sought to do away with deterrence. Now we seek to *enhance* deterrence. The President wanted to eliminate the need to threaten retaliation. Now we want to *increase* the threat of retaliation. The President wanted to be able to discard our offensive weapons. Now we want to *defend* them. The President sought to do away with MAD. Now we seek to make it just a little bit *MADder*. The President wanted to protect people and make nuclear weapons obsolete. Now we want to protect *nuclear weapons*—and make people obsolete.

Still, enhancing deterrence by protecting weapons of retaliation is a legitimate military objective. If it were necessary, however (and I do not believe it is, since we have thousands of invulnerable nuclear weapons to retaliate with), this objective could be achieved more easily and inexpensively. By simply reactivating the ground-based point defense we are allowed under the Anti–Ballistic Missile (ABM) Treaty, we could assure that many hundreds of land-based nuclear weapons survived any first strike— in addition to a few thousand cruise missiles and about seven thousand nuclear weapons from our invulnerable submarines. So if our objective is to enhance deterrence, we do not need Star Wars. We do not need weapons in space. We do not need to violate the ABM Treaty. We do not need to spend five or ten thousand dollars for every man, woman, and child in the country. And we do not need to put our survival in the hands of computers.

Star Wars is far more than is required to enhance deterrence—but far less than is required to do away with it. Star Wars is far more than is required to protect nuclear missiles—but far less than is required to protect people.

So what is its objective? Well, when I was directing Star Wars programs for the Air Force we never found one. But in all honesty it must be pointed out that there *is* a way that one might make a Star Wars system militarily effective. All you have to do is add one more layer. I call it the "pre-boost-phase defensive layer." It amounts to destroying enemy missiles in their silos *before* they are launched. We have the technology to do that: it is called MX, Pershing II, and Trident II. If we destroy 90 percent or so that way, there is a chance that a Star Wars system might actually be of some use against the few that remain. Of course, some people do not think that sounds like defense at all—it sounds like a first strike. And they are right. The most believable military use for Star Wars is to protect an aggressor from retaliation after his first strike. That is why we are so afraid of the Soviets getting one, and that is why they are so afraid of our getting one. And we are both right. We have every reason to fear a Star Wars system in the hands of an adversary.

Actually, there is another military use for a Star Wars system that has absolutely nothing to do with its questionable value in defending against ballistic missiles. It is to exploit its tremendous *offensive* potential against those far more vulnerable targets— satellites. Even a crude and ineffective Star Wars system would be extremely effective against space objects, manned or unmanned. Once a Star Wars system destroys all enemy space objects, it can prevent an adversary from ever launching anything else into space. Having thus gained absolute control of space (the ultimate high ground), the country with a Star Wars system could then fortify space even further, stationing such things as space bombers there. These systems, in turn, would seemingly give it absolute military control of earth. This is what the extremist supporters of Star Wars *really* want. Their talk of a moral alternative to MAD is nothing but an enormous con job. They have apparently taken in the President and many among the American people. But they will not fool the Russians. If we come even *close* to deploying a Star Wars system which might give us that capability, the Soviets are likely to initiate a desperation preemptive nuclear strike. And without its pre-boost-phase layer, our Star Wars "defenses" would be useless against such an attack.

If Star Wars systems on either side would lead to nuclear war, what about having them on *both* sides? Unfortunately, nobody has been able to figure out how to make such systems invulnerable to each other. In fact, the natural target for a Star Wars system is another Star Wars system. The minute both the United States and the Soviet Union were to have one, whoever shot first could disable the opposing system, rendering that nation again completely defenseless, while simultaneously launching a nuclear first strike and hoping for its own system to shield it from retaliation. If Star Wars systems on either side would greatly increase the likelihood of nuclear war, such systems on both sides practically guarantee it.

THE LIKELIHOOD OF WAR

Nuclear war can come about in two main ways: (1) the failure of deterrence, leading to a deliberate first strike by one side or the other, or (2) an accident, causing one side to strike in the mistaken belief that the other side has initiated hostilities.

Let us look at the second possible cause first. It is easy to see that Star Wars systems, being vulnerable to destruction by each other at the speed of light, reduce warning times dramatically, putting both sides on a hair trigger. They also put the "front line" in a position where it is difficult to observe. It is easy to tell the difference between an enemy attack on a missile silo and an accident, like a mechanic dropping a wrench and causing a missile to explode. But it would be almost impossible to tell the difference between an enemy attack on a Star Wars battle station and a failure due to impact with space debris, or even a mechanical failure. What is more, the extremely short time in which such systems must accomplish their mission demands that the decision to go to war must be delegated to computers. It thus seems obvious that Star Wars systems would greatly increase the chances of accidental war. But what about deliberate war?

In order to examine the effect of Star Wars defenses on deterrence, one has to understand how deterrence works. Defenses do not deter. Neither does the fear of failure. What deters is fear of the *consequence* of failure—retaliation. The only reason for protecting offensive weapons with strategic defenses is so they can carry out MAD. Defenses do not change the nature of the deterrent. They only change the details of the calculation, and they do that in a way that makes us *less* secure, not more.

Look at the impact of defenses on the usefulness of nuclear weapons. At the present time, thanks to arms control, the retaliatory capabilities of our nuclear arsenals far outweigh their first-strike capabilities. This is a stable situation which makes deliberate nuclear war extremely unlikely. How would defenses change this?

First, how would defenses affect the retaliatory role of nuclear weapons? The only nuclear weapons which deter an enemy attack are those which can both survive and penetrate to carry out their retaliatory mission. Consider a hypothetical example in which both sides have 50 percent-effective area defenses. This would enable about five times as many of our land-based missiles to survive (250 rather than the 50 which would survive without defenses), would increase somewhat the number of bombers surviving, would do little for submarines in port, and would have no effect on our already survivable submarines at sea (which contain the majority of our strategic warheads). Thus, the defenses would increase the number of surviving warheads from about 7,000 to about 7,700—a 10 percent increase. However, since we have assumed that the Soviets would also have similar defenses, only half of these would get through. Our net deterrent would thus decrease from 7,000 (the figure in the absence of defenses) to 3,850—a 45 percent decrease. And the better the defenses are, the greater the impact on the retaliatory capability of our forces. If both sides were protected by 95 percent-effective defenses, about 10,000 of our 10,500 strategic weapons could survive a first strike, but only 500 could penetrate—a 93 percent reduction in our deterrent.

The above scenario assumes that the defenses are just as effective in protecting the innocent party as they are in protecting the aggressor, who has the element of surprise on his side. That is unlikely to be true. Similar defenses could easily be only 10 percent effective against a massive surprise attack and yet be 50 percent effective against a smaller retaliatory force it was ready for. The difference would be even more striking if the aggressor used the offensive antisatellite capabilities of his Star Wars system to cripple critical elements of the other side's defenses at the same time he launched his nuclear attack. Under these circumstances, the missiles of the aggressor would have a free ride to the target, while the few surviving on the other side would have to penetrate alerted defenses in order to retaliate. Indeed, if they worked—a big "if"—Star Wars systems might reduce the usefulness of nuclear weapons in their retaliatory role. The irony is that by so doing, they would automatically increase their usefulness in a first strike. The inescapable conclusion is that Star Wars defenses would dramatically *increase* the likelihood of war.

THE CONSEQUENCES OF WAR

Limiting damage if deterrence should fail is often given as one of the justifications for Star Wars. How good a system would it take to accomplish that objective? If more than fifty warheads were to fall on the United States, we would lose most of our people and probably cease to function as a society. It might not take even that many. I think we could agree that unless a ballistic missile defense (BMD) system could reduce the number of warheads impacting to this level, it is probably not worth having. So we would be looking for a system that would stop 199 out of every 200 missiles. This is a 99.5 percent system. It would have technical requirements similar to those for the impossible system to replace deterrence. The strategic situation in which this system would operate, however, would be very different, for we would have retained our offensive forces.

Our adversaries, fearing that our Star Wars defenses might be 50 percent effective, would have doubled the number of offensive missiles in their arsenal. But they would also have implemented countermeasures that would reduce the actual effectiveness to perhaps 10 percent. The consequence in the event of war would thus be that nearly twice as many warheads would land on their targets in the United States. This is hardly a more "acceptable" outcome.

Neither would a Star Wars system protect us from nuclear terrorism. The proponents often raise its supposed value in protecting against Khomeini and Gadhafi. Yet if an international terrorist did get hold of a stolen or homemade nuclear weapon, the last thing he would do would be to initiate a fifteen-year development program to build an intercontinental ballistic missile (ICBM) to deliver it. He would simply float it up the Potomac on a barge or smuggle it into the country in any of the many ways people get marijuana and cocaine into the country today.

A COOPERATIVE TRANSITION

One of the popular scenarios for justifying Star Wars envisions a cooperative transition from an offense-dominated to a defense-dominated nuclear relationship between the superpowers. Unfortunately, nobody has the slightest idea how to bring this about.

The problem is that the transition between these extremes would involve passage through a very large unstable region. With the present offense-dominated stability, it is necessary for each side to have enough offense to be able to ride out an attempted disarming first strike and still have enough left to penetrate the other's defenses and wreak unacceptable damage. For a defense-dominated relationship to be stable, each side would have to have insufficient offense to penetrate the other's defenses even using the full power of its undiluted forces. Between these extremes lies the broad region of instability in which neither side has enough offense to retaliate effectively, but both sides have enough offense to carry out a successful first strike.

To bridge that gulf of instability successfully would require an unbelievable degree of cooperation and trust. Were it possible for the United States and the Soviet Union to cooperate to that extent, then it would also be possible (far more easily and inexpensively) for them simply to cooperate in the destruction of existing weapons. The fact is that the existence of Star Wars defenses would only complicate such a process.

CONCLUSION

Should "it" be done? This is a much simpler question to answer than, Could "it" be done? and a more important one. The latter question depends greatly on what "it" is and what you require "it" to do. Could "it" be done? is a question nobody can answer now, and seeking the answer is one of the justifications for the program. But the fact is we do not need to know! The answer to that question is immaterial, because the answer to the other is clear. Whatever "it" is and whatever requirements you place upon "it," "it" will:

1. Increase the likelihood of nuclear war.
2. Fail miserably at making the consequences of war more acceptable, possibly making them even worse.

3. Complicate any hope of a cooperative transition to a less threatening relationship between the superpowers, probably totally destroying the arms control process.

Does that mean we should stop all research on defensive weapons? Of course not. We now have a substantial lead in Star Wars technology. Still, a prudent level of true research to prevent technological surprise is necessary as long as the offensive threats on either side exist. But it should not take place within the framework of the Strategic Defense Initiative Organization or any bureaucracy having a vested interest in the continuation and growth of the program. It should take place within the existing services, where proposed systems must compete for funding with other approaches to enhancing our security. There is an old saying in the military: Put a dozen people in a suite of rooms in the Pentagon, give them $100 million a year to spend, and assign them no mission whatsoever, and in six months they will be back asking for more money and more manpower. This is not quite what we have done with Star Wars, but it does illustrate the importance of organization and bureaucracy in influencing the course of events. The SDI program must be cancelled and the SDI Organization abolished.

Besides, what we are planning in SDI is *not* research. It is precisely the kind of field testing prohibited by the ABM Treaty. And it is totally unnecessary. A verifiable treaty against space weapons testing is achievable and would greatly enhance our security. It would allow our critical early-warning space systems to continue enjoying the relative sanctuary from which they enhance stability. It would preserve the great benefits we have derived from the ABM Treaty and allow us to make progress toward the reduction of offensive weapons. And it would eliminate any hope of either side being able to launch a first strike and escape retaliation.

Avoiding an arms race in space also opens up exciting possibilities for cooperative peaceful space programs. Why initiate a new, costly, and dangerous round in the arms race in the futile pursuit of military superiority? The United States *and the Soviet Union have better things to do with resources, technology, brainpower, and creativity*. Together we can prevail in the hostile environment of space and, through it, better our lot on earth. Or we can export our instruments of death beyond the planet entrusted to us by God, and thereby destroy it. Let us choose life.

THE STRATEGIC DEFENSE ENVIRONMENT: POLITICS, STRATEGY, AND ARMS CONTROL
Alex Gliksman

The Kremlin's new leader has come out of the shadows in a skillfully orchestrated offensive, making it clear that the infusion of new blood into Moscow's leadership will present Washington with its most serious challenge in sustaining domestic and allied support for the Strategic Defense Initiative (SDI). Saying no to Soviet entreaties to bargain on the program may not be good enough.

THE POLITICAL CLIMATE

While Congress has voted to fund the SDI program, it has done so in deference to a popular President with a strong attachment to SDI, and in the belief that it is the chip that led Moscow back to the bargaining table. But congressional support is fragile. Many who voted for SDI have strong reservations about the concept and the money it could potentially involve. The Gramm-Rudman deficit reduction plan gives immediacy to the financial implications of the program.

Mr. Alex Gliksman is the Director of Strategic Defense Studies at the United Nations Association. His research is funded by a grant from the Carnegie Corporation of New York. This article expands upon and updates ideas presented by the author in an article for the *Christian Science Monitor*, Oct. 1, 1985.

Les Aspin, the Chairman of the House Armed Services Committee, and Sam Nunn, the ranking member of the Senate Armed Services Committee, share this perspective, in whole or in part. Soon after being named chairman, Congressman Aspin suggested that the Soviet reaction to SDI demonstrated that it, rather than the MX missile, was the "bargaining chip" that could bring about reductions. After travelling to Moscow, Senator Nunn indicated that an SDI trade should not be excluded. Despite his position as a member of the Democratic minority, when Nunn talks about national security, the Senate listens.

Within the defense community, SDI confronts critics with unimpeachable credentials who hold no stock in perfect defenses and believe it makes little sense to risk the Anti-Ballistic Missile (ABM) Treaty in pursuit of this phantom. To them, if SDI can be traded for deep reductions in offensive arms, then it will have achieved its goal of reducing the utility of nuclear forces without ever being deployed.

Two key administration advisors, former Defense Secretary James Schlesinger and former National Security Advisor Brent Scowcroft, are of this school. While Schlesinger has explicitly called for an SDI swap, Scowcroft sees the program as a wild card that could wreak havoc with arms reductions.

With the exception of industry, the Europeans are, at best, uncomfortable with SDI. France and Britain fear that strategic defenses might neutralize their small nuclear forces, even if they prove porous to superpower arsenals. More broadly speaking, Europe questions the value of ballistic missile defense (BMD) given the continent's exposure to a myriad of other nuclear and nonnuclear threats for which SDI will provide no relief.

Aside from the desire to acquire commercially relevant advanced technology from the United States, allies that have endorsed the program have done so for tactical reasons. These allies believe that European support for the program will assure that they have a voice at the critical moment in steering the administration toward an SDI arms control bargain.

In all these quarters, objections to SDI can be expected to grow if the price of maintaining the President's "vision for the future" is no reduction in nuclear arms today.

MOSCOW'S GAMBIT

The Soviets give high priority to derailing the Strategic Defense Initiative and they seem determined to use opportunities afforded by the West's political climate to advance toward this goal. Recent events are indicative of this, and they may provide a guide to likely future trends in Soviet arms control behavior designed to deal with the program.

At the January 1985 meeting between Secretary of State George Shultz and then–Soviet Foreign Minister Andrei Gromyko, the Soviets presented offense-defense linkage as a condition for progress in arms control and hinted that in exchange for a halt of SDI, Moscow would accept the deep nuclear arms reduction they previously resisted. Cuts ranging from 25 to 50 percent were mentioned.

Still, there was little substance to the Soviet position. While linkage was made explicit, it spoke of what the Soviets wanted but was silent about what they were prepared to concede. It is noteworthy that the hints of drastic cuts were made to the press, principally by unnamed sources. They were not brought to the table at Geneva until much later in the year. Of equal significance, the Kremlin failed to address the devilish problem of verification and omitted any reference to Moscow's own elaborate strategic defense efforts. But once Mikhail Gorbachev's position was firmly established, important changes in Soviet policy and tactics began to emerge.

Opening a dramatic September 1985 offensive, Gorbachev came forward with a negotiating concept whereby all but unverifiable experiments would be banned. If the United States agreed to limit itself to research, he was prepared to offer in return the "most radical" arms reductions proposals. But what went largely unnoticed, until some time later, was a masterful sleight of hand. The Soviet party chief had not only given, he had also taken something away. Before, the Soviets had insisted on the simultaneous solution of the nuclear and space components at the Geneva talks. Now, Gorbachev wanted Washington to renounce SDI first.

For Ronald Reagan, it was not much of a bargain. It asked the President to wager his Star Wars vision for the hope that Gorbachev shared his concept of what constituted drastic cuts.

But with Moscow determined to keep up the pressure as the November summit approached, this was not the end of the story. At a late September meeting between President Reagan and Soviet Foreign Minister Eduard Shevardnadze, the Kremlin went beyond hints to a specific offer that would cut nuclear weapons by 50 percent.

Gorbachev's proposal met some American concerns. For instance, Moscow's concept required some reductions in the Soviet's most threatening land-based missiles, the SS-18 and SS-19. Moreover, rather than hold all aspects of the European missiles talks hostage to the outcome of a space arms accord, the Soviets appeared ready to conclude an interim Euromissile agreement, though a final agreement on this issue would remain tied to a disposition of other elements of the Geneva arms control equation.

But in key areas the Soviet offer remained unsatisfactory to Washington. First, the Soviets define "strategic" systems in a way that captures some U.S. systems possessing only remote potential for use against the Soviet Union. As a result, the Soviets' plan would require disproportionate cuts in U.S. forces. For instance, the Soviet plan counted all carrier-based nuclear capable aircraft as strategic, including those based at U.S. ports. Similarly, nearly the entire inventory of U.S. nuclear capable aircraft in Europe could be subject to reduction, including dual-use systems with only marginal deep strike capabilities. This Soviet strategic definition conveniently excludes some 2,000 comparable and in some cases more capable Soviet systems.

Second, Moscow's formula called for cuts in strategic nuclear "charges" rather than warheads. This was a definition designed to encompass weapons on bombers required to penetrate Soviet air defenses, a form of strategic defense in which Moscow has a monopoly. Thus, by denying Washington compensation the Kremlin sought to preserve an advantage for itself.

Third, the Soviet plan would legitimize a disturbing aspect of recent Soviet arms control behavior. SALT II permits the United States and the Soviet Union to test and deploy only one "new type" of ICBM. In apparent defiance of the treaty, the Soviets are testing and deploying two new missiles, the SS-24 and the SS-25. An element in Moscow's 50 percent proposal would permit them to keep both.

Finally, and perhaps most important of all, Gorbachev's readiness to tolerate strategic defense research was an issue of Soviet public diplomacy and not of the private U.S.-Soviet negotiations. In Geneva, the demand that all SDI research cease continued to be Moscow's formal bargaining position.

Moscow's position has continued to evolve in the period since the first summit meeting. In January 1986, the Soviet leader announced a grand plan, calling for the total abolition of nuclear weapons by the year 2000. But this initiative contained all the hooks inherent in the earlier proposal. Much of this changed as pressure for a second summit began to build in spring 1986. By then, the Soviets seemed to realize that movement in arms control rested on meeting the concerns of Western security specialists including the negotiators across the table, rather than only those of world opinion.

In late May, the Soviets formally presented an offer providing for 40 percent strategic weapons cuts in exchange for a U.S. commitment to abide by the Anti-Ballistic Missile (ABM) Treaty for fifteen to twenty years. Though providing for more modest reductions than earlier proposals, the new Kremlin plan removed several important obstacles to an accord.

First, Moscow was ready to accept a less prejudiced definition of the kinds of weapons that should be regarded as strategic. Second, the Kremlin formally conceded a tolerance of SDI research. Moreover, in conversations with Western officials, Gorbachev hinted that some types of out-of-laboratory experiments might be permitted as well. At the same time, other officials suggested that Moscow would be willing to compromise on the length of an ABM Treaty extension.

The Soviet offer is still less than perfect. Some problems remain to be solved. But if the pattern of behavior established since Gorbachev's rise to power is repeated, it is fair to assume that we have not yet heard the Kremlin's final word. Over time, the Soviets are likely to refine their proposal in a way that will be increasingly attractive to the West.

Ultimately, if the Kremlin's offer becomes more equitable, the administration may be hard pressed to resist the forces who would trade the SDI chip for drastic cuts in strategic forces and theater-range nuclear weapons.

Rather than face this situation when it arises, the administration would be well advised to plan ahead. Careful preparation and hard bargaining can assure that U.S. security interests are advanced. But the President must first decide to negotiate. Besides political considerations, the need to address Soviet ballistic missile defense activities and the limitations of technologies likely to emerge from SDI are excellent reasons for doing so.

THE PRESENT DANGER

At Krasnoyarsk Moscow is building a radar that looks like an ABM Treaty violation in the making. Besides work on this and other elements of traditional missile defenses, the Soviets are developing the exotic weapons required for a Soviet SDI. An example is the high-power laser at the Sary Shagan test range, revealed in recent Defense Department publications. Over the past decade, Soviet spending on these advanced kill mechanisms is said to have been three to five times greater than that of the United States.

These Soviet activities have been central to the administration's justification of SDI. In their brief, U.S. officials note that while Washington's plans have held the spotlight of attention, Moscow's current strategic defense activities could upset the strategic balance long before any U.S. Star Wars system takes to the heavens.

Moscow's continuing failure to include these activities in its arms control pronouncements is significant. Does this mean that everything the Soviets do in strategic defense is fine and only U.S. activities are subject to criticism? It is possible that the Soviets will adopt this or a similar tack. Though there have been hints of some Soviet flexibility, they have previously done so when addressing U.S. concerns about Krasnoyarsk.

This is one area where negotiations are necessary. Through hard bargaining, the United States can assure that the Soviets seriously address developments that, in part, led to the President's defense initiative.

Moscow's strategic defense efforts appear to exploit loopholes in the ABM Treaty which, if not corrected, threaten to erode arms control at its foundation. Some prohibitions in the accord are so vaguely defined that Washington bears an unfair burden in challenging Soviet claims that developments like Krasnoyarsk will not give Moscow a BMD advantage over the United States. As part of an agreement on SDI, the treaty should be revised to place the onus of accountability where it belongs, on the potential violator rather than the victim.

The more exotic directed-energy weapons, such as lasers, pose a similar problem. A 1974 ABM Treaty protocol designed to constrain defenses permits the United States and the Soviet Union to have one hundred missile interceptors each. But this restriction may soon be rendered moot by emerging technology that could give a single weapon the firepower equivalent of one hundred older systems.

One possible remedy is a new protocol restricting such weapons to test ranges and limiting the number permitted at each location. But talks are required if this Treaty of the early 1970s is to be relevant to developments of the 1980s, the 1990s, and beyond.

THE PRESIDENT'S DILEMMA

What some proponents fail to recognize is that the success of SDI may hinge as much on arms control as on technology. While U.S.-Soviet agreement will require compromise on the program, the consequences of holding out could prove to be worse. This, in a nutshell, is the President's real dilemma.

Soon after President Reagan shared his vision with the nation, a group of technologists led by Dr. James C. Fletcher was impaneled to create a plan for proceeding. This group is widely identified as the architect of the five-year, $26 billion research program now called the Strategic Defense Initiative.

But what is less well known is that in the process of grappling with questions of technology, Fletcher and his colleagues examined the environment required for defenses to work. Perhaps because this issue was seemingly less spectacular than the research program, these findings have largely been ignored.

In the panel's judgment, strategic defenses can only be effective if they are "sized" to the dimensions of the Soviet offensive threat. At a minimum, this requires Soviet agreement to limit offensive forces. Deep strategic arms reductions would be even better. From this it is clear that strategic defense deployments and arms control agreements are inexorably linked and that the arms control process must run parallel to, if not precede, the technology program.

This conclusion has been reaffirmed in an exhaustive study by the Congressional Office of Technology Assessment (OTA) released at the end of September 1985. The OTA project was conducted under the direction of a high-level panel of experts representing the broad spectrum of opinions on strategic defense.

The only escape from reliance on arms control is the hope that science can reverse existing trends in technology which make it cheaper to deploy more nuclear weapons than to augment defenses to counter them. But prospects seem bleak, given that neither the President's own technology panel nor the OTA's experts were willing to stake their reputations on this hope.

GORBACHEV'S CALCULUS

Both history and current policy suggest that a Soviet Union faced with the prospect of SDI would seek to expand rather than reduce its offenses. Consequently, even the meager offensive limitations in place today could vanish. But there may be a way to alter Gorbachev's calculus. If very deep cuts in U.S. and Soviet offensive capabilities were in place first, Moscow could come to view advanced defenses as indispensible.

Suppose Washington and Moscow agree to reduce strategic offensive forces by 50 percent. Given the large number of weapons each side would retain, a violation in which a handful of weapons are secretly deployed in contravention of the accord would have a relatively minor effect on the superpower balance. On the other hand, if nuclear weapons are eventually limited to a few hundred on each side, the consequences of the same violation would be catastrophic. In this environment, both nations could guard against this risk if they were free to deploy defenses. In a world where there are few weapons left, defenses are essential as insurance.

Gorbachev claims to be ready to take the steps required to move toward a minimally armed world. Using SDI as leverage, President Reagan could push him toward this goal. Rather than limit his horizons to a one-time offensive-defensive trade, the President could negotiate a timetable of reductions and SDI research, testing, and deployment for the long haul.

For example, the President might propose a schedule for nuclear arms reductions involving a series of 40 to 50 percent cuts to be repeated at five-year intervals. In exchange, the President would agree to limit SDI to research until each side has fewer than 1,000 warheads. At that point, full-fledged development and testing could begin. Phased deployments could start once the weapons tally goes below 500.

Since what is suggested here is merely a concept rather than a proposal, a great amount of further elaboration will obviously be necessary. Clear definitions of what would constitute permitted levels of research, development, and testing will need to be developed and agreed upon. But in many instances the ABM Treaty and its negotiating history provide definitions of these activities that are more concrete than is generally assumed. These documents would provide a shortcut in this effort.

Much work will be required in addressing the sometimes devilish details of existing asymmetries in the American and Soviet offensive force structures. However, here also a great deal of the groundwork has already been done. For instance, well-developed formulas, like the "builddown," could be grafted onto this conceptual framework.

In his March 23, 1983, strategic defense address to the nation, President Reagan recognized that advanced defenses are unlikely to be available before the year 2000. The arrangement suggested here could permit a cautiously paced pursuit of more perfect defenses in a comparable time frame, while also offering several other advantages. Not only would it provide immediate nuclear weapons cuts and redress ABM Treaty compliance problems, but by drastically reducing nuclear arms in the future, it could assure that any defenses the United States might deploy would work.

THE ARMS CONTROL DIMENSION OF STRATEGIC DEFENSE
Warren Zimmermann

I would like to discuss some of the arms control background to strategic defense and some of the factors that will be important as the Geneva negotiations proceed.

The popular and misleading phrase "Star Wars" conjures up a futuristic vision of a world held in thrall to an arcane technology. The newness of it all seems overwhelming, and the prospects are either exciting or terrifying, depending on your point of view. That, however, is not the picture that we are dealing with in Geneva. What we are dealing with is much more familiar. We call it "strategic defense," and the Soviets call it "the militarization of space." But we are both talking about a subject that has a long history in force structures, in strategic doctrine, and in arms control.

When you think about it, the relationship between offense and defense is as old as military history. There is a tendency to assume that the offense always wins out, but there are plenty of examples of the reverse. In World War I, for example, the machine gun and barbed wire frustrated one attack after another, prolonging to four years what everybody thought would be a short war.

Ambassador Warren Zimmermann served as Deputy to the Chairman of the Nuclear and Space Arms Talks with the Soviet Union. He is currently Chief of the U.S. delegation to the Vienna Follow-up Meeting of the Conference on Security and Cooperation in Europe, beginning November 4, 1986.

Of all countries, the Soviet Union has the most reason to understand defenses. A vast continental landmass between the West and the Orient, Russia has experienced more than her share of invasions—from the Mongols in the east, from Napoleon and Hitler in the west. The last two, you will note, were overcome through a defensive strategy. The decisive battles—in the first, Borodino; in the second, Stalingrad—were fought deep within Russian territory.

To this day, Soviet strategists are no less dedicated to the concept of strategic defense. Let me quote from three of them. In 1964, N. A. Talenskiy, editor of a classified military journal, wrote that "the creation of an effective antimissile defense system by a country which is a potential target for aggression merely serves to increase the deterrent effect and so helps to avert aggression." In 1976, another Soviet military scholar, V. M. Bondarenko, wrote that "the history of military arms development is full of examples when weapons, which seemed irresistible and frightening, after some time are opposed by sufficiently reliable means of defense." And in 1982, then Chief of Staff Marshal Nikolai Ogarkov argued that "the experience of past wars convincingly demonstrates that the appearance of new means of attack has always invariably led to the creation of corresponding means of defense. . . . This applies fully even to the nuclear-missile weapons."

THE SOVIET STRATEGIC DEFENSE PROGRAM

The Soviet Union has practiced what it preaches about defense. I will cite four examples. First, the Soviet Union has the only operational antiballistic missile system in the world—the Galosh system around Moscow. The ABM Treaty allows one ABM site in each country; the Soviets chose to maintain (and are modernizing) theirs, while we dismantled our Safeguard ABM system at Grand Forks, North Dakota. Second, the Soviet Union has the most extensive air defense system in the world; the United States has nothing comparable. Third, the Soviet Union has spent enormous resources—far more than the United States—on passive defenses to protect its leadership, command and control systems, industry, and population; we have not.

Fourth, we know that the Soviets have been embarked for some time on a comprehensive research program on strategic defenses—far in excess of what we were doing and as ambitious as anything we contemplate in our SDI. Much of this research is highly sophisticated. Since the 1960s, the Soviets have been involved in research on high-energy lasers, particle-beam weapons, radio-frequency weapons, and kinetic-energy weapons. It is worth recalling that in the 1960s two Soviet scientists shared the Nobel Prize with an American scientist for the invention of the laser. In fact, some of the SDI research going on in our national laboratories is based on theoretical articles published in the 1960s by Soviet scientists, many of whom are still engaged in work on Soviet strategic defenses. In all, we estimate that the Soviets spend approximately as much on defense as on offense—a far larger share for defense than even full funding of our SDI research program would give the United States.

THE ABM TREATY

What I have said should indicate that, in both concept and application, strategic defenses are not new, and certainly not new to the Soviet Union. Nor are they new to arms control. Soviet propaganda about preventing the "militarization of space" should not obscure the fact that space is already highly regulated by arms control agreements. The Outer Space Treaty of 1967 prohibits the placing of weapons of mass destruction, including nuclear weapons, in space. The Limited Test Ban Treaty of 1963 prohibits the testing of nuclear arms in space. And the ABM Treaty of 1972 commits each party "not to develop, test, or deploy ABM systems or components which are sea-based, air-based, space-based, or mobile land-based." What is clearly unregulated is research. The SDI is a research program and can be no more than that for many years to come.

Against that background, let me look at the arms control implications of strategic defense—Soviet as well as U.S. strategic defense. In 1972, culminating the first round of Strategic Arms Limitation Talks (SALT I), the United States and the Soviet Union signed the ABM Treaty and the Treaty on Strategic Offensive Arms. The ABM Treaty put severe limits on defenses, the theory on our side being that our respective offensive nuclear forces would be capable of deterring a nuclear strike through their ability to retaliate. However, regardless of the new role that had been given to offensive forces, the United States did not consider large arsenals of offensive forces to be stabilizing. Thus Ambassador Gerard Smith, our SALT I negotiator, stated explicitly that the ABM Treaty depended crucially on significant reductions of strategic nuclear offensive arms.

Unfortunately, the Soviet Union did not pay much attention to those words. Instead, it launched a massive military buildup. Since the early 1970s, the Soviet Union has deployed three new types of intercontinental ballistic missiles (ICBMs), eight improved versions of existing ICBMs, five new types of nuclear ballistic submarines, four new types of submarine-launched ballistic missiles (SLBMs), five improved versions of existing SLBMs, and a new intercontinental bomber. By contrast, the United States has deployed no new types of ICBMs, one new type of nuclear submarine, one new type of SLBM, and no new type of heavy bomber. Well might Harold Brown, President Carter's Secretary of Defense, say, "When we build, they build; when we stop building, they build."

It was also assumed, back in 1972, that both sides would comply with the ABM Treaty. We have. But the Soviets have built an enormous radar near Krasnoyarsk, Siberia, in flat violation of the treaty. This radar, which can be used for ABM defense, as well as other Soviet actions, is causing concern that the Soviets may be actively preparing a nationwide defense against ballistic missiles in spite of their ABM Treaty commitment not to do so.

SDI AND GENEVA

These disappointments with the ABM Treaty, the continuing Soviet program on strategic defense, and the new possibilities for viable defense offered by technological advances have been at the heart of the SDI research program. It seems clear that the creation of that program by President Reagan played a major role in bringing the Soviets back to the negotiating table in Geneva, which they had left in November 1983, following the defeat of their campaign to prevent the Atlantic Alliance from carrying out its decision to deploy U.S. intermediate-range missiles in Western Europe as a balance to the threat of the Soviet SS-20 missile. Their primary objective in Geneva is almost certainly to scuttle the U.S. option of strategic defense. In view of the fact that so far they have pretty much had the field to themselves, they do not want us to catch up, and they are afraid that, with our technological prowess, we will. In Geneva, the Soviets have insisted that progress on reducing strategic and intermediate-range arms be a hostage to their demand that we abandon our strategic defense program.

What does this imply for arms control and for possible future cooperation between the United States and the Soviet Union on strategic defense? Prediction is impossible at this stage. On the one hand, some may ask why the Soviets would sacrifice a near monopoly on defenses and facilitate the application of feared American technology to strategic defense. On the other hand, with their historic interest and current commitment to defense, might they not in time see the value of a cooperative regime? Even now we are seeking to discuss with the Soviets in Geneva the offense-defense relationship and how we might work together toward a stable transition to a more defense-oriented environment, should SDI research prove out.

The U.S. position, at least, is clear. Let me conclude by citing its main points. First, strategic defense offers the possibility of a more stable world. Thus, as President Reagan has said repeatedly, we intend to continue our SDI research, which is sanctioned by the ABM Treaty and which the Soviets are doing as well. Second, our decision on whether to proceed from the research to the deployment stage is not imminent. That decision will depend on the meeting of two deployment criteria which we have set ourselves and which Ambassador Nitze described last February to the World Affairs Council of Philadelphia: that defenses must be both cost-effective and survivable. Third, we are committed to complying with the ABM Treaty, and we will do so. If our research is successful and we do decide to proceed with SDI, we will consult fully with our allies and seek to negotiate an improved strategic regime with the Soviet Union based increasingly on defense.

We are thus prepared at every step of the way to keep strategic defense fully within the context of arms control and of our overall objective of a safer and more stable world. But we are not prepared to accept the myths that Soviet spokesmen would have us swallow—most important, the myth that the U.S. strategic defense program is unique and that the Soviet Union itself is innocent of any activity on strategic defense. The prospects for arms control will undoubtedly improve if we can cut through the miasma of mythology to the real issues which divide us.

APPENDIX A
PEACE AND NATIONAL SECURITY
Ronald Reagan

The subject I want to discuss with you, peace and national security, is both timely and important. Timely, because I've reached a decision which offers a new hope for our children in the 21st century, a decision I'll tell you about in a few minutes. And important because there's a very big decision that you must make for yourselves.

This subject involves the most basic duty that any President and any people share—the duty to protect and strengthen the peace. At the beginning of this year, I submitted to the Congress a defense budget which reflects my best judgment of the best understanding of the experts and specialists who advised me about what we and our allies must do to protect our people in the years ahead. That budget is much more than a long list of numbers. For behind all the numbers lies America's ability to prevent the greatest of human tragedies and preserve our free way of life in a sometimes dangerous world. It is part of a careful, long-term plan to make America strong again after too many years of neglect and mistakes.

Our efforts to rebuild America's defenses and strengthen the peace began two years ago when we requested a major increase in the defense program. Since then, the amount of those increases

Televised address to the nation by President Ronald Reagan, March 23, 1983.

we first proposed has been reduced by half, through improvements in management and procurement and other savings.

The budget request that is now before the Congress has been trimmed to the limits of safety. Further deep cuts cannot be made without seriously endangering the security of the nation. The choice is up to the men and women you've elected to the Congress, and that means the choice is up to you.

Tonight, I want to explain to you what this defense debate is all about, and why I'm convinced that the budget now before the Congress is necessary, responsible, and deserving of your support. And I want to offer hope for the future.

But first, let me say what the defense debate is not about. It is not about spending arithmetic. I know that in the last few weeks you have been bombarded with numbers and percentages. Some say we need only a 5% increase in defense spending. The so-called alternate budget backed by liberals in the House of Representatives would lower the figure to 2%–3%, cutting our defense spending by $163 billion over the next 5 years.

The trouble with all these numbers is that they tell us little about the kind of defense program America needs or the benefits and security and freedom that our defense effort buys for us. What seems to have been lost in all this debate is the simple truth of how a defense budget is arrived at. It isn't done by deciding to spend a certain number of dollars. Those loud voices that are occasionally heard charging that the government is trying to solve a security problem by throwing money at it are nothing more than noise based on ignorance. We start by considering what must be done to maintain peace and review all the possible threats against our security. Then, a strategy for strengthening peace and defending against those threats must be agreed upon. And, finally, our defense establishment must be evaluated to see what is necessary to protect against any or all of the potential threats. The cost of achieving these ends is totalled up, and the result is the budget for national defense.

There is no logical way that you can say, let's spend X billion dollars less. You can only say, which part of our defense measures do we believe we can do without and still have security against all contingencies? Anyone in the Congress who advocates a percentage or a specific dollar cut in defense spending should be made to say what part of our defenses he would eliminate, and he should be candid enough to acknowledge that his cuts mean cutting our commitments to allies or inviting greater risk or both.

U.S. DEFENSIVE STRATEGY

The defense policy of the United States is based on a simple premise: the United States does not start fights. We will never be an aggressor. We maintain our strength in order to deter and defend against aggression—to preserve freedom and peace.

Since the dawn of the atomic age, we've sought to reduce the risk of war by maintaining a strong deterrent and by seeking genuine arms control. "Deterrence" means simply this: making sure any adversary who thinks about attacking the United States, or our allies, or our vital interests, concludes that the risks to him outweigh any potential gains. Once he understands that, he won't attack. We maintain the peace through our strength; weakness only invites aggression.

This strategy of deterrence has not changed. It still works. But what it takes to maintain deterrence has changed. It took one kind of military force to deter an attack when we had far more nuclear weapons than any other power; it takes another kind now that the Soviets, for example, have enough accurate and powerful nuclear weapons to destroy virtually all of our missiles on the ground. Now this is not to say that the Soviet Union is planning to make war on us. Nor do I believe a war is inevitable—quite the contrary. But what must be recognized is that our security is based on being prepared to meet all threats.

There was a time when we depended on coastal forces and artillery batteries because, with the weaponry of that day, any attack would have had to come by sea. Well, this is a different world, and our defenses must be based on recognition and awareness of the weaponry possessed by other nations in the nuclear age.

We can't afford to believe that we will never be threatened. There have been two World Wars in my lifetime. We didn't start them and, indeed, did everything we could to avoid being drawn into them. But we were ill prepared for both—had we been better prepared, peace might have been preserved.

For 20 years the Soviet Union has been accumulating enormous military might. They didn't stop when their forces exceeded all requirements of a legitimate defensive capability, and they haven't stopped now. During the past decade and a half, the Soviets have built up a massive arsenal of new strategic nuclear weapons—weapons that can strike directly at the United States.

As an example, the United States introduced its last new intercontinental ballistic missile, the Minuteman III, in 1969; and we're now dismantling our even older Titan missiles. But what has the Soviet Union done in these intervening years? Well, since 1969, the Soviet Union has built five new classes of ICBMs [intercontinental ballistic missiles] and upgraded these eight times. As a result, their missiles are much more powerful and accurate than they were several years ago; and they continue to develop more, while ours are increasingly obsolete.

The same thing has happened in other areas. Over the same period, the Soviet Union built four new classes of submarine-launched ballistic missiles and over 60 new missile submarines. We built two new types of submarine missiles and actually withdrew 10 submarines from strategic missions. The Soviet Union built over 200 new Backfire bombers, and their brand new Blackjack bomber is now under development. We haven't built a new long-range bomber since our B-52s were deployed about a quarter of a century ago, and we've already retired several hundred of those because of old age. Indeed, despite what many people think, our strategic forces only cost about 15% of the defense budget.

Another example of what's happened. In 1978, the Soviets had 600 intermediate-range nuclear missiles based on land and were beginning to add the SS-20—a new, highly accurate mobile missile with three warheads. We had none. Since then the Soviets have strengthened their lead. By the end of 1979, when Soviet leader Brezhnev declared "a balance now exists," the Soviets had over 800 warheads. We still had none. A year ago this month, Mr. Brezhnev pledged a moratorium, or freeze, on SS-20 deployment. But by last August, their 800 warheads had become more than 1,200. We still had none—some freeze. At this time Soviet Defense Minister Ustinov announced "approximate parity of forces continues to exist." But the Soviets are still adding an average of three new warheads a week and now have 1,300. These warheads can reach their targets in a matter of a few minutes. We still have none. So far, it seems that the Soviet definition of parity is a box score of 1,300 to nothing, in their favor.

So, together with our NATO allies, we decided in 1979 to

deploy new weapons, beginning this year, as a deterrent to their SS-20s and as an incentive to the Soviet Union to meet us in serious arms control negotiations. We will begin that deployment late this year. At the same time, however, we're willing to cancel our program if the Soviets will dismantle theirs. This is what we've called a zero-zero plan. The Soviets are now at the negotiating table; and I think it's fair to say that without our planned deployments, they wouldn't be there.

Now, let's consider conventional forces. Since 1974, the United States has produced 3,050 tactical combat aircraft. By contrast, the Soviet Union has produced twice as many. When we look at attack submarines, the United States has produced 27 while the Soviet Union has produced 61. For armored vehicles, including tanks, we have produced 11,200. The Soviet Union has produced 54,000—nearly 5 to 1 in their favor. Finally, with artillery, we have produced 950 artillery and rocket launchers while the Soviets have produced more than 13,000—a staggering 14-to-1 ratio.

SPREAD OF SOVIET MILITARY INFLUENCE

There was a time when we were able to offset superior Soviet numbers with higher quality. But today, they are building weapons as sophisticated and modern as our own. As the Soviets have increased their military power, they have been emboldened to extend that power. They are spreading their military influence in ways that can directly challenge our vital interests and those of our allies.

The following aerial photographs, most of them secret until now, illustrate this point in a crucial area very close to home: Central America and the Caribbean Basin. They are not dramatic photographs. But I think they help give you a better understanding of what I am talking about.

This Soviet intelligence collection facility less than 100 miles from our coast is the largest of its kind in the world. The acres and acres of antennae fields and intelligence monitors are targeted on key U.S. military installations and sensitive activities. The installation in Lourdes, Cuba, is manned by 1,500 Soviet technicians. And the satellite ground station allows instant communications with Moscow. This 28-square-mile facility has grown by more than 60% in size and capability during the past decade.

In western Cuba, we see this military airfield and its complement of modern, Soviet-built MiG-23 aircraft. The Soviet Union uses this Cuban airfield for its own long-range reconnaissance missions. And earlier this month, two modern Soviet antisubmarine warfare aircraft began operating from it. During the past 2 years, the level of Soviet arms exports to Cuba can only be compared to the levels reached during the Cuban missile crisis 20 years ago.

This third photo, which is the only one in this series that has been previously made public, shows Soviet military hardware that has made its way to Central America. This airfield with its MI-8 helicopters, antiaircraft guns, and protected fighter sites is one of a number of military facilities in Nicaragua which has received Soviet equipment funneled through Cuba and reflects the massive military buildup going on in that country.

On the small island of Grenada at the southern end of the Caribbean chain, the Cubans with Soviet financing and backing are in the process of building an airfield with a 10,000-foot runway. Grenada doesn't even have an air force. Who is it intended for? The Caribbean is a very important passageway for our international commerce and military lines of communication. More than half of all American oil imports now pass through the Caribbean. The rapid buildup of Grenada's military potential is unrelated to any conceivable threat to this island country of under 110,000 people and totally at odds with the patterns of the eastern Caribbean states, most of which are unarmed.

The Soviet-Cuban militarization of Grenada, in short, can only be seen as power projection into the region. And it is in this important economic and strategic area that we're trying to help the Governments of El Salvador, Costa Rica, Honduras, and others in their struggles for democracy against guerrillas supported through Cuba and Nicaragua.

These pictures only tell a small part of the story. I wish I could show you more without compromising our most sensitive intelligence sources and methods. But the Soviet Union is also supporting Cuban military forces in Angola and Ethiopia. They have bases in Ethiopia and South Yemen, near the Persian Gulf oil fields. They have taken over the port that we built at Cam Ranh Bay in Vietnam. And now for the first time in history, the Soviet Navy is a force to be reckoned with in the South Pacific.

Some people may still ask: Would the Soviets ever use their

formidable military power? Well, again, can we afford to believe they won't? There is Afghanistan. And in Poland the Soviets denied the will of the people and, in so doing, demonstrated to the world how their military power could also be used to intimidate.

The final fact is that the Soviet Union is acquiring what can only be considered an offensive military force. They have continued to build far more intercontinental ballistic missiles than they could possibly need simply to deter an attack. Their conventional forces are trained and equipped not so much to defend against an attack as they are to permit sudden surprise offenses of their own.

REPAIRING U.S. DEFENSES

Our NATO allies have assumed a great defense burden, including the military draft in most countries. We're working with them and our other friends around the world to do more. Our defensive strategy means we need military forces that can move very quickly, forces that are trained and ready to respond to any emergency.

Every item in our defense program—our ships, our tanks, our planes, our funds for training and spare parts—is intended for one all-important purpose: to keep the peace. Unfortunately, a decade of neglecting our military forces has called into question our ability to do that.

When I took office in January 1981, I was appalled by what I found: American planes that couldn't fly and American ships that couldn't sail for lack of spare parts and trained personnel and insufficient fuel and ammunition for essential training. The inevitable result of all this was poor morale in our Armed Forces, difficulty in recruiting the brightest young Americans to wear the uniform, and difficulty in convincing our most experienced military personnel to stay on.

There was a real question then about how well we could meet a crisis. And it was obvious that we had to begin a major modernization program to ensure we could deter aggression and preserve the peace in the years ahead. We had to move immediately to improve the basic readiness and staying power of our conventional forces, so they could meet—and, therefore, help deter—a crisis. We had to make up for lost years of investment by moving forward with a long-term plan to prepare our forces to counter the military capabilities our adversaries were developing for the future.

I know that all of you want peace, and so do I. I know, too, that many of you seriously believe that a nuclear freeze would further the cause of peace. But a freeze now would make us less, not more, secure and would raise, not reduce, the risks of war. It would be largely unverifiable and would seriously undercut our negotiations on arms reduction. It would reward the Soviets for their massive military buildup while preventing us from modernizing our aging and increasingly vulnerable forces. With their present margin of superiority, why should they agree to arms reductions knowing that we were prohibited from catching up?

Believe me, it wasn't pleasant for someone who had come to Washington determined to reduce government spending, but we had to move forward with the task of repairing our defenses or we would lose our ability to deter conflict now and in the future. We had to demonstrate to any adversary that aggression could not succeed and that the only real solution was substantial, equitable, and effectively verifiable arms reduction—the kind we're working for right now in Geneva.

Thanks to your strong support, and bipartisan support from the Congress, we began to turn things around. Already we're seeing some very encouraging results. Quality recruitment and retention are up dramatically—more high school graduates are choosing military careers and more experienced career personnel are choosing to stay. Our men and women in uniform at last are getting the tools and training they need to do their jobs.

Ask around today, especially among our young people, and I think you will find a whole new attitude toward serving their country. This reflects more than just better pay, equipment, and leadership. You, the American people, have sent a signal to these young people that it is once again an honor to wear the uniform. That's not something you measure in a budget, but it's a very real part of our nation's strength.

It'll take us longer to build the kind of equipment we need to keep peace in the future, but we've made a good start. We haven't built a new long-range bomber for 21 years. Now we're building the B-1. We hadn't launched one new strategic submarine for 17 years. Now we're building one Trident submarine a year. Our land-based missiles are increasingly threatened by the many huge, new Soviet ICBMs. We're determining how to solve that problem. At the same time, we're working in the START [Strategic Arms

Reduction Talks] and INF [Intermediate-range Nuclear Forces] negotiations with the goal of achieving deep reductions in the strategic and intermediate nuclear arsenals of both sides.

We have also begun the long-needed modernization of our conventional forces. The Army is getting its first new tank in 20 years. The Air Force is modernizing. We're rebuilding our Navy, which shrank from about 1,000 ships in the late 1960s to 453 during the 1970s. Our nation needs a superior Navy to support our military forces and vital interests overseas. We're now on the road to achieving a 600-ship Navy and increasing the amphibious capabilities of our Marines, who are now serving the cause of peace in Lebanon. And we're building a real capability to assist our friends in the vitally important Indian Ocean and Persian Gulf region.

THE NEED FOR DEFENSE RESOURCES

This adds up to a major effort, and it isn't cheap. It comes at a time when there are many other pressures on our budget, and when the American people have already had to make major sacrifices during the recession. But we must not be misled by those who would make defense once again the scapegoat of the Federal budget.

The fact is that in the past few decades we have seen a dramatic shift in how we spend the taxpayer's dollar. Back in 1955, payments to individuals took up only about 20% of the Federal budget. For nearly three decades, these payments steadily increased, and this year will account for 49% of the budget. By contrast, in 1955 defense took up more than half of the Federal budget. By 1980, this spending had fallen to a low of 23%. Even with the increase that I am requesting this year, defense will still amount to only 28% of the budget.

The calls for cutting back the defense budget come in nice, simple arithmetic. They're the same kind of talk that led the democracies to neglect their defenses in the 1930s and invited the tragedy of World War II. We must not let that grim chapter of history repeat itself through apathy or neglect.

This is why I'm speaking to you tonight—to urge you to tell your Senators and Congressmen that you know we must continue to restore our military strength. If we stop in midstream, we will send a signal of decline, of lessened will, to friends and adversaries alike. Free people must voluntarily, through open debate and democratic means, meet the challenge that totalitarians pose by compulsion. It's up to us, in our time, to choose and choose wisely between the hard but necessary task of preserving peace and freedom and the temptation to ignore our duty and blindly hope for the best while the enemies of freedom grow stronger day by day.

The solution is well within our grasp. But to reach it, there is simply no alternative but to continue this year, in this budget, to provide the resources we need to preserve the peace and guarantee our freedom.

COMMITMENT TO ARMS CONTROL

Now, thus far tonight I've shared with you my thoughts on the problems of national security we must face together. My predecessors in the Oval Office have appeared before you on other occasions to describe the threat posed by Soviet power and have proposed steps to address that threat. But since the advent of nuclear weapons, those steps have been increasingly directed toward deterrence of aggression through the promise of retaliation. This approach to stability through offensive threat has worked. We and our allies have succeeded in preventing nuclear war for more than three decades.

In recent months, however, my advisers, including, in particular, the Joint Chiefs of Staff, have underscored the necessity to break out of a future that relies solely on offensive retaliation for our security. Over the course of these discussions, I've become more and more deeply convinced that the human spirit must be capable of rising above dealing with other nations and human beings by threatening their existence. Feeling this way, I believe we must thoroughly examine every opportunity for reducing tensions and for introducing greater stability into the strategic calculus on both sides.

One of the most important contributions we can make is, of course, to lower the level of all arms, and particularly nuclear arms. We are engaged right now in several negotiations with the Soviet Union to bring about a mutual reduction of weapons.

I will report to you a week from tomorrow my thoughts on that score. But let me just say, I am totally committed to this course. If the Soviet Union will join with us in our effort to achieve major arms reduction, we will have succeeded in stabilizing the nuclear balance. Nevertheless, it will still be necessary to rely on the specter of retaliation, on mutual threat. And that's a sad commentary on the human condition. Wouldn't it be better to save lives than to avenge them? Are we not capable of demonstrating our peaceful intentions by applying all our abilities and our ingenuity to achieving a truly lasting stability?

I think we are. Indeed, we must. After careful consultation with my advisers, including the Joint Chiefs of Staff, I believe there is a way. Let me share with you a vision of the future which offers hope. It is that we embark on a program to counter the awesome Soviet missile threat with measures that are defensive. Let us turn to the very strengths in technology that spawned our great industrial base and that have given us the quality of life we enjoy today.

What if free people could live secure in the knowledge that their security did not rest upon the threat of instant U.S. retaliation to deter a Soviet attack, that we could intercept and destroy strategic ballistic missiles before they reached our own soil or that of our allies?

I know this is a formidable, technical task, one that may not be accomplished before the end of this century. Yet, current technology has attained a level of sophistication where it is reasonable for us to begin this effort. It will take years, probably decades of effort on many fronts. There will be failures and setbacks, just as there will be successes and breakthroughs. And as we proceed, we must remain constant in preserving the nuclear deterrent and maintaining a solid capability for flexible response.

But isn't it worth every investment necessary to free the world from the threat of nuclear war? We know it is. In the meantime, we will continue to pursue real reductions in nuclear arms, negotiating from a position of strength that can be ensured only by modernizing our strategic forces.

At the same time, we must take steps to reduce the risk of a conventional military conflict escalating to nuclear war by improving our nonnuclear capabilities. America does possess—now—the technologies to attain very significant improvements in the effectiveness of our conventional, nonnuclear forces. Proceeding boldly with these new technologies, we can significantly reduce any incentive that the Soviet Union may have to threaten attack against the United States or its allies.

As we pursue our goal of defensive technologies, we recognize that our allies rely upon our strategic offensive power to deter attacks against them. Their vital interests and ours are inextricably linked. Their safety and ours are one. And no change in technology can or will alter that reality. We must and shall continue to honor our commitments. I clearly recognize that defensive systems have limitations and raise certain problems and ambiguities. If paired with offensive systems, they can be viewed as fostering an aggressive policy; and no one wants that. But with these considerations firmly in mind, I call upon the scientific community in our country, those who gave us nuclear weapons, to turn their great talents now to the cause of mankind and world peace, to give us the means of rendering these nuclear weapons impotent and obsolete.

Tonight, consistent with our obligations of the ABM [Anti-Ballistic Missile] Treaty and recognizing the need for closer consultation with our allies, I'm taking an important first step. I am directing a comprehensive and intensive effort to define a long-term research and development program to begin to achieve our ultimate goal of eliminating the threat posed by strategic nuclear missiles. This could pave the way for arms control measures to eliminate the weapons themselves. We seek neither military superiority nor political advantage. Our only purpose—one all people share—is to search for ways to reduce the danger of nuclear war.

My fellow Americans, tonight we're launching an effort which holds the promise of changing the course of human history. There will be risks, and results take time. But I believe we can do it. As we cross this threshold, I ask for your prayers and your support.

APPENDIX B
ON THE ROAD TO A MORE
STABLE PEACE
Paul Nitze

Since the dawn of the nuclear age 40 years ago, there have been countless proposals to eliminate nuclear weapons from the face of the earth. That has been the professed objective of both the Soviet Union and the United States, but, until recently, it has not been a practical goal.

The President is determined to do more, to look even now toward a world in which nuclear weapons have, in fact, been eliminated. The present situation—in which the threat of massive nuclear retaliation is the ultimate sanction, the key element of deterrence, and, thus, the basis for security and peace—is unsatisfactory. It has kept the peace for 40 years, but the potential costs of a breakdown are immense and, because of continuing massive Soviet deployments of both offensive and defensive weaponry, are not becoming less. If we can, we must find a more reliable basis for security and for peace.

This concern prompted the President's decision to proceed with the Strategic Defense Initiative (SDI). He has directed the scientific community to determine if new cost-effective defensive technologies are feasible which could be introduced into force

Address by Ambassador Paul Nitze, Special Advisor to the President and the Secretary of State for Arms Reduction Negotiations, before the World Affairs Council of Philadelphia, February 20, 1985.

structures so as to produce a more stable strategic relationship. We envisage, if that search is successful, a cooperative effort with the Soviet Union, hopefully leading to an agreed transition toward effective non-nuclear defenses that might make possible the eventual elimination of nuclear weapons.

THE STRATEGIC CONCEPT

In preparing for Secretary Shultz's January meeting with Foreign Minister Gromyko, we developed a strategic concept encompassing our view of how we would like to see the U.S.-Soviet strategic relationship evolve in the future. That concept provides the basis for our approach to next month's talks in Geneva. It can be summarized in four sentences.

During the next 10 years, the U.S. objective is a radical reduction in the power of existing and planned offensive nuclear arms, as well as the stabilization of the relationship between offensive and defensive nuclear arms, whether on earth or in space. We are even now looking forward to a period of transition to a more stable world, with greatly reduced levels of nuclear arms and an enhanced ability to deter war based upon an increasing contribution of nonnuclear defenses against offensive nuclear arms. This period of transition could lead to the eventual elimination of all nuclear arms, both offensive and defensive. A world free of nuclear arms is an ultimate objective to which we, the Soviet Union, and all other nations can agree.

It would be worthwhile to dwell on this concept in some detail. To begin with, it entails three time phases: the near term, a transition phase, and an ultimate phase.

THE NEAR TERM

For the immediate future—at least the next 10 years—we will continue to base deterrence on the ultimate threat of nuclear retaliation. We have little choice; today's technology provides no alternative. That being said, we will press for radical reductions in the number and power of strategic and intermediate-range nuclear arms. Offensive nuclear arsenals on both sides are entirely too high and potentially destructive, particularly in the more destabilizing categories such as the large MIRVed [multiple independently targetable reentry vehicles] Soviet ICBM [intercontinental ballistic missile] and SS-20 forces.

At the same time, we will seek to reverse the erosion that has occurred in the Anti-Ballistic Missile (ABM) Treaty regime— erosion that has resulted from Soviet actions over the last 10 years. These include the construction of a large phased-array radar near Krasnoyarsk in central Siberia in violation of the ABM Treaty's provisions regarding the location and orientation of ballistic missile early warning radars.

For the near term, we will be pursuing the SDI research program—in full compliance with the ABM Treaty, which permits such research. Likewise, we expect the Soviets will continue their investigation of the possibilities of new defensive technologies, as they have for many years.

We have offered to begin discussions in the upcoming Geneva talks with the Soviets as to how we might together make a transition to a more stable and reliable relationship based on an increasing mix of defensive systems.

THE TRANSITION PERIOD

Should new defensive technologies prove feasible, we would want at some future date to begin such a transition, during which we would place greater reliance on defensive systems for our protection and that of our allies.

The criteria by which we will judge the feasibility of such technologies will be demanding. The technologies must produce defensive systems that are survivable; if not, the defenses would themselves be tempting targets for a first strike. This would decrease rather than enhance stability.

New defensive systems must also be cost-effective at the margin—that is, they must be cheap enough to add additional defensive capability so that the other side has no incentive to add additional offensive capability to overcome the defense. If this criterion is not met, the defensive systems could encourage a proliferation of countermeasures and additional offensive weapons to overcome deployed defenses instead of a redirection of effort from offense to defense.

As I said, these criteria are demanding. If the new technologies cannot meet these standards, we are not about to deploy them. In the event, we would have to continue to base deterrence on the ultimate threat of nuclear retaliation. However, we hope and have expectations that the scientific community can respond to the challenge.

We would see the transition period as a cooperative endeavor with the Soviets. Arms control would play a critical role. We would, for example, envisage continued reductions in offensive nuclear arms.

Concurrently, we would envisage the sides beginning to test, develop, and deploy survivable and cost-effective defenses at a measured pace, with particular emphasis on nonnuclear defenses. Deterrence would thus begin to rely more on a mix of offensive nuclear and defensive systems instead of on offensive nuclear arms alone.

The transition would continue for some time—perhaps for decades. As the U.S. and Soviet strategic and intermediate-range nuclear arsenals declined significantly, we would need to negotiate reductions in other types of nuclear weapons and involve, in some manner, the other nuclear powers.

THE ULTIMATE PERIOD

Given the right technical and political conditions, we would hope to be able to continue the reduction of nuclear weapons down to zero.

The global elimination of nuclear weapons would be accompanied by widespread deployments of effective nonnuclear defenses. These defenses would provide assurance that, were one country to cheat—for example, by clandestinely building ICBMs or shorter-range systems, such as SS-20s—it would not be able to achieve any exploitable military advantage. To overcome the deployed defenses, cheating would have to be on such a large scale that there would be sufficient notice so that countermeasures could be taken.

Were we to reach the ultimate phase, deterrence would be based on the ability of the defense to deny success to a potential aggressor's attack. The strategic relationship could then be characterized as one of mutual assured security.

COMMENTS

Having thus outlined our strategic concept, let me offer some comments and perhaps anticipate some of your questions.

First, the concept is wholly consistent with deterrence. In both the transition and ultimate phases, deterrence would continue to provide the basis for the U.S.-Soviet strategic relationship.

Deterrence requires that a potential opponent be convinced that the risks and costs of aggression far outweigh the gains he might hope to achieve. The popular discussion of deterrence has focussed almost entirely on one element—that is, posing to an aggressor high potential costs through the ultimate threat of nuclear retaliation.

But deterrence can also function if one has the ability, through defense and other military means, to deny the attacker the gains he might otherwise have hoped to realize. Our intent is to shift the deterrent balance from one which is based primarily on the ultimate threat of devastating nuclear retaliation to one in which nonnuclear defenses play a greater and greater role. We believe the latter provides a far sounder basis for a stable and reliable strategic relationship.

My second comment is that we recognize that the transition period—if defensive technologies prove feasible and we decide to move in that direction—could be tricky. We would have to avoid a mix of offensive and defensive systems that, in a crisis, would give one side or the other incentives to strike first. That is precisely why we would seek to make the transition a cooperative endeavor with the Soviets and have offered, even now, to begin talking with them about the issues that would have to be dealt with in such a transition.

My third comment is that we realize that a world from which nuclear weapons have been eliminated would still present major risks. The technique of making nuclear weapons is well-known; that knowledge cannot be excised. The danger of breakout or cheating would continue. Moreover, there would also be the potential problem of suitcase nuclear bombs and the like.

But even if all risks cannot be eliminated, they can be greatly reduced. Nothing is wholly risk free; one must compare the alternatives. It seems to me that the risks posed by cheating or suitcase bombs in a world from which nuclear arms had been eliminated from military arsenals would be orders of magnitude less than the risks and potential costs posed by a possible breakdown in the present deterrence regime based upon the ultimate threat of massive nuclear retaliation.

THE GENEVA TALKS

U.S. and Soviet delegations will meet in Geneva in roughly 3 weeks' time to begin negotiations on nuclear and space arms. In those talks, we will advance positions consistent with and designed to further the concept I have outlined.

At the end of January, I was asked by the press whether I was confident about the outcome of the upcoming talks. I replied that I was more confident than previously—that is, before the Geneva meeting between Mr. Shultz and Mr. Gromyko—but I still wasn't very confident. We must bear in mind that there are profound differences of approach between the two sides.

In Geneva, Mr. Gromyko stated the Soviet position clearly and unambiguously. It has, since then, been repeated by many Soviet commentators. The Soviets insist on the "nonmilitarization" of space; by that, they mean a ban on all arms in space that are designed to attack objects in space or on earth and all systems on earth that are designed to attack objects in space. They have expressed opposition to research efforts into such systems, in spite of their own sizable efforts in this field, which include the only currently operational ABM and anti-satellite systems.

As to offensive arms reductions, the Soviets have yet to acknowledge the legitimacy of our concern about the threat we see in their large, highly MIRVed ICBM force. They continue to demand compensation for British and French nuclear forces and assert that U.S. Pershing II and ground-launched cruise missiles somehow represent a more odious threat than that posed to NATO Europe by the hundreds of SS-20 missiles now deployed.

In addition, the Soviets maintain that the three subject areas— strategic nuclear, intermediate-range nuclear, and defense and space arms—must not only be discussed in their interrelationship, but that it is not possible to implement an agreement in one area without agreement in the others. We believe otherwise; if the sides come to agreement in the one area, we see no sense in a self-denying rule that would prevent the sides from implementing an agreement that would serve the interests of both.

There are obvious differences. We will present our views and listen carefully to Soviet proposals. We do not expect the Soviets to accept immediately our viewpoint or our concept as to how the future strategic relationship should evolve. The negotiators have their work cut out for them; the process will be complex and could well be lengthy. But with persistence, patience, and constructive ideas, we hope the Soviets will come to see the merits of our position—that it will serve their national interests as well asours.

CONCLUSION

At the beginning of my remarks, I noted that the elimination of nuclear weapons has often seemed an impractical goal, one which has received little more than lip service. As you can see, the United States is going beyond that; the President has initiated a serious effort to see how it can be accomplished.

We do not underestimate the difficulties in reaching that objective. Quite frankly, it may prove impossible to obtain; and, even if we do eventually reach it, it will not be for many, many years—perhaps well into the next century.

But we cannot be anything but uneasy about the current situation, in which the nuclear arsenals of the world total tens of thousands of nuclear weapons. We owe it to our children, our grandchildren, and—in my case—to my great-grandchild to hold out for and to work toward some brighter vision for the future.

ABOUT THE AUTHORS

Lt. Gen. James A. Abrahamson is the Director of the Strategic Defense Initiative Organization of the Department of Defense. He heads the nation's research and technology efforts relating to defense against ballistic missiles. General Abrahamson was educated at the Massachusetts Institute of Technology, the University of Oklahoma, and the Aerospace Research Pilot School, after which he served as an astronaut with the Air Force's Manned Orbiting Laboratory Program. He went on to direct the television-guided, air-to-ground MAVERICK missile and the F-16 air combat fighter programs, as well as the space shuttle program, which he guided into its operational era. He assumed his present duties in April 1984.

Dr. Robert M. Bowman is the President of the Institute for Space and Security Studies. He was educated at the Armed Forces Staff College, the Air War College, and the California Institute of Technology, where he received his Ph.D. Culminating a twenty-two-year Air Force career in 1978, Dr. Bowman became Director of Advanced Space Program Development for what is now the Air Force Space Division. In that capacity he controlled space programs for the Air Force and the Defense Advanced Research Projects Agency including what are now the strategic defense programs.

Mr. Andrew Cockburn is a writer on defense issues. He graduated from Oxford in 1969, after which he worked with British newspapers and television. He has worked for ABC News and ABC Documentaries. His film "Red Army," written for PBS, won the George Foster Peabody Prize for documentaries in 1982. His work has appeared in the *New York Times, Le Monde, Parameters, Harpers,* and *Defense Week,* of which he is a contributing editor. Mr. Cockburn published *The Threat: Inside the Soviet Military Machine* in 1983.

Dr. Stephen F. Cohen is a professor of politics at Princeton University. He was educated at Indiana University and received his Ph.D. from Columbia University in 1969. He has served on the faculties of Columbia and Princeton alternately since 1965, and on the staffs of *Slavic Review* and *World Politics.* Dr. Cohen was awarded a Rockefeller Foundation Humanities Fellowship in 1980, and an NEH fellowship in 1984. He is the author of a number of works, including *Bukharin and the Bolshevik Revolution: A Political Biography, 1888–1938* and, more recently, *Rethinking the Soviet Experience: Politics and History since 1917* and *Sovieticus: American Perceptions and Soviet Relations.*

Dr. Robert S. Cooper is the President of Pollard Road, Inc., and a consultant to the Secretary of Defense. Dr. Cooper was educated at the University of Iowa, Ohio State University, and MIT, where he was a Ford Foundation Postdoctoral Fellow. He has served as Vice President of Engineering for Satellite Business Systems, Director of NASA's Goddard Space Flight Center, and Director of the Defense Advanced Research Projects Agency.

Dr. Adam M. Garfinkle is a research associate and the Coordinator of the Political Studies Program at the Foreign Policy Research Institute. He is a member of the editorial research and review staff of *Orbis* and a lecturer in political science at the University of Pennsylvania, where he received his Ph.D. in 1979. He coordinated the Seventh International Arms Control Symposium, held in Philadelphia in May 1982, and has published *The Politics of the Nuclear Freeze,* "Violating SALT II," and "SALT and the MX."

Dr. Richard L. Garwin is an IBM Fellow at the Thomas J. Watson Research Center. He holds adjunct research and teaching positions at Harvard, Cornell, and Columbia Universities, and has served as a consultant to the U.S. government on matters of military technology and arms control. He received his B.S. in physics from Case Institute of Technology, and his Ph.D. in physics from the University of Chicago in 1949. Dr. Garwin has made contributions in the design of nuclear weapons, has published more than two hundred papers, and has been granted twenty-nine U.S. patents.

Mr. Alex Gliksman is the Director of Strategic Defense Studies at the United Nations Association. He studied at New York University and the University of Vienna, and pursued doctoral studies in international relations at University College in London. He has worked under contract for the Congressional Office of Technology Assessment, Sandia National Laboratory, Lawrence Livermore National Laboratory, and the Systems Planning Corporation. He is a contributing editor of *National Defense* magazine. Mr. Gliksman directed the staff of the U.S. Senate Foreign Relations Arms Control Subcommittee, where he was involved in hearings on space arms control negotiations and where he drafted legislation on antisatellite weapons programs and the Strategic Defense Initiative.

Dr. Colin S. Gray is the President and founder of the National Institute for Public Policy. Dr. Gray studied at the Universities of Manchester and Oxford and has taught at the Universities of Lancaster, York (Canada), and British Columbia. He was a Ford Foundation Fellow at King's College, University of London, and Assistant Director of the International Institute for Strategic Studies in London. Beginning in 1976, he was a staff member and then Director of National Security Studies at the Hudson Institute before founding the National Institute for Public Policy.

Dr. Franklin A. Long is Professor Emeritus of Chemistry and of Science and Society at Cornell University's program on Science, Technology and Society, and has long been actively involved in research on arms control and U.S. policies for national security.

He was educated at the University of Montana and received his Ph.D. in chemistry from the University of California at Berkeley in 1935. He served as Assistant Director for Science and Technology of the U.S. Arms Control and Disarmament Agency in 1962 and 1963, and participated in the 1963 negotiations resulting in the Limited Test Ban Treaty. Dr. Long has participated in many international studies of arms control, including several International Pugwash Conferences.

The Honorable Robert S. McNamara is associated with many non-profit organizations that work on the issues of nuclear arms, population and development, world hunger, and East-West relations. He is also a director of a number of companies, including Corning Glass Works, Royal Dutch Shell, and the Bank of America. He graduated from the University of California in 1937 and received an M.B.A. from the Harvard Graduate School of Business Administration in 1939. After serving in the Air Force, he joined Ford Motor Company and was elected its president in 1960. Mr. McNamara served as Secretary of Defense of the United States in the Kennedy and Johnson administrations and became president of the World Bank Group of Institutions in 1968, retiring in 1981.

Dr. Richard Pipes is a professor of Russian history at Harvard University and a senior consultant at Stanford Research Institute, and he serves on the Executive Committee of the Committee on the Present Danger. He attended Muskingum College, Cornell University, and Harvard, where he has been a faculty member since he received his Ph.D. in 1950. Dr. Pipes served on the National Security Council from 1981 to 1982 as the Director of East European and Soviet Affairs, and on the Government "Team B" to Review Intelligence Estimates as chairman in 1976. He received Guggenheim Fellowships in 1956 and 1965, and has written extensively on Russian and Soviet history.

The Right Honourable Francis Pym is a Conservative Minister in the British Parliament. He was educated at Eton and Magdalen College in Cambridge, and then served in Africa and Italy during World War II. Mr. Pym was elected to Parliament in 1961. During his career in Parliament, he served as Opposition Spokesman for Northern Ireland, Agriculture, House of Commons Affairs and

Devolution, and Foreign Affairs until the General Election of May 1979, when he was appointed Secretary of State for Defense. In 1981 he was appointed Leader of the House of Commons, and was then appointed Lord President of the Council. From April 1982 to June 1983 he was Secretary of State for Foreign and Commonwealth Affairs.

The Honorable James R. Schlesinger currently divides his time between Georgetown University's Center for Strategic and International Studies, where he serves both as a counselor and a member of the Executive Board, and the investment banking firm of Shearson Lehman Brothers, Inc., where he serves as Senior Advisor. He graduated from Harvard College in 1950 and subsequently received A.M. and Ph.D. degrees from Harvard. He taught at the University of Virginia from 1955 to 1963 and held several positions at the Rand Corporation, including the directorship of Strategic Studies. Mr. Schlesinger has held numerous government positions at the Bureau of the Budget, the Atomic Energy Commission, the CIA, and the Defense Department. He was appointed Secretary of Defense in 1973 and became the nation's first Secretary of Energy during the Carter administration.

Mr. Craig Snyder is the Program Director of the World Affairs Council of Philadelphia, a nonprofit, nonpartisan educational organization devoted to increasing citizen understanding of American foreign policy and global issues. He is also the producer of *WorldViews,* a radio newsmagazine broadcast daily in Philadelphia. He was educated at Yale University and the University of Pennsylvania, where he received his B.A. in philosophy and political economy, and currently attends the Temple University School of Law, where he is pursuing a J.D. degree as an evening student. Mr. Snyder was the coordinator for "Strategic Defense and American Security," the conference upon which this book is based.

Dr. Michael Vlahos is an adjunct professor and Co-Director of National Security Studies at the Johns Hopkins School of Advanced International Studies. He received his A.B. from Yale University and his M.A. and Ph.D. from the Fletcher School of Law and Diplomacy. He has served as a strategic analyst with the CIA as the primary specialist in Soviet naval doctrine, and he worked on a number of projects for the Defense Nuclear Agency and the Lawrence Livermore National Laboratory, and on the Joint Service Small Arms Program, and a consultant to the Rand Corporation. Dr. Vlahos is the strategic policy analyst for the Cable News Network and a research fellow at the Naval War College and the Foreign Policy Research Institute, and has been a visiting teacher at the National Security Agency and the Marine Corps Command and Staff College.

The Honorable Caspar W. Weinberger is Secretary of Defense of the United States. He graduated from Harvard College in 1938 and received an L.L.B. from Harvard Law School in 1941. Following law school, he served with the U.S. Army's 41st Infantry Division in the Pacific and as a member of General Douglas MacArthur's intelligence staff. He was a member of the Assembly of the California State Legislature, was appointed by President Nixon as Chairman of the Federal Trade Commission, and then became Director of the Office of Management and Budget. He served as Secretary of Health, Education and Welfare and continued to head that department under President Ford until he resigned to enter private business in 1975. He assumed his present position in 1981.

Mr. Leon Wieseltier is the Literary Editor of the *New Republic*. He received his B.A. in philosophy from Columbia University in 1974, after which he became a Kellett Fellow at Balliol College, Oxford. He then studied Jewish history at Harvard University, where he was a member of the Society of Fellows from 1979 to 1982. He is the author of *Nuclear War, Nuclear Peace* and has written essays on a wide variety of political and cultural subjects for *Foreign Affairs, Dissent,* and *Commentary,* among others.

Lt. Col. Simon P. Worden is the Special Assistant to the Director of the Strategic Defense Initiative Organization of the Department of Defense and advisor to the U.S. delegation to the Negotiations on Nuclear and Space Arms with the Soviet Union. Dr. Worden received his B.S. in physics and astronomy from the University of Michigan in 1971, and his Ph.D. in astronomy from the University of Arizona in 1975. After holding several positions in the Air Force, he served as the Executive Military Assistant to the Defensive Technologies Study, also known as the Fletcher Study, which provided technical guidance for the Strategic Defense Initiative. Dr. Worden is the author of over one hundred scientific papers in astrophysics, space sciences, and optics. He is a scientific co-investigator for NASA's Spacelab II and Shuttle Solar Optical Telescope programs, and has twice received the Air Force Outstanding Research and Development Award for his work in astrophysics and optics.

Ambassador Warren Zimmermann served in 1985-86 as Deputy to the Chairman of the Arms Control Talks with the Soviet Union. He is currently Chief of the U.S. delegation to the Vienna Follow-up Meeting of the Conference on Security and Cooperation in Europe, beginning November 4, 1986. He graduated from Yale University in 1956, and from Cambridge in 1958, where he was a Fulbright Scholar. He joined the Foreign Service in 1961 as a consular and political officer in Caracas. Subsequently, he held the positions of analyst on Soviet foreign policy at the Bureau of Intelligence and Research, speechwriter for Secretary of State Henry Kissinger, Special Assistant for Policy Planning at the Bureau of European Affairs, and Deputy Chief of the U.S. Mission in Moscow. He was awarded the President's Meritorious Award in 1984.

INDEX